Out of the East

Out of the East

SPICES AND THE MEDIEVAL IMAGINATION

Paul Freedman

YALE UNIVERSITY PRESS / NEW HAVEN & LONDON

Published with assistance from the Kingsley Trust Association
Publication Fund established by the Scroll and Key Society of
Yale College and from the Louis Stern Memorial Fund.

Epigraph in the Introduction quoted from Henry Hobhouse,
Seeds of Change: Five Plants That Transformed Mankind, copyright
1985, 1986, by Henry Hobhouse, reprinted by permission of
HarperCollins Publishers.

Designed by Nancy Ovedovitz and set in Adobe Garamond
by Duke & Company, Devon, Pennsylvania. Printed in the
United States of America.

Library of Congress Cataloging-in-Publication Data
Freedman, Paul H., 1949–
Out of the East : spices and the medieval imagination /
Paul Freedman.
     p.   cm.
Includes bibliographical references and index.
ISBN 978-0-300-11199-6 (alk. paper)
1. Spices—History—To 1500. 2. Spice trade—Social aspects—
History—To 1500. 3. Food habits—History—To 1500. 4. Trade
routes—History—To 1500. 5. Europe—Territorial expansion—
History—To 1500. I. Title.
TX406F75 2008
641.3'383—dc22   2007036412

A catalog record for this book is available from the
British Library.

The paper in this book meets the guidelines for permanence and
durability of the Committee on Production Guidelines for Book
Longevity of the Council on Library Resources.

10 9 8 7 6 5 4 3 2 1

For Alexandre Genís &

Montserrat Orriols de Genís

Contents

Preface

Working on this book over several years, more than I care to enumerate, I have accumulated many debts to colleagues, friends, and institutions that it is my pleasant obligation to acknowledge here. For a long time I have wanted to write about the medieval European desire for spices, a result of a fascination with changing fashions for different sorts of luxury products. I tried to understand why spices became the focus not only of medieval culinary taste but of an imaginative worldview of the exotic and the fragrant. I began serious research during the academic year 2002–2003 while a fellow at the New York Public Library's Dorothy and Lewis B. Cullman Center for Scholars and Writers. My time at the center was funded by the American Council of Learned Societies. I cannot adequately express my gratitude to the library and the ACLS for a marvelous year. I was helped in a great many ways by Peter Gay, the director of the Cullman Center at that time, and by Pamela Leo, the assistant director. I benefited from the friendship, knowledge, and encouragement of the other members of the Center that year and the staff of the library, especially Jeremy Treglown, Roger Keyes, and Amy Azzarito.

My research has also been supported by grants from Yale University, and I am grateful to many colleagues there who have read or listened to pieces of this book at different times. I'd like to thank specifically Howard Bloch, Traugott Lawler, Stuart Schwartz, Joshua Burson, and Christiane Nockels Fabbri for their advice with regard to literary references, medical aspects, the Portuguese explorations, and many other topics. Azélina Jaboulet-Vercherre, a graduate student at Yale, helped me with the illustrations. I greatly appreciate the help of Agnieszka Rec, an undergraduate student at Yale, who read and corrected the manuscript.

I gave papers on various aspects of the history of spices at Vanderbilt

University, the University of Toronto, the University of Pennsylvania, Johns Hopkins University, Fordham University, Louisiana State University, Arizona State University, and the City University of New York's Graduate Center. On all those occasions I received useful comments, suggestions of material to look at, and ways of changing how I thought about the problems connected with the economics and imagination of the spice trade. I spoke on the demand for spices at the Eighth Anglo-American Seminar on the Medieval Economy and Society, which met at Gregynog, Wales, in 2004. A version of what I have argued in Chapter 5 concerning medieval perceptions of rarity and high price was published as an article in *Speculum* (October 2005) with the title "Spices and Late-Medieval European Ideas of Scarcity and Value."

In the course of gathering information, including many odd bits of medical, gastronomic, and religious knowledge that make up so much of medieval thought about spices, John Friedman, emeritus professor at the University of Illinois, has aided me more than anyone. I am astonished by the depth and variety of his understanding of the Middle Ages, and touched by his willingness to help with requests for lore. I learned a considerable amount about the modern perfume and flavoring business from Robert Beller. He also afforded me the opportunity to appreciate ambergris, one of the most highly regarded medieval fragrances and medicines. I've also received valuable help and advice from Susan Einbinder, Mark Burde, Eric Goldberg, Ilya Dines, Ellen Ketels, Kurt Weissen, Alain Touwaide, Michael McVaugh, Christopher Woolgar, Walton Orvil Schalick, III, Christine Reinle, and Christopher Dyer.

Lisa Adams of the Garamond Agency helped me immeasurably in conceiving and placing the manuscript, as well as editing and revising it. I am grateful to Lara Heimert and Chris Rogers, editors at Yale University Press, for their encouragement, enthusiasm, and patience.

I began to study the Middle Ages in the 1970s and chose a topic in the history of medieval Catalonia for my dissertation. This book is dedicated to my Catalan friends Alexandre and Montserrat of Malla. Their hospitality, affection, and joie de vivre supported and inspired me at the start of my career and have sustained me over the decades.

INTRODUCTION

Spices: A Global Commodity

The starting point for European expansion had nothing to do with
the rise of any religion or the rise of capitalism—but it had a
great deal to do with pepper.

Henry Hobhouse
Seeds of Change: Five Plants That Transformed Mankind

This book is about the demand, really the *craving,* for spices in Europe
during the Middle Ages, from roughly A.D. 1000 until 1513, the year the
Portuguese finished their exploration of the Moluccas, or Spice Islands, the
source of nutmegs and cloves, in what is now eastern Indonesia. Through
their research on the spice trade, historians have shown how the supply of

spices was affected by price, warfare, and changes in trade routes. But there is less understanding about the demand side: *why* spices were so popular in the first place, why they were sufficiently sought after for traders to bring them to Europe from what seemed the farthest corners of the world. There was only the vaguest understanding of where India, the great spice source and entrepôt, was located and no knowledge at all until the fourteenth century about other lands where spices grew, such as Java, Sumatra, or the Moluccas, yet the desire of European consumers for spices was strong enough to draw precious aromatic commodities from distant and unknown places.

Much of their allure had to do with the use of spices to flavor a sophisticated cuisine. Medieval European food, or at least that enjoyed by the more economically comfortable classes, was perfumed with a great variety of spices. The recipe collections of the era provide evidence of a fashion for spicier food than Europe has ever enjoyed since the Middle Ages ended. The fierce demand for spices, however, was caused by needs beyond simply gastronomic preferences. Spices were considered unusually effective as medicines and disease preventives; they were burned as incense in religious rituals and distilled into perfumes and cosmetics. Prized as consumer goods by the affluent, spices were symbols of material comfort and social prominence. The medieval infatuation with spices, encouraged by their mysterious origins and high prices, stimulated attempts to find the lands where they originated and to take over control of their trade. The need for spices fueled the expansion of Europe at the dawn of the modern era.

Desire, fashion, and taste move empires. If, as Adam Smith plausibly claimed, the two most important events in world history were the nearly simultaneous voyages to America by Columbus and around Africa to India by Vasco da Gama, then the European desire to find a route to the spices is among the most significant forces the world has known.[1]

In the modern era too, consumer demand affects people across the globe, so that drug addiction in America has an impact in Afghanistan or Colombia; the value of diamonds has disrupted African countries, including the Congo, Angola, and Sierra Leone. The interaction of everyday preferences with great shifts in global economies was the background in the sixteenth to the nineteenth centuries for the rise of transatlantic slavery in order to supply Europe with sugar, indigo, tobacco, and cotton, just as the demand for oil drives so much of today's political balance or imbalance of power.

Of all the world's commodities, spices most dramatically affected history because they launched Europe on the path to eventual overseas conquest, a conquest whose success and failure affects every aspect of contemporary world politics. The passion for spices underlies the beginning of the European colonial enterprise, a force that remade the demography, politics, culture, economy, and ecology of the entire globe.

The desire for spices, however, was already waning before European colonial expansion reached its zenith. By the eighteenth century, European food preferences had dramatically changed in favor of a richer but blander taste, and spices were no longer associated with healing or the sacred. The spice trade became unimportant. Even though today spices have a role in fusion cuisine and in cutting-edge food trends, they long ago ceased to be of global economic significance. In the summer of 2004, Hurricane Frances destroyed the nutmeg crop of Granada, the largest producer of this spice, yet the world financial system did not tremble. In fact, it took no notice whatsoever. A once great commodity is now a mere flavoring. Timothy Morton put it cogently in his book *The Poetics of Spice:* "Yesterday's banquet ingredient becomes today's Dunkin' Donuts apple-cinnamon item."[2] It therefore requires some effort to understand why spices would have been so vitally important and so passionately desired in the past. This book is intended to depict cinnamon and other spices at the height of their fame, when they enchanted Europe and set in motion its creative and destructive campaigns overseas.

The most popular explanation for the love of spices in the Middle Ages is that they were used to preserve meat from spoiling, or to cover up the taste of meat that had already gone off. This compelling but false idea constitutes something of an urban legend, a story so instinctively attractive that mere fact seems unable to wipe it out.[3] Actually, spices don't do much to preserve meat compared with salting, smoking, pickling, or air curing. The bad taste of spoiled meat, in any event, won't be substantially allayed by spices, or anything else.

The myth of spices as preservatives runs up against the actual conditions of perishability. Americans usually assume that in the absence of modern refrigeration meat will spoil almost immediately, but, particularly in the cool climate that dominates much of Europe, this is simply not the case. Some meat, such as game, was in fact supposed to age before being ready to cook. Master Chiquart, chef to the count of Savoy in the early fifteenth century, instructed purveyors to get the game they had gathered to the court well enough in advance to allow it to hang sufficiently (up to a week or so) before preparation.[4] He was not worried about freshness or a just-in-time delivery system.

In the Middle Ages fresh meat was not, in any event, all that hard for the reasonably affluent to obtain. In an overwhelmingly agricultural society, where cities were surrounded by farms without substantial intervening suburbs, plenty of animals were available. People of even moderate means had their own land in the country and kept livestock. Butchers were closer to the wholesale side of processing than are their modern descendants. In back of the store, they slaughtered most of what was sold in the front. Medieval town ordinances all over Europe denounced and attempted to regulate (with apparently only limited effect) butchers who fouled the streets with blood or unwanted entrails of animals they dispatched. Anyone who could afford spices could easily find meat fresher than what city dwellers today buy in their local supermarket.

Spices were very expensive, and meat was relatively cheap. According to the household accounts of the earl of Oxford in 1431–32, an entire pig could be had for the price of a pound of the cheapest spice, pepper.[5] An account left by the steward of the Talbot family in Shropshire shows that the monthly cost of spices was almost exactly the same as expenditures for beef and pork combined. For the fiscal year 1424–25, the family consumed seventeen pounds of pepper, fourteen pounds of ginger, and seventeen pounds of other spices, including three of saffron.[6] Given the cost, trying to improve dubious meat with cloves or nutmeg would have been perverse, something like slicing Italian white truffles (currently upward of eight hundred dollars per pound) to liven up the taste of a fast-food cheeseburger.

This simple explanation for the popularity of spices doesn't work—it had nothing to do with the perishability of meat. A truer account involves the prestige and versatility of spices, their social and religious overtones, and their mysterious yet attractive origins. Versatility is especially significant because, as previously stated, spices were not used just for cooking. They were regarded as drugs and as disease preventives in a society so often visited by ghastly epidemics. Spices were considered not only cures but healthful in promoting the body's equilibrium. In particular they helped balance the internal fluids, or humors, that affected both wellness and mood, so they were not only medicinal but luxurious and beautiful. Spices soothed and cheered, creating a refined environment of taste and comfort. They could be consumed in edible form or breathed as perfume or incense. The odor of spices wafted through houses fumigated with burning aromatics, as a kind of predecessor to aromatherapy. Churches were also permeated by the odor of resinous spices, especially frankincense, used in the celebrations of the Christian liturgy.

The symbolic overtones of spices linked fragrance to health and even to sanctity. The holiness of saints was demonstrated by the wonderful odor of spices that they exuded in life and even, contrary to the usual way of corpses, in death. As Chapter 3 will show, the Garden of Eden, the terrestrial paradise, was supposedly perfumed with spices and functioned as the true home of these wonderful aromatic products.

The location of paradise in the East, according to most Christian geographers, contributed to the already alluring images of India and East Asia held in the West. That spices came from Asia was further evidence of their magical qualities, bolstering the attraction conveyed by their expense, mystery, and sacred overtones. According to medieval legends, the Three Magi who visited the newborn Jesus were kings of Oriental realms who brought with them two spices, frankincense and myrrh, along with gold as signs of tribute (wealth) and worship (sacredness). The attraction of the East as both exotic and sacred is apparent in a story told by Thomas of Cantimpré, a thirteenth-century encyclopedist who also wrote biographies of saintly contemporaries. He describes an unusually austere bishop who received a magnificent silver cup filled with nutmegs. The bishop sent back the silver goblet, but he made an exception to his rule of refusing gifts and accepted the nutmegs, saying that he did so because they were "the fruit of the Orient."[7]

Once the notion of spices as not merely useful but somehow wonderful took hold, their importance was enhanced by the need to show off. As with all prestigious consumer items, spices were effective in claiming, conveying, and confirming social status, but they therefore had to be consumed in a public and ostentatious manner.

Medieval levels of ostentation could be quite impressive. In 1476 a series of banquets marked the marriage of Duke George "the Rich" of Bavaria with Princess Jadwiga of Poland. Records of the feast describe the startlingly large quantities of spices that were required: 386 pounds of pepper, 286 of ginger, 207 of saffron, 205 of cinnamon, 105 of cloves, and a mere 85 pounds of nutmeg.[8] Some of these spices may have been given away as presents, and certainly the feasting went on for days, but the quantities are nevertheless staggering. Beyond cuisine preferences, and certainly beyond mere necessity (as in the preservation of meat), spices here represent a calculated display of wealth, prestige, style, and splendor.

The modern French philosopher Gaston Bachelard observed that "the conquest of the superfluous is more spiritually exciting than the conquest of what is necessary. Man is a creature of desire, not a being motivated by necessity."[9] The truth of such a statement depends on circumstance, specifically the ability to enjoy choices above mere subsistence, but the power of unnecessary desire is at the heart of any explanation for the appeal and cost of luxuries. Spices were not as conspicuous as clothes, fine horses, tapestries, and other medieval aristocratic props, but they were as important and delightful as symbols of noble graciousness and status. They were objects of desire but not simply frivolous. Just as with silk clothes, hunting accoutrements, or titles and lineage, spices were luxuries that conferred well-being but also social distinction. Only out of a kind of reverse snobbery or world-renouncing simplicity could a person of high rank fail to serve highly spiced meals to guests. It was not a preference but an obligation. Spices weren't necessary for subsistence, but they were required in order to demonstrate and maintain social prestige.

Part of the gratification afforded by aromatic products arose from their fragrance, flavor, and perceived healthfulness, but they were also items of conspicuous consumption, which can be defined as the enjoyment of things that are less satisfying when consumed in private than when displayed to one's friends and associates. Jean of Hauteville, a satirical poet of the late twelfth century, criticized spices in the course of a diatribe against both gluttony and pride. A Norman who resided in England, Jean wrote his *Archithrenius* (Prince of Lamentations) as a moralistic denunciation of contemporary customs in the form of an imagined allegorical journey. His young protagonist visits the land of Venus and then the territory of gourmandise, where the "stomach-worshippers" live. According to Jean, the already vicious excessive love of food is made even worse by adding to it the passion for status seeking. Cooking is judged by the expense involved, he lamented, not on the basis of flavor. The best condiments are those that are the most costly, so that gluttony (a base but natural instinct) is further corrupted by arrogance or pride (a perverse, unnatural vice).[10]

However much moralists and advocates of simple and sensible living complain, the flaunting of fashionable and expensive goods is a constant social fact. What changes is the nature of such goods. What provides status and pleasure in one historical period may not carry over into the next. True, there are some enduring forms of prestige objects, such as fine clothing or jewelry, that mark class distinction even when specific fashions change: there has never been a time when rubies weren't precious. Most goods, however, rise and fall in perceived social value. Sometimes this is the result of a more generalized affluence or a price decline, so that a freezer was an emblem of prosperity in the 1950s but is no longer, and chicken is now cheap whereas it was considered a treat in the 1920s. As this is being written, flat-screen televisions are making the transition from show-off to routine items.

In some cases fashions simply change. Cuban cigars are still prized (and expensive), but most tobacco products and their accompanying paraphernalia including pipes, ashtrays, and lighters have lost their status over the past twenty years. Fur coats are not what they once were, because of changing attitudes toward animals. Hot chocolate was all the rage in the eighteenth century and has left souvenirs of its importance in fine porcelain collections, but elegance in the world of chocolate has moved to exclusive or artisanal candies, while the beverage is now mostly just for children.

Spices in the Middle Ages were marks of status and success, but they occupy this position no longer, and have not for several centuries. Serving a highly spiced meal in Europe today might show cooking skills or a willingness to try out risky dishes, but the spices themselves confer no particular social distinction. Some medieval luxuries (silk, jewels, and gold) retain their prestige in the contemporary world, while the allure of others (saints' relics or unicorn horns, for example) requires from us an effort at conceptual reconstruction. Some of the magic of spices was the intrinsic appeal of fragrances and the pleasurable flavor sensations they offered. The desire for spices was additionally stimulated by external factors, by their rarity. Even if spices were readily available, for a price (markets, spice sellers, and apothecaries carried all manner of exotic products), they were seen as rare because they came from far away and their origins were mysterious. Above all, they were expensive, ranging from merely costly (pepper) to the fabulously expensive (ambergris and aloe wood).

IMPORTED AND DOMESTIC AROMATICS

In the Middle Ages in Europe, spices were aromatic items of commerce with a high unit cost (that is, price per pound) imported from distant lands. They were not bulk goods like salt or lumber, nor were they domestic European items, such as herring or woolen cloth. Because of the time it took for spices to arrive from their usually unknown sources, people conceived of them as dry: as leaves, fruit, bark, or resins whose fragrance was not destroyed by the long voyage. This is a crucial difference between spices and herbs, with which they are often categorized both in cooking and in medicine. Herbs as well as spices impart flavor and aroma, but herbs were thought of as green and fresh even if they might be dried on occasion. Herbs like parsley, sorrel, or borage were used in both cooking and medicine. Many, such as mandrake, digitalis, or rue, were exclusively or primarily medicinal. Some were gathered in fields and woods, while others were cultivated, but they were above all familiar, literally part of the European landscape.

Spices, on the other hand, arrived in dried or semiprocessed form. Until the end of the thirteenth century, when Marco Polo visited India and other parts of southern Asia, Europeans were completely unfamiliar with pepper, nutmeg, or cloves in their botanical form or fresh state. Even ginger and its cousins like galangal and zedoary must have been considerably dried out after a journey that would have taken at least a year. Manuals of drugs, now often known as "herbals," contained illustrations that were accurate as far as European herbs were concerned, but completely fanciful in their depiction of tropical spices.

Because they were gathered or cultivated locally, herbs did not have great commercial value. They were sold at markets, so they were not completely

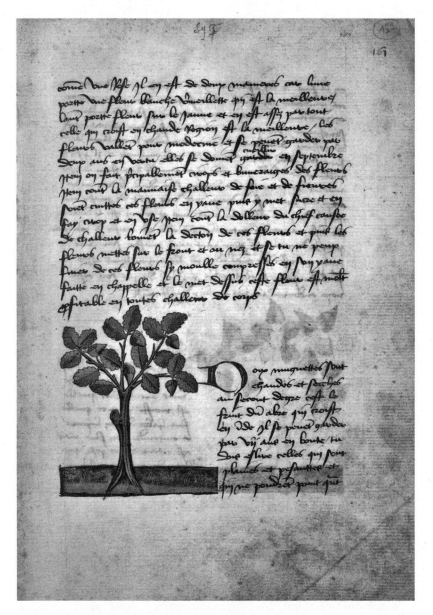

A fanciful depiction of a nutmeg "tree," from the *Livre des simples médecines,*
manuscript copy made in the fourteenth century.
(Copyright Bibliothèque Royale, Brussels, MS IV 1024, f. 149)

devoid of economic significance, but herbs were not comparable in price to spices, which were imported, sold in special stores, and measured out in small, expensive quantities to all save those, such as the stewards of George the Rich, who could buy them by the wagonload. Chapter 2 examines spices used as drugs, discussing the curative properties of spices and how these differed from herbs. Suffice it to say here that both spices and herbs were considered powerful medical tools, but applicable to different areas of need, with herbs having a wider use in such things as love potions and poisons.

Saffron is an exception to the definition of spices as imported aromatic products, since it grew locally but was nevertheless viewed as exotic and was breathtakingly expensive. The dried stigmata of a variety of crocus (*crocus sativus*), saffron probably originated in the Middle East (Iran and Kashmir are the leading growers of saffron now). In the Middle Ages saffron grew throughout the Mediterranean world and was particularly associated with Tuscany, where there were major markets in Pisa and San Gimignano.[11] At the end of the period, the eastern part of Spain started to gain the reputation it continues to hold as the source of the best-quality saffron. Unlike almost all other medieval spices, the saffron crocus was easily adapted to different soils and climates. As the English place name Saffron Walden attests, even northern Europe could produce a crop. The difficulty with saffron and the reason for its expense is in the tedious labor of harvesting just the stamen and the astronomical number of tiny threads necessary to make up a standard unit of measurement. Saffron was used as it is now in flavoring various dishes, but also as incense, as a coloring agent, and, probably most importantly, for its medicinal applications.

A few spices were native to Europe, but usually in very restrictive ecological zones. Mastic, for example, an aromatic resin, is produced by a species of acacia that grows only on the Aegean island of Chios. Most spices, however, came from much more distant climes, from "India" as conceived in the European imagination, but, as will become apparent, that geographical term could encompass a tremendous amount of real and imagined territory.

SPECIAL SPICES OF THE MIDDLE AGES

The best impression of what exactly the term "spices" meant to medieval traders comes from handbooks of how to do business composed by experienced merchants. These compendia of weights and measures, proverbial wisdom, and market lore tend to include lists of spices and advice on how to assess their quality in wholesale transactions. The longest such list appears in a commercial manual composed shortly before 1340 by Francesco Pegolotti, a Florentine banker who had experience in Cyprus, a great center for European imports of Eastern spices. Pegolotti's *La pratica della mercatura* itemizes 288 spices (*speziere*) amounting to 193 separate substances (many come in several forms: three kinds of ginger, two grades of cinnamon, and so on).[12] For our purposes we can leave aside some of the so-called spices such as alum (used to fix dyes so that the colors won't run), or wax (eleven varieties). Pegolotti included these because he tended to consider any nonperishable imported good as a spice. Ninety percent of Pegolotti's list consists of fragrant plants and a few animal products, some edible, some used more commonly as medicines or perfumes. Without exhausting ourselves in the minutiae of this spice directory, it is worth exploring its categories to see some of the less familiar exotics and the aura of desire and value surrounding them.

Edible Spices

The four major spices in commercial terms were black pepper, cinnamon, ginger, and saffron. Nutmegs and cloves were very expensive, but they were also ubiquitous in medieval recipes. These spices account for a large percentage of what was imported into Europe and sold for culinary purposes, but there are many spices that were common, if not as prevalent as these, that are almost or completely unfamiliar now outside their homelands. Pegolotti mentions an astounding range of spices even by today's sophisticated culinary standards. His list includes galangal, for example, an aromatic root related to ginger, now barely known in Europe and North America, and only through Thai cuisine at that. In the Middle Ages this was an expensive but widely available spice used in sophisticated cooking, and at the same time featured in pharmaceutical handbooks. According to another commercial manual, this one from Catalonia, the buyer of galangal should make sure the root is "heavy" (meaning probably not completely dried out), yellow in color both inside and out, and, most important, that the flavor is strong when bitten into, "otherwise it is worthless."[13] Another spice often called for in medieval recipes is long pepper, which is not in fact related to black pepper. Its dried fruit is extremely pungent, black, and rather large, the size of dry catfood or kibble. Beyond East and South Asia it is now completely unknown, having dropped out of European cuisine by the eighteenth century. Zedoary, another aromatic root related to turmeric, has also vanished outside India, but it was mentioned in medieval European cookbooks and its aroma was thought sufficiently attractive for it to be included among the fragrant plants in the magical garden of love at the opening of the popular allegorical poem *The Romance of the Rose*.[14]

Among the new and fashionable spices of the medieval period was what the French called "grains of paradise," known more prosaically as malagueta pepper. Like long pepper, this spice is not in fact related to black pepper. It is sharp and peppery, dark red, and grows in West Africa. It was first mentioned in Europe in the thirteenth century, and the designation "grains of paradise" seems to be an early example of a commercial marketing and branding campaign. Grains of paradise enjoyed a tremendous vogue in the fourteenth and early fifteenth centuries. By the time the Portuguese found the African regions where it grows, the fashion was waning; grains of paradise were headed for European oblivion by the close of the sixteenth century.[15]

The most important new spice (that is, a spice unknown to the ancient world) was sugar, destined for a prominent life of its own as a commodity, but an expensive import during the Middle Ages. Although sugar is not exactly aromatic, it qualified as a spice according to the medieval classification of imported goods and drugs since it was exotic, sold in small quantities, valuable, and credited with marvelous properties.

The Greeks and Romans had relied on honey, a much less powerful sweetener than cane sugar (obtaining sugar from beets and other plants is a modern development). Sugar began as another import from India, but by the fifteenth century sugarcane was being cultivated in Spain, Sicily, the Canary Islands, and the eastern Mediterranean. In the modern era sugar has become a cheap, fundamental ingredient in sodas, desserts, and candy, and a critical additive for processed foods from salad dressings to barbecue sauce. In the medieval period it was a luxury, first considered a medicine but later frequently enhancing a great variety of dishes, not just desserts, which were not yet distinct from other courses by reason of their sweetness.

Pegolotti lists thirteen varieties of sugar commonly sold, including rock candy, sugar scented with roses or violets, and sugar from Damascus, Babylon, and Caffa (a Genoese port in the Crimea). Sugar has a seductive flavor that retained its importance in medicine even as it was becoming accepted and later required in cuisine. Then as now, sugar disguised the bitter taste of medicine, but it was also useful as a way of preserving the often volatile ingredients of drugs. Medicines were combined with sugar and by heating and cooling rendered into a variety of textures: gummy, hard, paste-like, soft, or chewy. These sugared medicinal preparations, known as "electuaries," are the origin of candy and many similar confections combining sugar and spice.[16]

Beginning with the eighteenth century, sugar ceased to be considered a drug and changed from a mere food flavoring (what we understand as a spice) to an essential basic ingredient. At the same time, the end of medieval culinary practices meant that sweet dishes were separated from savory ones, so that the last course (dessert) came to be defined as sugary. In some respects, therefore, the Middle Ages used sugar more widely across the menu than now, but overall in much smaller quantities.

Drugs

While medieval lore taught that every edible spice had some purported medical use, the spices so far mentioned were all most often found in food preparations. There were other spices that were predominantly for medical purposes. Lists of medicines and their uses do not limit themselves by any means to common condiments, but rather demonstrate a fascination for strikingly exotic "spices"—dried, fragrant, and expensive imports with attributed medical value. Thus Pegolotti cites among his spices two kinds of opium and a botanical known as dragon's blood (extracted from the plant genus *Dracanea*), a medicine and red dye. A commonly mentioned panacea was "tutty," charred scrapings from inside chimneys. According to Pegolotti, tutty was imported from Alexandria, so obviously a routine European chimney would not suffice. Tutty was considered a spice as it was nonperishable, imported, fragrant (after a fashion), sold in small quantities, and expensive.

Among the strangest of Pegolotti's spices is *momie*, also known as *mumia* and informally in English as mummy. The fundamental drug handbook known from its first (Latin) words as *Circa instans* (dating from 1166) defines mummy as "a kind of spice collected from the tombs of the dead"—but not just any dead people, only those whose bodies have been specially embalmed. Mummy, which was thought to be effective in stopping bleeding, was an exudation from the head and spine of the corpse resulting from decay combined with the spices used in the preservation process. The meaning of mummy is therefore not wrapped-up corpses from the era of the Egyptian pharaohs, but rather a substance produced by embalmed but not completely dried-out corpses that were old, no doubt, but not necessarily ancient. In its way mummy was definitely aromatic, if not particularly delightful in its fragrance. Indeed, Pegolotti notes that mummy should have a foul odor and a pitchlike consistency, or else it's inferior. Mummy was imported from Egypt and the East, regions whose embalming techniques were perhaps considered more medically effective.

Medicinal Perfumes

The border between fragrance and drugs was porous and ill-defined. Among the rarest and most expensive spices listed in herbals and merchant's handbooks are perfumed substances used primarily as medicines, things like balsam, an aromatic resin from a plant native to Arabia. Its sap was credited with marvelous healing properties but also with high spiritual powers. Balsam was called for in Christian rites involving anointment, such as baptism, the ordination of priests, and the consecration of bishops.[17] Another Arabian resin, frankincense, was (and remains) the principal ingredient in the censing rituals of the Catholic and Orthodox churches. In keeping with the versatility characteristic of spices, frankincense was also used as a medicine, to scent houses, and to perfume banquets.

The most esteemed (and staggeringly expensive) medicinal perfumes were four animal products: ambergris (from sperm whales), castoreum (from certain kinds of beavers), musk (from a small Tibetan deer), and civet (from a kind of wild cat). Of these, ambergris was the most important and the most mysterious.[18] Ambergris was coughed up by sperm whales and could be found washed up on Indian Ocean beaches (usually in East Africa because of the winds and tides). The connection with whales was dimly and

A Medical "Spice": Mummy

Mummy is hot and dry in the second degree, according to Constantine's testimony. Some say that it is cold because it binds, but this is not true, for many cold and dry substances relax while many hot and dry substances bind. Mummy is a spice or confection found in the tombs of people who have been embalmed with spices, as they used to do in ancient times, and as the pagans near Babylon still do. This mummy is found near the brain and the spine. You should choose that which is shining, black, bad smelling, and firm. On the other hand, the white kind, which is rather opaque, does not stick, is not firm and easily crumbles to powder, must be refused.

Mummy has binding qualities. If a compress is made of it and the juice of shepherd's purse herb, it stops excessive nasal bleeding. . . . Furthermore, to treat spitting of blood through the mouth because of a wound or a malady of the respiratory organs, make some pills with mummy, mastic powder, and water in which gum arabic has been dissolved and let the patient keep these pills under the tongue until they have melted, then let him swallow them.

From the *Livre des simples médecines*, the fifteenth-century French translation of *Circa instans*.

---

inconsistently understood. Some Arab authorities ignored whales altogether and asserted that ambergris came from a fountain at the bottom of the sea or that it was a kind of marine fungus. In the *Arabian Nights*, Sinbad says it comes from an island spring but is then consumed by sea monsters and vomited up. Pharmaceutical manuals, such as *Circa instans* and its French translation from the 1400s, the *Livre des simples médecines,* were more confident that it was produced by whales. Marco Polo informs his readers on the basis of his knowledge of the Indian Ocean that ambergris comes from whales, and in one version of his travels he describes whale hunting off the island of Socotra.[19]

Ambergris tends to be gray and surprisingly lightweight in relation to its mass, resembling an aromatic version of pumice. It has a compelling smell that seems to combine perfume, the sea, and some primordial animal

Gathering nonbotanical medicines, including
a whale representing ambergris, as shown in an
illustration by Robinet Testard in the *Livre des
simples médecines,* ca. 1490. (National Library of
Russia, St. Petersburg, MS Fr. V. VI., fol. 143v)

scent. It was often confused with amber, another lightweight substance
often found on beaches. The word for "amber" and "ambergris" is the same
in most languages, and our term "ambergris" comes from the French for
"gray amber." Ambergris was supposed to be helpful in combating epileptic
seizures, but its main use was as a hygienic perfume. According to medical
treatises, it relieves suffocation of the womb and helps in childbirth just
by the effect of its wonderful scent. Ambergris was especially prominent
in attempts to ward off the plague by resisting the foul miasma thought to
be its cause.

☙

At this point, with such strange and fabulous animal substances as ambergris, we may seem to have strayed far from the narrow definition of spices as condiments, but the point of the chapters that follow is to trace the many complementary but diverse meanings spices held in the medieval period. They were not just for cooking but were employed in different ways as health and consumer items. In Chapter 1 we begin with their most obvious use, in cooking, showing what sorts of flavors were held in esteem by medieval connoisseurs and what kinds of spiced dishes were considered standard. The second chapter describes spices in their medicinal applications, as drugs to cure illness and as aromatic preventives. Beyond their direct utility in treating or repelling illness, spices were ingredients for perfume in an age that was dazzled by fragrances. Spices were credited not just with healing but with a kind of spiritual power. Chapter 3 concerns fragrance, describing how the mysterious origins and aromatic powers of spices were associated with paradise, religious transcendence, and the immaterial world.

Having established the basis for the medieval love of spices, the remaining chapters look at the consequences of this infatuation. Chapter 4 considers the spice trade, the routes of supply and how merchants, scholars, and economic strategists thought of the lands beyond the familiar borders of Europe. Chapter 5 focuses on medieval theories about rarity, scarcity, and why spices were expensive. Here geographical theories were mobilized to further the desire to obtain spices directly from the still mysterious territories where they were grown and to avoid the Muslim intermediaries who were not only economic rivals but religious enemies.

The image of spices as marvelous and their links to spiritual refinement were contested by those who believed their expense and seductiveness were emblematic of human foolishness, even sinfulness. Chapter 6 shows how moralists and literary writers viewed the passion for spices as a triumph of greed and pride in social status over modest restraint and common sense. That spices came from so far and at such cost, yet were consumed in a matter of moments, made them perfect symbols of wasteful ostentation. The final two chapters describe the denouement of the medieval love of spices, a desire that continued despite the warnings of moralists and that directly inspired the voyages of the fifteenth and early sixteenth centuries that concluded the Middle Ages and began the process of European expansion.

In all of this the mysterious was mixed with the practical. Spices were used in cookery and in medicine, but their popularity and importance went beyond utility. They were marvelous and mysterious—aspects of the world's secrets and miracles along with saints, strange animals, extraordinary natural events like earthquakes, or mythical natural phenomena including rivers of stones or lands of darkness. The quest to discover the lands where the spices grew was practical in an economic sense, but also part of the medieval desire to fathom the secrets of the earth.[20] The story of spices is about how people lived in the past, their views of the marvelous, and how they thought they could discover and exploit the beauty of the world.

ONE

Spices and
Medieval Cuisine

MEDIEVAL RECIPES

A fifteenth-century English cookbook gives a recipe for haddock in a
sauce known as "gyve," which includes cloves, mace, pepper, and "a grete
dele" of cinnamon along with raisins, saffron, sandalwood, and ginger. The
same collection also includes a recipe for Pork Tarts in which ground pork
is combined with all sorts of spices (including again lots of cinnamon),
along with eggs, cheese, figs, dates, and then baked in a covered pastry.
To enhance the elegant effect, the tarts might be covered with a mixture
of saffron and almond milk before baking to give them a golden color (a
process called "endorring"). Another English compendium has a recipe for
swan prepared simply (roasted and cut up), but served with an elaborate

sauce involving the swan's entrails, ginger, galangal, and bread colored with the swan's blood.

Spices were everywhere in medieval gastronomy. In European cookbooks for the thirteenth to fifteenth centuries, spices appear in 75 percent of the recipes. Medieval English cookbooks call for spices in no less than 90 percent of their recipes.[1] By the term "spices" we don't mean merely one or two common condiments like pepper or ginger. According to Taillevent, chef to the king of France in the late fourteenth century and author of the *Viandier,* the best-known and most widely imitated cookbook of its time, the cook's standard repertoire of ingredients included twenty separate spices (not to mention mixtures, combined powders, and prepared sauces).[2] Spices were used in ways that would seem alien now to all but the most adventurous palates, in dazzling combinations and across the entire menu, from fish to dessert and even beyond to candied confections and wine.

Much of our information about medieval food comes from around 140 cookbooks that survive from the thirteenth century to the end of the fifteenth, sometimes in manuscripts that also contain medical works, sometimes forming part of miscellanies that include observations about pastimes, such as hunting, or scientific and astrological texts.[3] Most of these cookbooks were written in French, English, and other vernacular languages, but there are some Latin cookbooks that make an implicit claim that cooking is a higher form of knowledge.

Cookbooks were not so much manuals of instruction as reports of the customs or aspirations of the taste-making courts of Europe. They were composed primarily by the highest ranking chefs, men like Taillevent, chef to King Charles V of France. His English rival, chef to the English monarch Richard II, was the author of *The Forme of Cury* (The Way to Cook), which became authoritative in the English-speaking world. By the late fourteenth century, books put together by experts of less stellar status appeared, and there was also more geographical and linguistic diversity. Important recipe collections were composed in German, Spanish, Catalan, and Italian. France was, as usual, the arbiter of cuisine, but it did not quite have unquestioned hegemony in defining elegance and fashion in the way that it would in the eighteenth through twentieth centuries. The French enthusiasm for West African grains of paradise, for example, was met elsewhere with only tepid regard.[4]

There are other sources besides cookbooks that give an impression of what was eaten, including descriptions of real banquets in chronicles and imagined ones in chivalric literature. The account books of great households, listing expenses and quantities of provisions bought or otherwise acquired, provide detailed information about what was required for both everyday meals and special occasions. Books of advice, ranging from denunciations of gluttony to medical treatises, also convey a sense of what was consumed along with what people thought they should or should not eat for either prestige or health.

These various texts show us a cuisine whose color, innovation, and love of display are at once intriguing and alien. The fact that a variety of spices was used, and used in significant quantities, separates medieval European taste from its modern counterpart in which spices other than pepper (and that in small amounts) have been almost entirely banished, or at best relegated to desserts. Along with pepper, the most important medieval spices were cinnamon, ginger, and saffron, none of which are used anymore in significant quantities in European main courses, except for saffron in some kinds of paella and occasional novelties like Lotte au Safran (monkfish in saffron sauce). Cloves, nutmeg, and mace, which cost considerably more than other culinary spices, were greatly valued and, if anything, more prestigious, though not as common as the four principal spices. What is most striking, however, is the medieval ubiquity of spices like galangal and grains of paradise that have been unknown in Europe for centuries.

From the cookbooks it is apparent that spices turn up in every aspect of food preparation and seasoning, but also that the most common vehicle for spices was in sauces to accompany meat or fish. Meat might be prepared rather simply: roasted or (more commonly than one would think) boiled. Sometimes meat was ground up either before or after a preliminary cooking, and then heavily spiced before being further fried or sautéed or otherwise put through additional processing. Where the spices are most visible, however, is in an array of sauces, such as the above-mentioned gyve sauce for fish. Some other standard examples were a sharp black sauce, made primarily but not exclusively with black pepper; *cameline* (whose name is derived from its camel color), based on cinnamon but with admixtures of long pepper, grains of paradise, nutmeg, and mace; and *jance,* a ginger sauce made with almonds and ginger. Sauces tended to be rather thinner than what we are accustomed to, the thickening agent being usually just toasted breadcrumbs and the underlying flavoring often vinegar or its cousin verjuice (made from unripe grapes). The closest modern parallel in consistency and look might be the bright green mint sauce sometimes served with roast lamb, but of course medieval sauces would have been sharply flavored with spices rather than herbs.

These sauces might or might not also be sweetened with sugar. From our point of view, one of the most peculiar aspects of medieval cuisine is the use of what we would consider dessert items (such as figs, raisins, sweets in general) to accompany or make up main courses. Some of this aesthetic survives in such dishes as Canard à l'Orange or Chinese-American Sweet-and-Sour Pork.

Besides sauces, the other main place for spices in medieval cooking was in after-dinner confections. Spices not only appeared in meat courses but were highlighted in two particular forms: in sweetened and spiced wine (served both before and after the meal), and in such confections as spices in crystallized sugar. A celebration given in 1458 by the count of Foix (in the foothills

Two Recipes for Spiced Wine

Potus Ypocras [Hippocras]

Take a half lb. of canel [cinnamon] tried [select]; of gyngyuer tried, a half lb. of greynes [grains of paradise], iii unce [3 ounces]; of longe peper, iii unce; of clowis, ii unce; of notemugges, ii unce & a half; of carewey, ii unce; of spikenard, a half unce; of galyngale, ii unce; of sugir, ii Lb. Si deficiat sugir [if you don't have sugar], take a potel [a small pot] of hony.

Piment [Pigmentum]

If you wish to make piment, take one ounce of cinnamon, one ounce of ginger, a dram each of cloves, nutmeg, lavender, cubebs, long pepper, galangal. Add two drams of grains of paradise and a half ounce of round [black] pepper. Once these have all been pounded (in a mortar) and well pulverized, put them in two pounds of brandy (aygardant) that has been distilled twice. Stir well and keep for at least 15 days. After this time has elapsed, pour off gently the liquid from the bottle that is above the spices. And then, when you wish to make piment, put three or four drops of this liquid in a bottle filled with good wine and it will become good and fine quality piment. And this is a proven recipe as many can attest.

Hippocras recipe from *Curye on Inglysch,* ed. Constance B. Hieatt and Sharon Butler (London, 1985), pp. 148–49. Piment recipe edited from a record in the cathedral archives of Girona, Catalonia, and published in Pep Vila, "El piment, una beguda confegida a la Catedral de Girona durant el segle XIV," *Annals de l'Institut d'Estudis Gironins* 40 (1999): 91–92.

of the French Pyrenees) for envoys from Hungary began with white hippocras (spiced wine) and ended with red hippocras served with rolled toasted wafers. Among the desserts was a presentation of heraldic animals sculpted in sugar with embedded whole spices. Rampant and couchant candied animals held the arms of the king of Hungary in their mouths or paws.[5]

Sugar and spiced sweets of this sort were wildly popular. The first surviving English menu for a feast, included in the late-thirteenth-century "Treatise of Walter of Bibbelsworth," concludes with "white [sugared] powder, large dragées [sugared spiced confections of various sorts], mace, cubeb, cloves, and enough other spices, not to mention wafers." Just before a papal election at Avignon in January 1371, the small assemblage of cardinals ate twelve pounds of candied spices before entering the electoral conclave.[6] The prestige of spiced sweets is also shown casually in tales of chivalric adventure, such as *Sir Gawain and the Green Knight* or the first of the grail legends, Chrétien's *Perceval*. Gawain celebrates Christmas at a mysterious castle with a hospitable lord and his beautiful and strangely flirtatious lady. They dine on fish in spiced broth (*fyschez . . . in sewe saured with spyces*) followed by wine and spices. Perceval arrives at the Grail Castle and is served peppered venison followed by candied fruit, nutmeg, cloves, Alexandrian "gingerbread," and sugared medicines (electuaries) along with after-dinner cordials such as *pliris,* a concoction of musk and camphor. These castles have a supernatural, other-worldly atmosphere, but the hosts are realistically up-to-date on what sort of entrées and desserts befit knights.[7]

Spices were featured in regular meals—at least for the comfortable classes—not just in ostentatious festive set pieces. The Catalan *Libre del coch* (The Book of Cooking), composed in 1500 for the king of Naples, offers 200 recipes. Of these, 154 call for sugar, 125 require cinnamon, and ginger is mentioned in 76.[8] Unlike the authors of modern cookbooks, medieval compilers didn't try to divert their readers by images or fantasies of a beautiful manner of life reflected in cooking. No medieval cookbook is lavishly presented with drawings or painted (let alone illuminated) decoration. The recipes are often complicated and intended to produce spectacular effects in flavor and color, but their format is rather plain. As books of instruction for experts, the cookbooks seldom give quantities of ingredients and assume a high degree of familiarity with technique and proportion. As a result, it is impossible, or at least difficult, to determine just how much clove, nutmeg, or cinnamon actually went into a classic dish, such as the stewed poultry presented in the *Viandier* of Taillevent. Anything from a quarter teaspoon to a quarter cup of each is theoretically possible.[9]

What *is* certain is that a person of even modest affluence consumed impressive quantities of spices, especially by modern European standards. This is confirmed by records of what kinds and amounts of food were dispensed to people whose maintenance was provided for by such institutions as royal or noble courts. In the early fifteenth century, for example, retainers and staff of the household of Beatrice of Hungary, mother to Humbert II, ruler of the Dauphiné in the French Alps, went through four pounds of spices per year, according to the court account books. By contrast, the average French adult now consumes just a few ounces of pepper per year, and even less of other spices.[10]

CULINARY FASHIONS

How did this taste for sharp and piquant flavors arise, especially if the spoiled meat theory doesn't work? The closest familiar modern equivalents to medieval European food are the cuisines of India, North Africa, and the Middle East, which use spices in substantial quantities and mix them together in complicated blends like curry powder. What Westerners now consider sweet spices, such as cinnamon and cloves, appropriate only for desserts, are found in South Asian and Middle Eastern meat and seafood dishes. Traditionally European and American cuisine uses one spice at a time: cloves to stud baked ham, cinnamon to sprinkle on French toast, a little nutmeg to enhance Italian sauces. The medieval palate preferred overlapping fragrant taste sensations, much as is the case in India, Persia, or the Arab world.

All this might encourage the conclusion that medieval Europe acquired its culinary tastes from the richer, more alluring if infidel world of the Muslims of the Middle East and North Africa. Contact between Christians and Muslims in Spain and the Crusader kingdoms stimulated the diffusion of citrus fruit, rice, paper, and other products of the East, along with such culinary practices as the use of almond milk, saffron, rosewater, even the widespread use of sugar. Fulcher of Chartres, a chronicler of the First Crusade, observed shortly after 1100 with an air of wry condemnation that the attractions of life in the East meant that settlers in Crusader states "have become Easterners rather than Westerners and have forgotten our native land."[11] Over a century later the German emperor Frederick II was denounced by the pope for keeping a virtually Saracen court, with a private army of Sicilian Muslims, and even a menagerie of exotic animals. An entire style of Spanish architecture under the Christian conquerors of Spain, particularly in Aragon and Andalusia, imitated the Muslim style, even in the structure and decoration of the royal palace in Seville.

Yet the habit of using large amounts of spices was not borrowed from the Muslim world—rather, it antedated the beginning of Islam and the Arab expansion. As far back as the Romans the taste for strongly flavored cuisine dominated in Europe. The Romans lacked certain spices that became popular in the medieval centuries, especially cloves and nutmeg, which at the time were cultivated only in the Molucca Islands in what is now Indonesia, but they had a fondness for a North African spice called silphium (which they managed to render extinct), and for asafetida and fish paste (now considered completely alien to European tastes). In the sole surviving Roman cookbook, purporting to be by Apicius, fully 80 percent of the recipes require pepper, and in substantial quantities. In the first century A.D., Pliny the Elder asked with exasperation why pepper, which is not actually very pleasant tasting but rather pungent, should excite such enthusiasm among his contemporaries. Who, he asked, was the first to decide that food required such additional inducement over and above normal hunger? It was appropriate for people in India to consume ginger and pepper since the plants grow wild there, but for the Romans to expend gold and silver on this passion for piquancy seemed to Pliny a measure of popular folly. Archaeological research has demonstrated that in the era of the Roman Empire, the southern coast of Egypt along the Red Sea had an intense, direct trade with India, much of it devoted to the importation of pepper.[12]

The collapse of Roman power severely hampered trade, but spices and exotic drugs continued to find their way from southern and eastern Asia to Europe, and in fact the first mentions of such spices as cloves, nutmeg, or galangal come from after the end of the Western Empire but before the spread of Islam, from the fifth to the seventh centuries.[13]

The degree to which medieval European gastronomy was indebted to Muslim influence remains controversial.[14] It seems by reason of ingredients and general culinary principles (such as the liberal use of spices) as if there should be a close connection, but there is surprisingly little to link European recipes directly to Arab or Persian antecedents. Sauces described as "Saracen" in Western cookbooks are often merely red (regarded as the color of Islam in medieval art), or they are unusual but have nothing to do with anything from the East. One recipe from a Neapolitan cookbook in the Morgan Library from the mid- or late fifteenth century actually calls for a Saracen sauce made with wine and pork fat, both forbidden under

Muslim dietary rules.[15] Even something that does have an Arab origin, the common medieval European dish known as *mawmeny* or *mamonia,* derived etymologically from the Arab *mamūniyya,* took on a very different texture, color, and flavoring. What had been a white dish of boiled rice and sweetened chicken (sometimes perfumed with musk and camphor) became on the Christian side of the Mediterranean a cold puddinglike affair made with raisins ground up in almond milk and wine with a great variety of spices and sugar, to which ground-up chicken or mutton was added. The mawmeny could then be colored in every possible hue.[16]

Rather than assuming that Western Europe acquired its culinary tastes from Muslim or other influences, we should see the love of spices as a long-term general preference shared by most of Europe and Asia over centuries. The real mystery is not where the idea of preparing food with so many condiments originated, but why Europe gave the practice up in the modern era in preference for other culinary effects, a mystery to be considered toward the end of this book.

Within medieval Europe, a taste for highly spiced food was an international style, something found from one end of the continent to the other. Piquant cuisine was as characteristic of medieval taste as Gothic architecture, heraldry, or chivalric literature. France exerted the most influence in cooking, but local preferences modified gastronomic trends rather than being submerged by them. The English used sugar extensively in cooking in the fourteenth century, when in France sugar was considered a medicine. Among the most pungent spices, the English liked cubeb while the French opted for long pepper. Italy was less interested in ginger than either France or England but devoted to saffron.[17]

Medieval cuisine had an autonomous set of rules and sense of what was appropriate. It was not simply an importation or even an adaptation of cues from the older and more sophisticated gastronomic traditions of the East, but rather a specific set of tastes emphasizing, in addition to spices, magnificent display, color, surprise, and special effects. This was a splendid, even vulgarly ostentatious cuisine whose aesthetic principles were based on delight and innovation. In the history of gastronomy, the cuisines of wealthy societies tend to oscillate between artifice and authenticity. Medieval cooking is firmly in the former category and represents the triumph of virtuosity over simplicity. Cooks of the Middle Ages had no interest in letting the basic ingredients speak for themselves, preferring complex dishes of multiple flavors and highly processed ingredients that often involved several methods or stages of cooking.

The overwhelming preponderance of dishes consumed by members of the upper classes—though not limited exclusively to them—were meat (with a preference for game and exotic poultry) or fish (required for the many fast days on which meat was prohibited). The love of artifice and spices, along with dislike of vegetables even when supposedly featured, are evident from a recipe for what is called a Cretonnee of New Peas in the *Viandier* of Taillevent. The peas are cooked, but then pureed, fried in bacon fat (considered the key step because *cretonnee* is derived from the Latin word for frying), and combined with chicken that has been boiled and then fried with ginger and saffron. Egg yolks are added to the mixture, forming a kind of thick soup.[18] Interesting, to be sure, but hardly designed to take maximum advantage of the flavor of new peas.

Spices played a central role in the medieval preference for strong flavors, display, and artifice. There was very little affectation of simplicity, so not only were spices permitted to distort or at least distract attention from the basic ingredients of a recipe, the entire dish was meant to surprise and astound. The splendor of medieval cuisine, along with its combination of variety and fixation on meat and fish, is evident from accounts of banquets. These are preserved both in chroniclers' descriptions and in more mundane records of what sorts of supplies had to be furnished. There were supplemental dishes of vegetables, soups, custards, even pasta (usually with cinnamon and sugar sprinkled on it before serving), but the banquet menus read like extreme examples of a high-protein diet. Two fifteenth-century English celebrations for the installation of important ecclesiastical officers reveal the passion for various species of birds and meat, but with little of the creative use of other kinds of ingredients characteristic of Chinese banquet menus. In September of 1465, Richard Neville was enthroned as archbishop of York, a position in the English church second only to the archbishop of Canterbury. The banquet that followed went on for several days, possibly as long as an entire week, and there were between two and three thousand guests and servants to feed. Neville was the brother of Warwick "the Kingmaker," who at this point in the Wars of the Roses was allied with the Yorkist king Edward IV.

This is an event of some fame and later notoriety because of the extraordinary amounts of food required, but it is unusual more by reason of its length than the elaborateness or novelty of what was actually served, which falls into the standard luxury display category. We have a better idea of what was ordered than the manner of preparation. The category of flesh (non-game) meat was relatively modest: 104 oxen, 1,000 sheep, 304 "veales," 2,000 pigs, 304 piglets, 4,000 rabbits, 204 kids, and 6 wild bulls. This works out to something like twenty-one pounds of meat per person (assuming three thousand were eating). Large game animals were well-represented in quantity, but not variety: 504 stags, bucks, and roes along with cold and hot venison pasties. The real attention of the hundreds of chefs involved in this production was given over to birds, from small game birds such as bitterns (200) to large splendid fowls including swans (400), peacocks (400), and cranes (204). There was room also for domestic chickens (2,000), pigeons (4,000), and capons (7,000). There were also four porpoises and eight seals, along with unspecified amounts of turbot, eels, sturgeon, lobsters, and other seafood served during whichever fast days were included during the course of the celebration. Some of the more exotic animals may have been served only at the principal tables, but still, 400 peacocks is quite impressive.[19]

The setting was the castle of Cawood, near the city of York on the River Ouse. As was customary, the seating at the feast was organized hierarchically. There were seven principal tables for the most honored guests. The newly enthroned archbishop presided at a High Table set above the others, facing out to the other tables from one end of the castle's hall. Here sat bishops, dukes, and earls. A second table accommodated the higher monastic officials—abbots and priors. Noble lords and knights occupied the third table. Clergy associated with York cathedral, led by the dean, were seated at table four, with the officials of the city of York at a fifth. The sixth table included the men of law, such as judges and officials of the Exchequer. At the last table in the hall sat sixty-nine "esquires," young men of some prominence in the royal court who wore the livery of the king. This was only the first banquet chamber. Other rooms beyond the great hall were occupied by the great ladies of the region, and several smaller chambers accommodated the lesser notables, ladies and gentlemen, and important local landowners, and a gallery included the many servants of the various guests.

The grandeur of the occasion was perhaps enhanced by the fragility of the political situation. Within months of the event, the Nevilles changed sides and briefly held Edward IV captive. Warwick fled England and attempted to return with the previously deposed Henry VI, the hapless Lancastrian monarch, but in April 1471 the Lancastrians were definitively defeated at Barnet and Warwick was killed. His brother the archbishop, despite his efforts to adapt to the new regime, was arrested and died in 1476.[20]

For the enthronement of Bishop John Chandler of Salisbury in 1414 we are better informed about the order of service and the presence of dishes other than game and birds.[21] The first course of *frumenty*, wheat porridge with scrambled eggs often served, as here, with venison, was a standard medieval item. In addition to the capons, swans, pheasants, and peacocks that one would expect, the first course also included a dish typical of the medieval affection for surprise and illusion, Pomys en Gele, which literally translates to "apples in aspic." In fact these were meatballs colored green with parsley sauce, made to look like brilliant green apples, and served in aspic. Also notable in all three courses were preparations of minced poultry or ground pork flavored with spices and combined in white soup or spiced wine, including a version in the third course of the aforementioned pseudo-Islamic mawmeny (here "mammenye").

Each course in Bishop Chandler's banquet was concluded by a "subtlety," or *sotelty*, a theatrical representation of a sacred or historical figure, an animal, or often a historical event. The subtlety, known on the continent as an *entremet*, formed a kind of intermission in the service of the banquet but could also be integrated in the meal, even at times serving as a surprise addition to the courses or at least a theoretically edible sculpture. Here the subtleties represented the Lamb of God, a leopard, and an eagle. They may have been made of pastry and decorated, but there is no evidence that they were actually intended for consumption. At a reception for French emissaries given by Cardinal Wolsey in 1520, a subtlety was prepared that consisted of a chessboard made of spiced sweetmeats (such as perhaps gingerbread) with chessmen made of sugar and spices much like those served earlier by the count of Foix to the Hungarian emissaries.

The subtleties show how much the visual aspect of the banquet counted in creating an effect of entertaining grandeur. Music might also accompany the meal, not just as a pleasant background but to herald the arrival of courses. In *Sir Gawain and the Green Knight*, the New Year's celebration

*Menu for the Feast Marking the Enthronement of
John Chandler as Bishop of Salisbury in 1414*

First Course (including boiled meats)
Frumenty (wheat porridge with scrambled eggs) with venison
*"Vyaund cyprys" (wine with sugar and spices, thickened with flour, and
ground pork or chicken)*
*Boiled capons, Swan, Pheasant, Peacock, "Pomys en gele" (meatballs in
aspic), "lechemete" (sliced meat), tart royal. Finished by a subtlety (tableau)
representing the Lamb of God.*

Second Course (including roasted meats)
"Vyand ryal" (sweetened and spiced wine, thickened with rice flour)
"Blandyssorye" (white soup with almond milk and ground poultry)
*Piglets, Kid, Crane, Roast venison, Heronsews (young herons), Stuffed pous-
sins, Partridge, "Un leche" (a tart?), "Crustade ryal" (resembling a quiche, with
an egg-based filling). Finished by a subtlety representing a leopard.*

Third Course (including fried meats and delicacies)
*"Mammenye ryal" (probably minced poultry in almond milk and/or spiced
wine)*
"Vyand" (here probably a soup)
*Bittern, Curlew, Pigeon, Young rabbits, Plovers, Quails, Larks, "Vyaunt
ardent" (something with brandy-like spirits), "Lechemete" (again), "Frytourys
lumbard" (fritters or filled pastries), "Payn puffe" (filled pastry), Jelly. Finished
by a subtlety representing an eagle.*

From C. M. Woolgar, *The Great Household in Late Medieval England* (New Haven, 1999),
p. 160.

at King Arthur's court begins with a trumpet fanfare as the first course
is brought into the hall, followed by kettledrums accompanied by fife.[22]
Visual and musical effects were sometimes combined. At the Feast of the
Pheasant in 1454, an event held to publicize a planned Crusade to take back
Constantinople from the Turks, the duke of Burgundy and his guests were

entertained by an immense pie that, when the crust was removed, revealed a group of musicians.

An illuminated manuscript picture made in 1378 depicts a banquet given some decades earlier by King Charles V of France in honor of the Holy Roman emperor Charles IV and his son (and successor) Wenceslaus. We are shown a conventional if unusually splendid array of banquet requisites and accoutrements. The king is seated high on a dais between his royal and ecclesiastical guests. In front of them are elaborate gilt saltcellars and spice vessels fashioned in the form of ships. These *nefs*, as they were termed (that is, ships), would adorn the table throughout the meal, not only fulfilling the function of holding condiments but also serving as centerpieces. A submissive servant in bi-colored hosiery is carving bread while, on either side of him, entremets are being performed in which a ship is brought in floating on a stream and a Muslim city is stormed by Crusaders. In addition to nefs, grand tables might be adorned with small fountains or *probae* used to detect poison. Gems, coral, or certain kinds of animal teeth or horns were supposed to change color or otherwise warn of poison, and they were formed into goblets or fancifully ornamented sculptures.

MEDIEVAL CULINARY TASTE

The events described thus far were all grand state occasions, which may seem in their gorgeous vulgarity divorced from anything resembling normal life. Yet, then as now, the merely affluent were able to offer a smaller-scale imitation of the spectacles of the great. The food eaten by people who were prosperous rather than fabulously wealthy was as highly spiced and as full of display and surprises as could be managed. The Franklin in Chaucer's *Canterbury Tales* is a well-off rural landowner with a particular liking for rich food. In the Franklin's Tale, one of the characters evokes a grand dinner in a great hall where magicians entertain and barges are rowed around in water as diversions, an experience the Franklin himself would have been likely to remember.[23] But let's look more closely at the order of service and how some of the dishes were prepared. Meals consisted of a series of courses, but each course was less distinct than is now the case. The menus seem to accept repetition, so that capons, venison, or wild birds might appear more than once. The organizing principle of the meal was not the nature

A banquet given in 1378 by King Charles V of France with
chivalric spectacles, showing elaborate golden salt and spice cellars and
a tableau of the siege of Jerusalem, from the Grandes Chroniques de France.
(Bibliothèque nationale de France, Paris, MS fr. 2813, fol. 473v)

of the primary ingredients (soup, fish, meat) but rather the manner of their preparation. Medical theories conceived of the stomach as a kind of oven in which food was "cooked," or processed for the body's use. The stomach had to be prepared, or warmed, as it were. This dictated that the easier to digest boiled dishes came near the beginning of the meal, followed by the more challenging, if succulent, roasted dishes, and then by what were thought of as more delicate preparations (fried food and sweets).

If every course seemed to involve meat, game, and fish, there was nevertheless an extraordinary variety of animals considered desirable to eat. Our own era, with its technologies of preservation and transport, makes available an entire world of exotica, but however innovative we may consider ourselves, our menus are comparatively impoverished, either because of unwillingness to consider certain medieval luxuries edible, or because of the depletion of the natural world. We don't seem to be interested in peacocks, dolphins, lampreys, herons, or small songbirds (larks, ortolans), but these were virtually required for a medieval menu of any pretension. Our oceans are sadly overfished and many of our rivers and lakes are polluted, so the extraordinary variety of medieval sea and freshwater fish is hard to duplicate, but environmental degradation aside, there are some medieval enthusiasms we simply don't share. Lampreys, large marine creatures like giant eels, were among the most prized dishes seven hundred years or so ago, now largely forgotten. The city of Gloucester, which used to be famous for lamprey pies, presented one ceremonially decked out to Queen Elizabeth II at her coronation in 1953. Lamprey survives as a dish characteristic of the Bordeaux region. Just as in medieval recipes, Lamproie à la Bordelaise requires eviscerating a live lamprey and letting its blood drain into red wine for a couple of hours before cooking. Other giant eels, such as conger or moray eels, also appear routinely on medieval banquet menus along with porpoises and dolphins.

Sea and river creatures were licit food on fast days (as were spices), and the interpretation of what fasting meant did not exactly require abstemiousness but rather the avoidance of meat, so that "lean" (fast-day) menus were every bit as elaborate as those for meat days. Lean items, according to Master Chiquart, cook to Duke Amadeus VII of Savoy, include roast lampreys, fresh and salted dolphins, fish pies, cinnamon-flavored bouillabaisse, fried eels in a different spiced fish broth, fish-tripe sausages, and fish jelly. In 1483, a Friday meal served in the Tower of London as part of the three-day coronation banquet for Richard III included salted lamprey, pike soup, plaice in Saracen sauce, sea crabs, fried gurnard, and baked conger eel, followed by a second course of grilled tench, bass in pastry, salmon in pastry, sliced sole, perch in pastry, shrimp, trout, roast porpoise, and gurnard again (this time baked with quinces). The spices accompanying this meal were pepper, ginger, cloves, "grains" (of paradise), mace, and a considerable amount of sugar.[24]

Game offered a similar diversity of species, many now either too rare or considered too unusual to make an appearance at table. Large animals like stag or bear were display pieces, but so were very small birds. At this time Europe was teeming with game compared with now, and its rulers devoted self-interested effort to conserving the habitat of wild animals against the encroachment of agriculture and the amateur efforts of poachers. As we have seen, Master Chiquart pointed out that the requisite supply of game for a grand feast needed to be sought out well in advance of the event. Chiquart instructed his purveyors to set out with forty horses six weeks or even two months before a two-day banquet to acquire deer, hares, partridges, pheasants, small birds ("whatever they can find of these without number"), doves, cranes, and herons. In keeping with this magnificence, Chiquart also required several hundred pounds of spices (pepper, two kinds of ginger, cinnamon, grains of paradise, and smaller quantities of nutmeg, cloves, galangal, and mace). He also ordered eighteen pounds of gold leaf for decoration.

The spices, wild animals, and gold leaf are all tokens of the festive excess typical of the high medieval culinary culture. We are dealing here with a sophisticated, ostentatious style. Nothing is more distorted than the popular idea of medieval notables feasting on crudely spit-roasted carcasses. The table was elaborately set, with great attention given to table linen, knives, salt-cellars, plates, cups, small sauce boats, and bowls. Bread was often laid at places before guests were seated and might itself serve as a kind of plate or as a sop to dip into sauces. Forks were not as completely unknown as is widely believed, but they were uncommon. Piers Gaveston, the favorite of Edward II of England, had a set of forks used just for eating pears, but he was perhaps given to showing off even by the standards of his time (the early fourteenth century).[25] The knife was the main implement, used to carve, to offer food, and to move it around the plate, sometimes supplemented by a spoon.

Courtesy books instructed diners to make genteel conversation and to avoid spitting and licking the fingers. Contrary, once again, to common belief, great attention was given to washing before the meal, an activity that might take place before sitting down, using bowls set near the dining table for that purpose, or while seated using special containers with pouring spouts called *aquamaniles,* of which a number have survived, often in the form of real or mythological beasts or representing moral or comical observations.[26]

The meal had a number of ceremonial aspects, and the relative social status of the guests was indicated by where they sat and what they were served. To the degree that the meal was a public occasion, a select group of poor people might be fed. Particularly emblematic of the medieval respect for craft and also love of rule making are the ceremonies involved in carving. Important courses made with difficult or at least challenging animals were brought to the table and carved according to the directives set down in various treatises, such as the fifteenth-century English *Boke of Kervynge.* This instruction manual, directed to higher servants, shows how to carve and serve meat, fish, and especially luxury poultry and lists the sauces to accompany them appropriately. Probably equally important as doing the job right was knowing what verb to use, a system of classification that depended on what creature was being operated on. One should not just say generically, for example, "carve up that heron"—herons are *dismembered.* The *Boke of Kervynge* puts the different formulations in the imperative, so that the lord should order his carver to "unbrace that mallard," but "barb that lobster," and "tranche that sturgeon." Knowledge of the right term showed assurance and connoisseurship—mistakes indicated ignorance or confusion.[27] Of course some animals were more difficult than others. John Russell, author of a more general late-medieval book on how to serve meals, says with a concise frustration that seems based on experience: "Crabbe is a slutt to kerve & a wrawd wight [ungodly creature]." Crab takes so long to deal with that, by the time it has been dissected and vinegar and spices have been added, it will have to be returned to the kitchen to be reheated, he says.[28]

Punctilious attention to ceremony does not mean there was no fun in medieval cuisine. Quite the reverse—the rituals of the table were part of a spectacle in which solemnity mingled with foolishness, and vulgarity often trumped elegance (at least to our way of thinking). Special visual and gustatory effects were sought after. Then as now certain kinds of dishes were expected at a high social level, in this case such delicacies as swan, peacock, or boar's head, but what was really most eagerly anticipated was the unexpected, presentations that emphasized the theatrical, or at the very least the whimsical. Cooks and their patrons were enamored of experiments with color and especially trompe l'oeil, the art of making one dish look like something else—as with the green ground-meat "apples" we have already encountered. More cleverly, Eggs in Lent consisted of eggshells emptied of their contents (prohibited during Lent) and replaced by almond milk, for the white, and cinnamon mixed with saffron to mimic the yolk. Sturgeon could be made to resemble veal; cooked meat was made to look as if it was raw by means of dried and powdered hare's blood. Birds like pheasants or mallard ducks could be cooked and then reassembled in their original plumage and so served ready-to-eat but looking alive.[29]

Such tricks are not unknown in our time but are usually employed to make inexpensive ingredients look like expensive ones, as with Chinese Mock Duck (made with bean curd), or the American Depression staple Mock Apple Pie, made with Ritz crackers. At the frontiers of contemporary cuisine, the reverse is sometimes accomplished and, in a more medieval style, something expensive is made to look humble: at El Bullí, Ferran Adrià's celebrated restaurant in Catalonia, foie gras is frozen and then powdered to resemble the humble Latin American grain quinoa (and served with broth).

Color, shape, and spectacle were as highly regarded as taste and smell. Much of the pleasure of stylish meals and proof of the cook's skill lay in how strikingly and skillfully the courses were presented. The variety and brightness of colors were dazzling. As already seen, pork tarts were given a golden hue ("endorred") achieved by the use of saffron, which was important also for flavor. Yellow, a color of opprobrium when it came to clothes, was very desirable for food. The most grandiose way to give food a golden look was to wrap gold foil around it—hence Master Chiquart's need for those eighteen pounds of gold leaf for the two-day banquet mentioned in his cookbook. Among his grand offerings is an entremet consisting of wild boar's head served with the boar's feet, the head having one side glazed with green sauce and the other covered with gold foil. This heraldic-looking dish was to be brought to the table breathing fire by means of a wick soaked in camphor and set alight.[30]

Red was also considered a distinguished color for food. A spice known as red sandalwood (a tasteless cousin to aromatic yellow sandalwood) was used in various "Saracen" dishes that, as we have seen, had little to do with any actually Arab antecedent. Color fashions changed, however, and so well-known dishes might undergo revisions over time. Mawmeny seems to have been deep indigo in 1325, yellow in 1380, and orange-red in 1420. Lete Lards, a sliced cold custard made with lard, came in all imaginable, or at least practical, colors. Great effort went into a common showpiece that combined love of difficulty with display: Fish Cooked Three Ways and in Three Colors. By means of deft handling and with the fish remaining whole, the tail section was boiled while the middle was roasted and the head was fried. The boiled portion was to be covered with green sauce while the roasted middle was given an orange sauce. The fried head was swimming in cameline sauce. Sometimes the fish too was brought out "breathing fire."

Edible pastes could be sculpted to look like animals or objects. Glazed "hedgehogs" (often called "urchins" in England), appear in many menus and cookbooks. These consisted of ground meat stuffed into a sheep stomach and then formed into a hedgehog shape. Stuck in a line along its back were sliced almonds (sometimes colored with different dyes), giving it what a modern observer might think is the look of a small Stegosaurus rather than a hedgehog. Another comical production was Coqz Heaumez, a roasted rooster set on an orange-glazed suckling pig as if riding a horse. According to the recipe in Taillevent's *Viandier,* the bird should have a lance with a flag and a tiny metal helmet.[31]

An edible entremet shaped as a castle with four towers, described by Master Chiquart, represents the height of both the medieval cult of culinary artifice and the love of entertaining special effects. Atop one of the towers is a pike prepared according to the above-mentioned recipe: cooked three ways and with three different colors. A glazed boar's head, a glazed piglet, and a skinned and redressed swan guard the other towers. All of them, it is probably unnecessary to add, should be breathing fire. In the courtyard of the fortress Chiquart placed a "fountain of love" spouting rosewater and mulled wine. A goose dressed in peacock feathers was set beside the fountain. Along the battlements were sculpted meat and bean-paste figures including hunters, horns, stags, lobsters, "hedgehogs," dolphins, and crossbowmen.

Wild boar's head glazed with parsley sauce on one side and covered
with gold foil on the other, and breathing fire. (From Master Chiquart,
Du fait du cuysine, as re-created and reproduced in *Fêtes gourmandes
au Moyen Âge,* ed. Jean-Louis Flandrin and Carole Lambert, p. 121;
photograph by Raude Huyghens)

SPICES, FOOD, AND STATUS

In describing all these impressive ceremonies and tableaux, we may seem
to have left spices behind, but in fact the glamorous flavor of spices, their
rarity and expense, formed part of the medieval culinary culture of display
and complexity. Spices are prominent and necessary in all of the traditional
banquet set pieces. The castle of Chiquart, for example, requires spices for
the wine flowing from the fountain of love, and for the ground meat made
into the hedgehogs and other denizens manning the battlements. The sauces
for the fish cooked three ways are essentially spices and herbs thickened
with bread crumbs.

Grand meals offered by important people had to involve spices, both
because of a real preference for piquant food and as a socially required mark
of status. Spices were luxurious, exotic, foreign, and expensive. They were attributes of grace and sophistication, but they also afforded sensual pleasure.

There had to be a real physical, gustatory affection for spices to sustain such a strong fashion preference over so many centuries. Nevertheless, their role in making social judgments and attributing appropriate class behavior is undeniable. Spices were among the many indices of class distinction, including manners, dress, speech, bearing, and physical appearance.

In considering spices and other aspects of medieval gastronomy, we are looking at the taste of the wealthy, at people who used food to distinguish themselves from the common mass or from the merely affluent. Every culture has a hierarchy of foods deemed appropriate to the upper classes and tends to depreciate others as betraying poor taste, poverty, or ignorance. A modern household with a reasonable claim to good taste would hardly serve guests fish sticks or canned wax beans. There are certain perennial prestige foods: truffles, lobster, or caviar, for example, that are generally expensive and in high demand. There tend to be stable social distinctions among foods—canned deviled ham has always been less prestigious than Smithfield or Black Forest ham—but class markers and fashions undergo sometimes quirky changes. Organ meats, for example, were shunned for a long time in the United States and thought of by the middle classes as food for poor people, but at the moment stylish restaurants like Babbo in New York or St. John in London have made them emblematic of serious culinary discernment. So-called comfort foods, such as meatloaf or mashed potatoes, have experienced a paradoxical vogue as jaded sophisticates rediscover the home cooking of the 1950s. As a rule, however, the boundaries separating the food of the well-off from the food of the poor are firm and clearly marked.

The foods that carried the most prestige in medieval Europe were meat, game, and fish. There were categories of food consumed by both peasants and nobles, but status was clearly marked off by quality or what was perceived as qualitative difference, most obviously the consumption of cereals. White loaves made from wheat were the only generally acceptable kind of bread for the wealthy. Peasants consumed very little bread of this fine sort and were much more likely to make do with rye, barley, millet, oats, or other less valuable and coarser grains made into either bread or its poorer cousin, pottage.

Dairy products were also regarded as peasant food. The elite idea of the rustic condition is shown by the chorus of a song written at the time of a great Flemish peasant insurrection (between 1323 and 1328), according to which peasants thrive on curdled milk, bread, and cheese. Anything better would render them incapable of work.[32] In fact, however, as far back as the thirteenth century a few cheeses were acknowledged as stylish. Brie, Comté, and Roquefort had enough prestige that they were known outside their regions of origin, but only in fifteenth-century Italy do we find a discussion of cheese addressed to an audience of gourmets. In Pantaleone da Confienza's "summa" on dairy products, cheese is for the first time a delicacy worthy of comment and discrimination.[33]

Another common food seldom found at the tables of the wealthy was sausage or any meat flavored and made less perishable by means of salting, drying, smoking, or pickling. Even if spices had been used to preserve meat (which they were not), the resulting products, today considered delicacies, would have been regarded as hopelessly rustic or at best middle class. Although a tremendous amount of attention is now given to various Iberian, Italian, and German hams like *jamón jabugo, Bündnerfleisch,* or prosciutto, these were originally designed to save meat over the winter and so not favored by those with the resources to serve fresher meat during the normally hard months. Sausages were thought of as typical of prosperous urban nobodies (merchants and the like), or of affluent peasants. It seems that in every late-medieval or Renaissance woodcut depicting a peasant wedding (and there are many), the guests are gobbling up sausages while a dog is running off with a string of them snatched from a table.

Fruit was in a peculiar category of its own. Dried and sugared fruits were greatly admired, especially those preserved in sugar syrup or made into jams or pastes (resembling the modern Spanish flat quince-paste *membrillo* or the Middle Eastern "apricot leather"). A Catalan treatise devoted solely to such "comfits" includes sugared preparations of quinces, apples, dates, pine nuts, almonds, and so on.[34] Fruit could also be cooked or roasted, but raw fruit was supposed to be avoided. The medical consensus regarded all fruit as dangerous unless cooked or sugared, because the body was thought to find it impossible to digest raw fruit fully. There was therefore a fear that fruit would putrefy inside the stomach and so lead to disease. Cherries and berries might sometimes be served fresh, and probably more fruit was eaten this way than the cookbooks and menus show us. By the fifteenth century, melons had become fashionable in Italy, but doctors opposed this dangerous trend, considering melon especially prone to internal decay. Popular approval eventually swept away these objections.[35]

Vegetables were the most consistent edible sign of rusticity, even more than dairy products or sausages. As with fruit, we can surmise that nobles and affluent townspeople actually ate more vegetables than the sources allow us to see, but there is no doubt that the upper-class diet was quite unbalanced in the direction of meat and protein. One calculation, using 1,466 recipes from various medieval cookbooks, figures that only 48 of them, or 3.3 percent, involved vegetables (including beans).[36] Among vegetables, strongly scented root crops like turnips, onions, and parsnips were regarded with particular contempt as characteristic of the diet of the rural poor. The biographer of the tenth-century monk St. Odilo of Cluny recalls how he was rebuked by the saint while they were traveling to Rome for distancing himself conspicuously from a peasant who was a member of their party because he was carrying an unpleasantly pungent food supply that included overripe onions and garlic.

The degraded life of the peasantry is symbolized by many things, according to their betters: bedraggled clothing, coarse features, dirt—but also by what they eat. A thirteenth-century German comic poem tells of a village lad popular with all the girls. His swaggering confidence is soon curbed, however, as he marries a wife who scolds and worries him. The emblem of his servitude is that he has a diet of cabbage and horseradish to look forward to. Contemptuous terms for peasants included several that focused on their lowly diet: "turnip eaters" in Germany, "pea eaters" in France.

According to the opinion of the well-off, it wasn't just that rustics had to settle for unpleasant food, they actually preferred it and couldn't appreciate decent food even when given the opportunity to consume it. There is a French story about a farmer who prospers and marries above his station. His new bourgeois wife prepares various delicacies, but, true to his peasant origins, the husband finds this refined food doesn't agree with him. Once his wife realizes the cause of his discomfort, she changes the family menu and serves things like beans, peas, and bread soaked in milk. Her husband feels much better and is considerably more cheerful. Such fare is appropriate for the laboring classes even if they rise above their origins.

Spices, preferred by persons of distinction, were potentially dangerous for the lower orders, or so the wealthy believed. Another comical French story involves a peasant who is driving a dung-cart through downtown Montpellier, one of the most famous European spice emporia. Going through the spice market, the simple countryman is overcome by the unfamiliar aromatic perfumes and faints dead away. All efforts to revive him fail until someone cleverly thinks to put a few pellets of cow dung under his nose. Immediately revived by the comforting odor of home, the peasant drives off and the free flow of traffic is restored.[37]

In fact, contrary to this image of the rustic completely baffled by spices, we know that when afforded the opportunity peasants did use imported spices, not just garlic and herbs, to flavor their food. Even in very small towns in England there were spices for sale to a largely rural clientele.[38] Pepper was the overwhelming favorite for ordinary people and the cheapest spice available. It became so widely popular that by the fifteenth century it was identified as the seasoning typically favored by the lowly and so was in danger of losing its position within the sphere of upper-class taste. A fifteenth-century medical writer stated that pepper was an appropriate condiment for rustics.[39] In the *Viandier* of Taillevent, pepper plays a lesser role in recipes than the more expensive and prestigious ginger and grains of paradise. In the poetry of Eustache Deschamps, a French moralizer, traveler, diplomat, and court poet who died in 1404, pepper is as much a sign of rusticity as vegetables. He complains about inns in the country where all that was available to eat were such disgusting things as cabbage and leeks seasoned with black pepper.[40]

All this says more about fashion and the unsettling affordability of pepper than about its actual use. The immense quantities of pepper imported in the fifteenth century show that it remained popular with all classes, but there is a connection between food prices and social prestige. As its cost declined in the twentieth century, chicken ceased to be a luxury appropriate to special occasions and came to epitomize the most ordinary of meals. In general, first class loses some of its allure if ordinary people can upgrade to it easily; a "gold" credit card means nothing if everyone possesses several of them.

Although certain foods remained firmly regarded as lower class, hence out of the question for affluent palates, it was possible to dress up plebian favorites in what might have been a momentary nostalgia for the medieval equivalent of comfort food. A fifteenth-century Neapolitan cookbook offers a recipe for humble fava beans made more sophisticated by being seasoned with spices and sugar. This was just barely plausible in Italy, but in northern adaptations of the cookbook, the recipe was left out. The exceptions made for certain cheeses and dishes, such as the Cretonnee of New Peas, are also examples of accepting or transforming ordinary, modest ingredients.[41]

If we concentrate on what people of higher status consumed, there are further gradations and distinctions between the acceptable and the truly desirable. Other than game, meat was not endowed with unusual prestige. Beef was not, contrary to what might be expected, sought out although it was certainly respectable. Pork was important in the diet of everyone above a modest level of affluence (witness all the pigs and piglets slaughtered for the archbishop of York's enthronement), but salt pork, common among ordinary people of a certain humble prosperity, was proscribed for the higher orders.

All sorts of poultry, on the other hand, were acceptable even if there was a distinct hierarchy. Ordinary domestic fowl such as chickens were consumed in great numbers at the coronation banquet of King Richard III (where, to be sure, they were gilded) and also at the Neville banquet. Capons were at the top of the domestic poultry pecking order. Among game and other "outdoor" birds, the larger and more gorgeous ones like peacock and swan were extremely prized. So well regarded was peacock that it was widely believed that its flesh was nearly incorruptible, requiring no effort to preserve, an idea that goes back to the authoritative word of St. Augustine. Peacocks are identified with courage and are the quintessentially appropriate nourishment of the brave, according to a famous "vowing" poem of the fourteenth century in which knights at a banquet pledge great deeds in the name of this bird set on a platter before them.[42]

The birds most often regarded as the natural sustenance of the nobility were partridges. In 1404, for example, Ser Lapo Mazzei, a Florentine notary, wrote to the great merchant Francesco de Marco Datini, thanking him for the gift of some partridges, but reminding Datini that these birds were really too elegant for a man in Ser Lapo's modest social station. It is true that at one time Lapo Mazzei had been a member of the Florentine government and then, he says, it had been not only his privilege but a *duty* to eat partridge, but now as an ordinary man it was inappropriate. For those of truly low status, partridge might be downright unhealthful. A physician of Bologna in a dietary treatise claimed that rustics find partridge harmful when eaten. Nobles, on the other hand (according to Florentin Thierriat, a French stylist of aristocratic tastes), eat more partridges than non-nobles, "and this gives us a more subtle intelligence and sensibility than those who eat beef and pork."[43]

What happened if, despite all these warnings, the not-so-brave people of ordinary rank but sufficient financial means started demanding peacock and partridges, going against the supposedly natural food preferences of their social position? Throughout the Middle Ages, but especially toward their end and into the early modern era, attempts were made by governments to limit the ostentatious and wasteful display of wealth, especially on the part of those deemed newly rich and hence not entitled to such tokens of privilege by ancestry. Concern over ruinous competition played a part in such sumptuary legislation, but even more important was anxiety over the erosion of social boundaries and a desire to avoid the perceived moral decay arising from indiscriminate consumption of luxuries. Most of the regulations enacted by cities and states dealt with clothes: what sorts of jewelry could be worn (or, more to the point, *not* worn) by different classes, with fur trimming and silk also coming in for special attention. Consideration was also given to banquets and the dishes served at them, to prohibit the lower orders from inappropriately showing off culinary creations symbolically higher than their status permitted (hence Ser Lapo's anxieties about the gift partridges). English sumptuary regulations of 1517 allowed cardinals, for example, to serve nine dishes at a meal, while those with property providing an income between forty and five hundred pounds were limited to three. These rules expressed obsessive concern regarding poultry and how many of the different kinds of birds might be deployed in any one service. One crane, peacock, or swan was an absolute limit. In addition, cardinals might have six small luxury birds (partridges, woodcocks), but other lords had to content themselves with four. Secular nobles might be consoled, however, with up to eight quail and a dozen larks. All this seems rather severe, but it is quite unlikely to have been effective in any event.

One would expect to find more regulation of spice usage in sumptuary legislation, but it was not a major concern. Spices were an important fashion item and a form of conspicuous consumption, but it was easier to control jewelry, clothing, or, for that matter, main courses than the purchase of spices, expensive though they were. What is important to emphasize is that the passion for spices was not confined to the highest levels of society; it was by no means limited to royal or princely courts. Moreover, this was not a passing fancy of a few years or decades. The popularity of spices and the taste for a piquant and highly seasoned cuisine did not wane until well after the end of the Middle Ages.

A revealing example of well-off but non-noble taste is a book known as *Le Ménagier de Paris* (The Parisian Book of Housekeeping), a compendium of household advice dating from the 1390s that includes more than four hundred recipes. The anonymous author of *Le Ménagier* was a well-educated, elderly Parisian gentleman, probably a member of the high bourgeoisie but perhaps a knight.[44] He begins by saying he is responding to his young wife's request that he help her learn to run a household. He acknowledges her superior birth and diffidently, even poignantly, defers to her beauty, youth, and rank while providing her with far more instruction than she probably had expected.

She was indeed very young, just fifteen at the time of their wedding. So far, according to her husband, all she knows is how to dance, sing, and make flower garlands, charming if not particularly useful pastimes that he wants to supplement rather than discourage (Prologue, 1–4). The "supplemental" result forms an exhaustive body of information and advice accumulated by someone more knowledgeable about housekeeping than any European man before or since. He has instructions on shopping for fish, dealing with servants, bleaching salt, and getting rid of fleas. He tells his wife how to recognize good-quality ginger and galangal. His tone will strike the modern reader as patronizing and hectoring, but there is a real urgency, even pathos, when he acknowledges that his wife will presumably long survive him and marry again. He wants her to be expert in satisfying the needs of a future husband and able to pass on household wisdom to her future daughters (Prologue, 4; 1.6.43, 61).

The book is a kind of album representing a decades-long assemblage of knowledge, like the series of recipes, hints, observations, and clippings a modern parent might put together as a wedding gift or a life's summary. It was not intended for public circulation and so represents, without great artifice or concern for posterity, the realistic ambitions of an affluent but not socially distinguished house. The author of *Le Ménagier* seems to have had about a dozen full-time, live-in servants. Others were hired for special occasions, so that, at least for festive meals like wedding banquets, there were something on the order of ten or twelve people working just in the kitchen and at serving. This is not the simple life, but nevertheless, on the scale of things in the preindustrial world, it is not more than would be expected for the class he belongs to.

The recipes occupy about 40 percent of the book. They are preceded by advice about such things as judging the quality and age of poultry, the seasons for trout and shad, and how best to kill capons and chickens. The recipe collection includes luxury items and elaborate preparations typical of the court, and many can be traced to grand cookbooks such as the *Viandier,* although they are not quite as complicated or showy. Partridges are to be served with a sauce consisting of rosewater, orange juice, and wine. The difficult preparation Swan Redressed in Its Plumage makes an appearance (2.5.156–58). Poussins can be made to look like partridges, but this is accomplished not by means of elaborate trompe l'oeil cleverness but simply by making the legs appear shorter (2.5.241). Beef can be made to look like venison or bear (2.5.86, 87, 147). The author advises that wild boar when fresh should be eaten with pepper, and to accompany salted boar, mustard is preferable (2.5.89), but in place of heraldic boar's head we have a sensible, minimally decorated sheep's head (2.5.358). Aristocratic lamprey and sturgeon are included, but so are modest cabbage and sausage. The author specifically rejects certain dishes as too expensive or time consuming: no stuffed mutton (not worth the effort) or "hedgehogs" (very costly and a lot of work for small result); no stuffed and gilded chicken, "which requires an enormous labor and is not the work appropriate to a chef for a bourgeois or simple knight, so I am leaving it aside" (2.5.364–66). In keeping with his opposition to mere display, the author of *Le Ménagier* offers some money-saving ideas, such as flavoring mustard with spices that have already been used to flavor hippocras (2.5.272).

Yet the author is by no means a consistent advocate of unpretentious simplicity. His banquet menus are quite impressive. A dinner of twenty-three plates in six services includes sausages, but also roast partridge, capon, minced spiced eels, veal, shad and eel pâtés, and a final course of cooked pears, spiced dragées, nuts, wafers, and hippocras (2.4.28). For a grand banquet he envisages buying cameline sauce and hippocras already made, but also plenty of sugar, saffron, two kinds of ginger, cloves mixed with grains of paradise, long pepper, and a half pound of cinnamon (2.4.55). For other meals white spice powder (one pound) and "fine" spice powder (half a pound) need to be procured.

The importance of spices in the culinary system of *Le Ménagier de Paris* can hardly be overstated. Whatever economies the author suggests, spices have to be purchased routinely and in large quantities. Even if he bought it ready-made sometimes, the author presents cameline sauce in two versions, distinguishing winter and summer varieties. His green sauce is no mere parsley or herb preparation but a complex concoction that includes lightly boiled ginger, grains of paradise, and cloves ground up together along with marjoram, parsley, and sorrel. At the beginning of his prologue to the section giving specific recipes he states succinctly: "know your spices" (*cognoistre espices*). The recipes employ about twenty different spices, including galangal, grains of paradise, zedoary, and a few others beyond the usual repertoire. In his shopping instructions the author of *Le Ménagier* gives us a good idea of what basic and prepared spices and spiced products might be bought from a spice seller (*especier*): delicacies including pomegranates, rock-crystal sugar, candied nuts, citron, and a popular sweet known as Manus Christi (the hand of Christ), a white confection made with sugar and ginger with a soft consistency, the length of a finger. A separate sauce merchant provided mustard and cameline sauce (2.4.59). Such purchases were made for special events, to save time and effort, not because they were impossible to make at home. The author in fact gives recipes for homemade versions of all these items except for the Manus Christi.

The significance of *Le Ménagier* is that the author was in conformity with the grand tradition of cookery represented by Chiquart, Taillevent, and the like, including in his use of spices for both ordinary and festive dishes. The taste for spices in cuisine was not the affectation of a tiny court elite, but rather a basic attribute of the medieval culinary aesthetic.

That culinary aesthetic embraced notions of health and balance as well as of display and fashion. This may seem strange given the importance of ostentation in the Middle Ages and what would seem to modern standards a brilliantly unhealthful set of preferences. Behind the recipes and banquet menus, however, there stands a body of theoretical knowledge and medical practice that attributed to spices a role in both the preservation of health and the cure of disease. The following chapter looks at spices as protectors of the body's equilibrium, especially their place in the theory of bodily fluids, or humors. We will then consider how spices could be considered drugs—their supposed curative properties once the balance of health had become disturbed by disease. The world of food and enjoyment shades off into preoccupations about what is now termed "wellness," in addition to worries about disease. It is a measure of their importance in the Middle Ages that spices were simultaneously emblems of pleasure and of health; symbols of luxurious display and yet medicines as well.

TWO
Medicine: Spices as Drugs

DIET, HEALTH, AND HUMORS

Food is a source of pleasure but also of unease, even guilt. The ability of reasonably affluent people to choose widely and to eat excessively creates real and imagined consequences ranging from mild indigestion to chronic illness. Overindulgence also prompts moral judgments about appetite, self-control, and the body's form. In the medieval Christian tradition, gluttony was one of the seven deadly sins, along with what now seem the more serious transgressions of pride, sloth, anger, envy, covetousness, and lust. Not only are the other sins more dangerous than gluttony to people beyond the individual sinner, but traditionally there is something a little comical about overeating. Yet gluttony, however frivolous it may seem in comparison with the dangers of greed, for example, is if anything a more prominent pre-occupation now than during the Middle Ages. The average affluent person today spends more time worrying about what might be broadly defined as the category of gluttony (diet, body fat, nutrition versus self-indulgence) than about pride and covetousness (which are perhaps not even vices now according to general opinion).

The worries in each society are different, however. Medieval gluttons were certainly portrayed as fat. As with any exaggerated physical characteristic, corpulence was regarded as undesirable, but the people of the Middle Ages were not particularly worried about weight gain. The upper classes were supposed to be reasonably trim, pale, well-proportioned, and graceful while, according to artistic and literary depiction, their inferiors were gross, misshapen (often fat), dark, and not especially clean, but thinness as such was neither so distinctively upper class nor as hard to achieve as is now the case. The life of even the wealthiest was comparatively rigorous and athletic. In a world where hunger was widespread, thinness was also not a mark of well-being.

Beyond the immediate obsession with weight, current fears about diet concern long-term consequences, such as the relation of cholesterol level to heart disease or the carcinogenic properties of certain kinds of food. Medieval preoccupations were not about the effects of bad nutrition over a span of years but rather more urgent; doctors taught that certain foods were immediately dangerous. Illness was not the result of repeated exposure over time in the manner of trans fats and heart disease, but something that would occur quickly unless countervailing measures were taken. As was earlier observed, fruit was the object of considerable apprehension because it was thought to putrefy in the stomach and produce awful vapors within the body leading to disease. Lampreys were a distinctively upper-class food but regarded as extremely dangerous because of their cold and wet nature. King Henry I of England died in 1135 a week after eating lampreys in defiance of his doctor's orders, and this became well enough known to serve as a cautionary although ineffective story. Lamprey remained de rigueur at aristocratic and even, as the author of the *Ménagier* demonstrates, bourgeois tables.[1]

Ideas of digestion also differ then and now. Spices were regarded as neutralizing many of the dangers of food and so considered important aids to digestion, a notion that might seem strange given the current Western opinion that spices are irritants that make it harder to process food in tranquility. According to medieval medical and popular opinion, however, gastrointestinal calm was not greatly valued. There was a purgative idea of how the body should digest food and the main worry was stagnation: the failure of the system to absorb what was nourishing and to expel expeditiously what was not. To the degree that spices stimulated the bowels, this was all for the best. The perceived cleanliness of the body's interior was perhaps more important than its exterior, rather than vice versa as today; the laxative more important than the moisturizer.

The importance of spices in the diet, according to theories of health in the Middle Ages, was their role in harmonizing the body's primary fluids, or humors, liquids that caused moods and affected character, and whose imbalance was a major cause of disease. A significant difference between medieval and modern opinions about diet is the importance ascribed to bodily equilibrium in the Middle Ages. The closest modern parallel is perhaps Chinese medicine and its teachings about balance in cuisine. Certain foods are complementary, offsetting the negative or extreme qualities of others. These qualities have to do with physical states, such as degree of heat or moisture, as well as with points of orientation (yin versus yang). It is not just that gustatory sins can be compensated by restraint in another direction—this would be more in keeping with the American practice of having a diet soft drink to offset a cheeseburger. Rather it is a notion of harmony and complementarity, linking foods and ingredients that belong together for reasons of both taste and balance, or even that medical balance is what lies behind the achievement of beautiful gastronomic effects, something Chinese cuisine certainly has accomplished, within its theoretical constraints.

For medieval Europe, which inherited the medicine of classical Greece as modified by Arab physicians, health as well as personality were governed by four bodily fluids, the four humors: blood, yellow bile (or simply bile), black bile, and phlegm. The goal of preventive medicine and a regimen for healthy living had to be based on avoiding giving any one of the fluids an excessive influence over the individual physiology. Disease was the result of humoral imbalance, and so the failure to adjust diet to suit the body's humoral temperament would increase susceptibility to illness, indeed inevitably lead to illness.

Humoral pathology—the theory that disease is the result of this humoral disequilibrium—was based on ideas transmitted by ancient Greek physicians, notably Hippocrates and Galen, and enjoyed unquestioned authority in the Middle Ages and the Renaissance. Humoral theory elaborates two instinctually appealing concepts: the need for bodily equilibrium (that health is a kind of moderation or balance), and a correspondence between how the individual and the cosmos are put together. The fluids of the body, according to Greek science, match up with the basic categories of matter, the four elements of earth, water, fire, and air. The elements in turn combine fundamental qualities of degrees of warmth and moisture, so these qualities are even more basic than the elements. Humors combined qualities and replicated the nature of the elements. Blood is warm and moist and is linked to the element of air. Regular or yellow bile is warm and dry and its element is fire. Phlegm is cold and moist like water, while black bile is cold and dry and conceptually and physically corresponds to earth. As in Chinese medicine, therefore, diet is not just a limited field of medical practice, but a philosophical and scientific body of knowledge, part of the fundamental order of nature. A natural and even cosmic logic runs through all living things. Human beings, according to this worldview, stand above the animals but below the level of the divine and are microcosms of earthly and cosmic harmony. Disruption of that harmony within the individual body provokes illness.

There is no such thing as a completely humorally neutral person. Everyone was thought to favor one humor or another or a combination, giving them a particular profile, referred to as a "temperament" or "complexion," words still retained for mental and physical types even if now divorced from their original physiological context. Language and thought patterns preserve certain vestiges of a relation between character or mood and skin coloration. Paleness or freckles still carry certain assumptions about personality, for example. The word "temperament" can also imply physical manifestations of character type, as with supposedly sanguine or melancholy personalities. The meaning of "sanguine" comes from the Latin word for blood (*sanguinis*) and the notion that a preponderance of blood means an essentially optimistic and extroverted nature. The word "melancholy" is related to the troublesome humor black bile (*melan* meaning "black" and

French tile depicting a man of phlegmatic temperament. The pig symbolizes wet and cold, the combination characteristic of the phlegmatic humor. According to the inscription, he is a realist and mild-mannered. Pointing to his head shows the thoughtful nature of phlegmatic people, and his carrying a purse suggests a tendency to spend money. (From D. A. Wittop Koning, *Art and Pharmacy*, vol. 3 [Deventer, 1964], plate 8)

khole meaning "bile" in Greek). Other words, such as "bilious," "choleric," and "phlegmatic," are also remnants of humoral categories.

In common with all foods, spices possessed humoral properties.[2] According to the received learning, spices were mostly hot and dry and therefore effective at counteracting the moist or cold properties of many kinds of meat and fish. Diet affected health because food influenced the humors and could either improve equilibrium, when consumed wisely, or contribute to humoral imbalance and thus illness. Certainly there were acknowledged to be many other factors affecting health such as sleep, exercise, and climate, but the most direct and immediate impact on physical well-being was thought to come from food.

General rules about humoral properties and complementarity had to be adjusted to an individual's humoral condition. A healthful regime should calibrate the qualities of various foods to the individual temperament. Beef is cold and dry, so someone inclined toward melancholy because of a preponderance of black bile should not be eating a lot of beef. For such a person pork and fish would be somewhat better because, although they are cold, they are at least moist. There were quite a lot of complexities, however. Game animals were thought to be warmer and drier than their domestic counterparts. Wild ducks would be more harmful to a person of bilious temperament than domestic ones. Young animals are moister than adults; females moister than males.

Cooking methods also brought out or tempered the humoral properties of food, and one manner of cooking was usually preferable in offsetting the natural qualities of the primary ingredients. Roasting and frying were supposed to make food warmer and drier. Pork thus lends itself to roasting because this counteracts its cold and moist qualities, but roast beef was considered less healthful because beef is already dry in its natural state. Beef should be boiled, it was thought, because this process warms and moistens at the same time. Vegetables tend to be humorally dry, so they should be boiled and chopped if they are going to be used at all, but onions are an exception as they are moist, so it is a good idea to fry them.

Dietary theories became even more complicated because humoral properties were measured by degrees. Fruit is moist in the second or third degree; the perilous lamprey is cold and moist in the fourth, or highest, degree. Pepper is hot in the fourth degree and dry in the second. Some of this is intuitive: it's not surprising that pepper is hot or that eels and fish are cold. But seemingly similar ingredients could vary greatly in their humoral qualities. Wine, vinegar, verjuice (made from unripe grapes), and must (slightly fermented grape juice) are close cousins, but according to medieval lore they possessed quite different properties. Wine tended to be warm and dry with white wine less warm than red (hence the convention of killing lampreys in red wine); vinegar, however, was cold in the third degree and dry in the first. Must was warm and moist in the second degree, while verjuice was cold in the third degree and dry in the second.

Because spices were for the most part hot and dry, they were especially appropriate for beef, goose, crane, brains, tongue, and other humorally cold meats. These required vigorously spiced sauces like cameline to temper them, whereas chicken, considered nearer to humorally neutral, needed only the milder *jance* sauce. Jance is also the appropriate accompaniment for fried fish, but boiled fish (which retains an essentially moist and cold character) should really be accompanied by cameline or perhaps a green sauce. Eels, and lamprey especially, get special treatment. Part of their danger is humoral, part is that they resemble snakes and so were thought to have poisonous properties.[3] To be on the safe side, after being killed by immersion in wine, lamprey should be dried, boiled in wine and water twice, and prepared either roasted, baked (in pastry or with a nutmeg in its mouth and cloves around its neck), or prepared in aspic and then served with an appropriately strong spiced accompaniment, such as black-pepper sauce.[4]

Spices and spiced sauces were most effective when the meat they were complementing was ground up, so that both could be digested at equal consistency. Poultry, which was less humorally charged, could be eaten simply cut up in pieces with spiced sauces, but one of the reasons for the often highly processed nature of meat dishes, in which the meat is cooked in several ways and combined with other ingredients, is to make sure that the humoral properties mix appropriately.

Within the category of spices, just as among meats and different sorts of fish, there was a certain humoral diversity. Mace and nutmeg were considered hot and dry in the second degree. Pepper was even hotter but similar in its degree of dryness. Ginger was also quite hot (in the third degree), but unusual among spices in that it was moist (in the second degree). Spices could themselves be tempered if they seemed to be too hot for the food they were seasoning. Vinegar, which was humorally cold, was especially useful to accompany spices in the summer.

Sugar, although considered a spice, was moderate, merely hot in the first and moist in the second. It was regarded as unusually wholesome, not just as offsetting opposed humoral properties but in and of itself. It conferred a benign charm on whole categories of food, such as semi-medicinal comfits (sugared confections of nuts, fruit, or spices) and even fully medicinal electuaries in which the sugar was a preservative and also served (as is still the case) to make bitter ingredients palatable.

All of these theories had some real effect on the nature of medieval cooking. The piquant, sweet-and-sour flavor and the highly worked ingredients reflect medical notions about the best way to prepare and present food. At times, however, theories yielded to popular preference, as in the persistent consumption of lampreys, or were dealt with by a kind of compromise. The habit of eating prosciutto with melon began in late-medieval and Renaissance Italy because the salty, humoral warmth of the ham would allay some of the danger posed by the cold, moist melon. Initially, however, salty cheeses, pickled herring, or caviar were recommended.[5]

The complex structure of this theory held a certain amount of flexibility or at least left room for debate and amelioration. The vogue for spiced wine could have seemed dangerous because it exaggerated the already hot and dry properties of wine. Yet doctors approved of such spiced wines as hippocras, claret, or piment. The prestigious Catalan physician Arnau de Vilanova recommended spiced wines to be taken after meals in winter because they heat the entrance to the stomach and comfort the digestion. He warned against the misuse of these "inflammatory" substances (spices and wine), but offered his own recipe for piment with his own special mixture of spices.[6]

There was a dialogue between doctors and chefs. The author of the English *Forme of Cury* states that he compiled the collection of recipes with the assent and advice of "maistres of phisik and of philosophie." Cookbook authors usually included a section on dishes suitable for invalids and gave recipes for restorative broths. An outstanding example of the latter is furnished by Chiquart, who recommends what is essentially a very elaborate chicken soup, made in a special glass container like a double boiler. The chicken or capon is simmered with gold and jewels wrapped separately in linen bags. The jewels that might be used are listed, but the actual selection is to be according to the doctor's orders, since jewels too have various health-giving properties.[7]

When the duke of Burgundy dined, doctors counseled him about what dishes were most "profitable" for him to partake of, a rather unappealing privilege of rulership.[8] Medical and dietary advice were allied, then as now, but the ambiguous frontier carried over into the genre of what constituted a cookbook. The physician Maino de Maineri (also known as Magninus of Milan) was the author of a handbook of diet and health written around 1330 in which he paid a great deal of attention to food. In fact, one part of the book was spun off and expanded as a separate list of recipes for spiced sauces. In this "little book of sauces" (*Opusculus de saporibus*), Maino de Maineri asserts that sauces are intended only for those who have delicate and humorally unbalanced constitutions. Grudgingly he admits that sauces were first invented for pleasure rather than for health, but eating sauces is not advisable for healthy people because the seductive tastes induce overeating, and moreover (here perhaps a dim basis for the later legends about spices and spoiled meat) tend to hide the use of inferior ingredients.[9]

Maino de Maineri implicitly admits that the lay public does not always follow professional advice, and that appetite and pleasure tend to trump prudence and dietary orthodoxy, something all doctors understand. It's worth asking, therefore, whether medieval people really were guided by the counsel of doctors in deciding what to eat. Did the duke of Burgundy eat the lampreys anyway? In terms of tastes and preferences, medieval diners probably strayed as often from medical advice as their modern counterparts do. The devotion to meat contradicted Greek teachings about the virtues of abstemiousness. Eels, melons, and other "dangerous" foods continued to be consumed. Such responses amounted not to defiance or rejection of medical opinion but to something more like creative or selective acceptance. In medieval Europe, as now, people adopted those aspects of medical opinion that they found tolerable. They embraced enthusiastically what they already found congenial with their own likes, dislikes, and assumptions, such as using spices to counteract excessively cold and moist foods. What they didn't like they evaded, positing their own sense of what was good for them, what "agreed" or "disagreed" with them, whatever their doctor's warnings.

In our own era certain foods have achieved largely unsubstantiated reputations as healthful. Consider the widespread belief that chicken is "light" and therefore beneficial, despite the reality of its unpleasant and unhygienic industrial mass production, or the high reputation of fish despite the dangers of pollution, the difficulty of keeping it fresh, and its often fraudulent mislabeling. People select the dietary advice they are willing to go along with. They are selective both in the sense of what they acknowledge as valid and whether or not they plan to act even on the accepted advice (for example, "I don't believe there's anything wrong with French fries," versus "I know French fries are bad for me, but I can't give them up").

A comic medieval example of reconciling personal preferences with official expertise was created by the Catalan moralist Francesc Eiximenis, a

Franciscan friar of the fourteenth century who wrote extensively about sin. In a disquisition on gluttony, he makes up a satirical portrait of an affluent priest, a gourmand who believes he is a thoughtful follower of medical knowledge.[10] The moral purpose of the discourse exaggerates the hypocritical and ludicrous greed of this grand clerical figure, but it accurately reports standard beliefs about what might be called healthful self-indulgence. The high-ranking clergyman writes to his doctor because, he claims, he has lost his appetite. He lays before the doctor his usual regimen, not only what he does and does not eat, but also his careful way of life. He likes dancing and avoids thinking about death; he claims he needs to shave often and to enjoy sexual intercourse with young women (which, it is strongly implied, he has to pay for). The importance of an optimistic attitude and the physical and mental benefits of sex (if not shaving) contradicted Christian teachings, but they were topics of conventional medical advice.

The cleric's diet is reasonably orthodox, up to a point. He eats copious amounts of poultry. His meals have lots of spices and he is especially devoted to spiced wine with wafers, although, again in keeping with medical opinion, he limits his consumption to the winter months. The cleric seasons his meat with spiced sauces, especially those made with cloves and green ginger. He indulges in a lot of spiced items between or after meals, including Manus Christi (the soft white finger-shaped candies), gingerbread (regarded as an aphrodisiac), egg yolks flavored with both cinnamon and cubeb (another aphrodisiac), and sugar-covered larks to help the liver. He also plies himself with sugared medicines in the form of electuaries.

Given all these good habits, why has he lost his appetite? The doctor's response is predictably censorious, combining outraged expertise, moral condemnation, and social judgments, as the doctor reminds the cleric of his lowly origins and hence the even greater absurdity of his pretensions. His whole manner of existence is a scandal. His diet is ridiculous. To recover his appetite and find a way out of his gluttony, the grand ecclesiastic should return to the peasant diet of his youth, the typical rustic foods such as barley, bread, and salted meat flavored with onions and garlic rather than spices.

The gluttonous cleric is obviously intended as an example of vicious behavior, but his way of pretending to be up-to-date with regard to medical fashion would have been familiar. Eiximenis was an expert on the excuses people use for their sins. Elsewhere in his long and incomplete treatise on being a Christian, Eiximenis listed typical rationales for gluttony: "Doctor's orders prevent me from eating more abstemiously," or "If I don't eat well, I'm not good for anything."[11]

What was different in the Middle Ages is that one category of food—spices—was considered both sensuous and health giving. Spices were extravagant luxuries, yet good for you, a combination that no food now duplicates. In both the medieval and modern conventional ideas about diet, things that are thought delicious are usually bad for you—melons or doughnuts; humorally cold versus foods made with trans fats. In recent times such things as oat bran or flaxseed oil have been praised as healthful, but although their proponents claim they don't taste too bad, no one already regarded them as delicious before they became identified as beneficial. There is no modern equivalent to spices in their medieval sense as luxuriously healthful. It's not widely believed that lobster, ice cream, or chocolate are both delicious and prevent disease except in the (slightly comical) sense of helping one's mood. And few would pay extravagant prices and consume as much oat bran or flaxseed as they could in the absence of the conviction that they have curative or preventive properties.

MEDICINES, EXOTIC AND DOMESTIC

If spices had this dual allure, both luxurious and healthful, it was because they were considered at one and the same time delightful flavors, prestigious commodities, and, in effect, drugs.[12] They tempered the dangerous tendencies in the foods they seasoned and complemented, but spices were also medicines, endowed with curative powers in their own right. Conceptually the difference between condiments and medicines is much wider today than in traditional preindustrial societies. This is partly because of the theories of balance and health related to food already discussed, but also because exotic botanical products were thought to have medicinal value by virtue of their rarity.

In the Middle Ages food and medicine, spices and drugs, were closely related and often (to our way of thinking) confused. The difference between a spice merchant and an apothecary was never very clear and at times nonexistent in medieval Europe. The "spicer" (as such merchants were often called) sold medicines while the apothecary often provided spiced sweets and materials for cooking. One of the basic Arab spice mixtures, *adwiya*, is the plural for what in its singular form (*dawa*) means medicine. There are some modern parallels of substances that began as medicines but later became food products, the most notorious being Coca-Cola, first sold as a healthful tonic. From Coca-Cola's transformation at the end of the nineteenth century through the 1950s, American "drugstores" all had soda fountains even after the fizzy beverages had shed their medicinal antecedents. In certain respects the proliferation of herbal medicine, of various teas and infusions of botanical products that are supposed to calm, soothe, or promote some sort of healthful state represents a return to the ambiguity of medicinal flavoring.

In the field of medicine, as in cooking, there was a fairly clear perception of spices and herbs as important and useful, but an equally clear sense of the difference between them. Spices were considered "exotics" according to the lore of apothecaries, as opposed to domestic European herbs such as rosemary, rue, borage, or thyme. Both Asian spices and domestic herbs figured in drug manuals and physicians' recommendations. There was some debate about their relative powers. Spices were considered stronger and certainly more prestigious, but not necessarily more effective. A whole branch of medical recipes dealt with what were called *Euporista* (the title of a book by Oribasius, physician to the fourth-century emperor Julian), instructions for using and identifying common efficacious herbs. According to the theory of substitution, "quid pro quo," local plants could replicate most of the curative properties of the imports.

In addition to their value as substitutes for spices, herbs had certain properties of their own that spices did not possess. Herbs were especially useful in medicine for women, particularly in obtaining what were considered illicit effects. Pennyroyal, rue, and artemesia were believed capable of preventing conception, even inducing abortion. The only spice in this category is myrrh, but inconsistently as some medieval authorities considered it an aid to conception.[13] Herbs, not spices, constituted the active ingredients in potions to aid against spells made by malevolent witches or by benign wise women. In the romance *Tristan et Iseut*, the Irish princess Iseut is given a love potion by her mother to assure mutual love with her future husband. The potion contains herbs, flowers, and roots; thus even a queen turned to

European herbs rather than imported spices for making up a magical beverage. Things went badly awry because the servant inadvertently administered the drink before Iseut met her intended, King Mark. Instead of the king of Cornwall, Iseut fell fatally in love with the royal emissary, Tristan, so that, although her marriage to King Mark was unsuccessful (to understate the case), there is no question that the herbal recipe worked, in fact like a charm. On an even more sinister level, herbs were more versatile and effective than spices as poisons. Aconite (hellebore), hemlock, and digitalis were known to be poisonous, whereas spices did not have this danger (although arsenic, known in the medical manuals as *realgar* could be listed as a spice in merchant handbooks).[14]

Both spices and herbs contributed to the large number of medieval remedies described in pharmaceutical manuals, our most useful source of information about medieval medicines. These lists of drugs and their effects are a genre of medical and botanical writing that goes back to the Greek model established in the first century A.D. by Dioscorides, a physician who elaborated an extensive list of medically useful substances, mostly but not exclusively plants. Subsequent compendia of materia medica, now often known as "herbals," were organized by type—animal, vegetable, mineral—or alphabetically, or by some other system. The basic form of these handbooks was a list of single ingredients with medicinal properties, known as "simples," as opposed to compound medicines that were combinations of these. Other handbooks known as "antidotaries" give instructions to pharmacists on how to compound diverse ingredients to form drugs that might have multiple properties. A third kind of manual was formed by books in the *Euporista* tradition of substituting common herbs for expensive exotics. Such books as *The Treasure of the Poor* by Petrus Hispanus (who became Pope John XXI) were intended to show ordinary people without expertise how to find medically useful plants. This handbook contains 526 simples, of which 366 are botanical, 111 are derived from animals, and 49 are minerals.[15]

Medieval Europe obtained its knowledge of drugs largely through Arabic and Byzantine intermediaries rather than directly from Greek texts. The Arabs were the first to consider pharmacy a separate profession or trade. Islamic learning enriched the text of Dioscorides, so that in one of the most renowned treatises on simples, that of Ibn al-Baytar, there are no fewer than 2,324 substances listed. The Arabs introduced new exotics unknown to the classical world, especially ambergris and other perfume-like ingredients. They developed new techniques of preparing medicines, including the use of sugar and the concoction of syrups, juleps (both words of Arabic derivation), comfits, and electuaries. Islamic science also advanced the cause of the humoral theories in what has been called a "new Galenic revolution." Some 300 medical texts were translated from Arabic into Latin in the course of the twelfth and thirteenth centuries.[16]

Among medieval annotated lists, the most widely diffused basic compendium of simples was the Latin treatise *Circa instans,* attributed to Mattheus Platearius, written around 1160 and later translated into French as the *Livre des simples médecines* (The Book of Simples). *Circa instans* lists 270 substances, most of them obtained from plants. It favors spices and other exotics, but gives some place to such European herbs and flowers as parsley, peonies, cypress, roses, and sage.

All of the standard cooking spices appear in *Circa instans,* and the author discusses their humoral properties, how long they may be kept, and what they are good for. Black pepper, for example, is effective at removing phlegm from the chest (especially when cooked with figs and wine) and is a treatment for asthma. It also heals sores when ground into a powder. Cinnamon is good for digestive problems like "weakness" of the stomach and liver and loss of appetite. It freshens the breath and can be cooked in wine to arrest gum decay. Nutmeg is also effective against gastric distress, especially when cooked with wine and mastic (the resinous gum from the Greek island of Chios that has a somewhat piney flavor). Mixed with cumin, anise, and wine, nutmeg relieves gas pains and flatulence.[17]

Culinary spices were of value in balancing diet and as medicines in themselves, but equally or more important as drugs were exotic imports used primarily for fragrance rather than flavoring. Their wonderful scent was thought to be a token of medical efficacy and to bring a kind of healing. We have already described certain of these aromatic products, considered spices by merchants and apothecaries: resins like frankincense, myrrh, mastic, and balsam, along with the four perfumed animal secretions: ambergris, civet, castoreum, and musk.

The animal products were certainly exotic. They came from far away and their distant and curious origins showed how complex the divine order of nature was, with marvelous aromatic and medical products hidden in animal glands and effluvia. The two components, wonderful fragrance and unusual provenance, gave an aura of almost miraculous curative power to these substances, an image aided by their fabulous expense. Ambergris was considered the sovereign preventive drug against the plague. In one of the first treatises written in response to the catastrophic Black Death of 1348, an epidemic that killed between one-quarter and one-third of the population of Europe, the Catalan physician Jacme d'Agramunt, addressing the king of Aragon, recommended that aromatic pills be burned as incense to ward off the disease. Ingredients of the pills, intended "for great lords," included ambergris, aloe wood (not to be confused with the common plant known as aloe vera, still used in soaps, handcreams, and the like), myrrh, frankincense, storax, dried rose petals, and sandalwood. The fragrance of ambergris combated the foul miasma that was thought to cause epidemics, especially the plague. In a similar but more exhaustive investigative report in the aftermath of the Black Death, the medical faculty of the University of Paris recommended carrying around sweet-smelling ingredients in what were called "ambergris apples" (*pommes d'ambre*, the origin of the English word "pomander"). These were openwork metal balls that could be filled with various combinations of aromatics that varied according to recipe, availability, and budget. They were portable and so could accompany the bearer around the dangerous infested streets, an advantage over medical incense.

The University of Paris "house blend" for pomanders calls for storax, myrrh, aloe wood, ambergris, mace, and sandalwood. Some pomander recipes involve dozens of ingredients producing a complex combination of aromas. As is often the case, however, the highest level of prestige (and presumed efficacy) was in the form of quiet and expensive simplicity. The king and queen of France, according to the Paris doctors, should carry lumps of pure ambergris in their pomanders.[18]

In addition to culinary and fragrance spices, the herbals contain a small but impressive group of animal and mineral substances. These figure as spices because of their high unit value and exotic origins. Lapis lazuli, a semiprecious stone imported in the Middle Ages from Afghanistan, was a regular item in pharmaceutical guides and listed as a spice in Francesco Pegolotti's merchant handbook—along with "dragon's blood," musk, and mummy, as we have already seen.

A copy of the *Livre des simples médecines* in St. Petersburg and another

> ### A Prescription Against the Corrupt Air of the Plague
>
> *The regimen to be observed against pestilential air, in seven parts, the first of which concerns the rectification of rotten and corrupt air. . . . Great lords can benefit from a perfume made of the following ingredients: lignon aloes and ambergris (two drams each); the best select myrrh and pure frankincense (1 oz.), camphor, storax (1 oz.), dried rose petals (2 drams), "Makassarene" sandalwood and leaves of myrtle (1 oz.). Pulverize these more or less together with resin* [lapadano *in the original, probably a resin derived from* Cistus creticus, *which grows in Cyprus, Crete, and Turkey; not to be confused with the opiate* laudanum] *or rosewater of Damascus in which camphor has been dissolved. These can be made into pills or troches.*
>
> From Jacme d'Agramunt, *Regiment de preservació de la pestilència* (Lleida, 1998), p. 62, written in Catalan in 1348, the year of the Black Death.

in Paris probably copied from the same manuscript illustrate the perceived medical importance of nonbotanical substances. Both copies include two pictures of apothecary shops where shelves behind the counter are filled with labeled substances not, as one might expect, hidden away in jars but rather in their pristine form. A few aromatic botanicals are displayed, such as mastic, myrrh, mace, and Indian dried plums called "myrobolans," but the illustrator, the great French illuminator Robinet Testard, has here emphasized remedies with more shape, color, and visual drama, things like coral, cuttlefish cartilage, green vitriol (ferrous sulfate), pearls, azurite, glass, and solidified lynx urine (*pierre de lynx,* thought to be related to amber). Mummy is depicted in its bulk or "wholesale" form, an entire corpse reposing in its opened coffin.[19]

Gems were another type of valuable (in this case extremely valuable) nonbotanical object of exotic origin credited with curative powers. The supposed healing properties and occult strength of gems gave rise to an entire learned genre of books called "lapidaries" that catalogued precious stones and their powers. Like spices, jewels had humoral qualities of hot, cold, moist, and

Apothecary shelves showing various nonbotanical medical substances,
including mummy, in an illustration by Robinet Testard from the
Livre des simples médecines, ca. 1490. (National Library of Russia,
St. Petersburg, ms. Fr. V. VI., fol. 166v)

dry. Their different colors were also signs of the various forces they conveyed, similar to the diversity of planetary influences in astrology. According to Marbode, bishop of Rennes in Brittany and the author of an eleventh-century lapidary, the power of precious stones resembles that of spices and herbs. Jewels with medical uses included topaz to soothe hemorrhoids, and bloodstone, which when ground up and mixed with pomegranate juice was considered good for the eyes. The black semiprecious crystal jet was ground up and spread around a room as a fumigant to provoke menstruation (providing reassurance against unwanted pregnancy). It was also a test for virginity and an antidote to the effects of evil incantations.[20] Pearls were especially important as they are softer than other precious stones and could be crushed and swallowed to staunch hemorrhages, recover from fainting, and alleviate diarrhea. Crushed pearls were also good for stimulating the flow of milk in nursing mothers.[21] According to a late-medieval manuscript falsely attributed to Arnau de Vilanova, a medicine to ensure the perpetuation of youthfulness, to be taken twice a day, includes both spices (ambergris and musk) and tiny pieces of gemstones (pearls, sapphires, rubies, and coral).[22]

That gems have healing properties may seem absurd to those of a reasonably scientific turn of mind, but it remains a widely accepted idea, especially the belief that crystals can cure disease or improve mood and insight. Shimmering substances seem to project ideas of health. Just one of many examples: a recent issue of a supposedly hard-nosed business publication touts a "microdermabrasion system" (facial scrub) made with ground-up gemstones and sold under the label "Healing Gems."[23]

All of these substances—plants, animal products, gems—were "simples" and could be combined to form various compounds. Pharmacists had to know how to grind up mixtures of simples according to medical instructions or their own ingenuity. Pounding and grinding together these aromatic products was a tedious task and became a symbol of the art and labor of the medical or culinary expert in spices, the cook and the pharmacist. The mortar, an emblem of sophisticated cooking in the Middle Ages because of its use in grinding spices, has remained the preeminent symbol of pharmacists, just as the word "recipe" in most languages means both instructions for cooks and prescriptions for druggists, a reminder of the conceptual similarity of the two professions.

Compounds were catalogued in antidotaries such as the thirteenth-century *Antidotarium Nicolai,* a tract that led to many imitations and elaborations. In its different versions the *Antidotarium Nicolai* gives between 110 and 175 compound remedies. An antidotary composed by Armengaud Blaise in about 1300 lists between 49 and 73 medicines (according to different manuscripts) and was organized by the form of medicine: syrups, electuaries, pills, and so on. Some of these compounds appear to be elaborate and expensive ways to relieve routine complaints. A *potio muscata,* musk and sea coral in a decoction of anise and dried figs, was effective against gas pains. A compound known as *yera pigra abbatis* combines aloes, lapis lazuli, and bitter apple (colocynth) and is good for stomach pains and melancholy. Pills made from dragon's blood, sumac, and opium are good for insomnia.[24]

The queen of all compound preparations was "theriac," a panacea by reason of the extraordinary number, quality, and, in many cases, peculiar nature of its ingredients. Theriac began in the classical era as an antidote to poison and then became credited with the power of curing diseases as well as preventing their onset. The most celebrated medieval variety of theriac came from Montpellier, site of one of the most famous medical schools. Montpellier theriac contained no fewer than eighty-three ingredients, mostly aromatic exotics, and there was an annual ceremony in which these were displayed and then solemnly mixed to assure the public that only genuine substances were used.[25]

Intimidating "medicines" of these sorts have given the Middle Ages a bad reputation for perverse strangeness, but it is worth remembering that modern medical experiments have produced such things as Byetta, a recently approved drug for diabetes derived from gila monster venom; horseshoe crab blood (which detects bacteria that can infect implants, such as artificial heart valves); and cadaver skin (used in cosmetic treatments to fill in wrinkles). What is really different about the Middle Ages is that all of these spices, jewels, potions, and electuaries were luxury items as well as medicines. Medicine remains expensive today, certainly, but no one leaves their prescription drugs out on the piano or coffee table to display their good taste and ability to afford them. In certain circles illegal drugs may be subjects of snobbish discussion, but because they are illicit they are hard to show off to the world at large.

Medicine may be allied to personal satisfaction in such specialties as cosmetic surgery or sports medicine, and some people talk or even boast about their psychotherapy, but this is hardly in the same category as jewels, clothes, gadgets, or other consumer items. By contrast, even in the midst of epidemics, medieval elites displayed their status and discrimination through such devices as beautiful silver pomanders and the healthful aromatic haze of perfume, incense, and medicine. The boundaries between wellness and luxury were nonexistent.

Chivalric romances, too, created an appropriate aristocratic but also attractively mysterious atmosphere through the presence of medical luxuries. As mentioned earlier, Perceval at the Grail Castle was served sugared medicines (electuaries) along with after-dinner cordials of compound medicines. In the chivalric poem *Girart de Roussillon,* French princes negotiate to serve the Byzantine emperor in Constantinople, and he treats them with great dignity and consideration. At the emperor's orders they are lodged near the great church of Hagia Sophia, and their rooms are strewn with silks and scented with burning balsam, tokens of the emperor's generosity as well as his ability to dispense largesse, "for no other king matched his wealth." In addition he bestows gifts of spices, gems, sable pelts, rings, brooches, and vases of balsam and theriac.[26] Even mummy had a certain consumer cachet. Shakespeare's Othello, a Moor and so familiar with the East, possessed a handkerchief (in fact the fatal handkerchief given to Desdemona) "dy'd in mummy."

From these dizzying heights of costly imports, we turn to humble domestic herbs to get an idea, partially by contrast, of what spices could and could not do. Doctors distinguished between herbs and exotics and acknowledged that their practice was to prescribe modest local ingredients for the poor and fine expensive spices for the rich. According to an eleventh-century Latin verse, "in return for mere words [of gratitude] we use mountain herbs, but for real money we recommend spices and aromatics."[27] It's not that herbs were less likely to work—after all, many compound drugs contained herbs as well as spices, and the manuals of drugs itemized European leaves, grasses, and flowers. Expensive ingredients were sometimes considered stronger or more reliable, but they were deemed appropriate for the wealthy simply by reason of their cost. This may reflect the desire of doctors to make a profit from what they prescribed, but these sorts of ingredients were what the wealthy expected. Why recommend sage when dragon's blood is available at ten times the price? Why buy a fifty-dollar watch when a five-thousand-dollar model will keep accurate time equally well?

The rich sometimes evinced a contemptuous pity for the inability of the poor to afford the best medicines. In a French poetic version of the Paris physicians' plague advice, Olivier de la Haye (writing in 1426) says that the poor, who can't buy the pomander mixture recommended by the medical faculty, will just have to make do with prayer.[28] In general, however, herbs were considered effective "generic" substitutes for spices and, as with poisons and love potions, there were also some things herbs could do better. A summary of the quid pro quo between exotics and herbs is contained in a letter written in 1147 by Wibald, the abbot of several important monasteries (Stavelot, Corvey, and Monte Cassino) to a friend suffering from a cold. The abbot promises to send a medicine known as *dicalamentis* (a mixture of such common garden plants as parsley, catmint, lovage, celery, pennyroyal, wild thyme, and fennel) to combat the effects of winter. He also promises that this dicalamentis, "although cheap, has the same effectiveness as *diamargariton*," a more expensive compound of powdered pearls, cloves, cinnamon, galangal, aloes, nutmeg, ginger, ivory, and camphor.[29]

Another example of substitution is found in the directions for an operation given by John of Arderne, a fourteenth-century English surgeon who perfected a treatment for anal fistulas, a condition that was thought in the Middle Ages to be extremely dangerous. Once the fistula was laid open, there was the problem of stopping the flow of blood. The surgeon could employ the standard exotic styptics, such as dragon's blood, Armenian bole (a kind of yellow compacted earth), or Arabian hepatic aloes. Or he might have recourse to more homey remedies: the herb walwort (*Parietaria officinalis*), burned chicken feathers, or powder made from a hare burned with old linen cloth. John tells surgeons to use more expensive and "noble" medicines for the aristocracy, but he says explicitly that the domestic products will work equally well if not better. He credits walwort in particular with excellent healing powers. In his various works, John instructs the reader how and where to find herbs in the English countryside based on his own experiences. Clearly the practitioner himself is expected to do a certain amount of botanical foraging.

In the later stages of healing from the anal fistula operation, John calls for using a compound medicine known as blood of Venus. Garden-variety blood of Venus is based on an herb called alkanet (*Alkana tinctoria*), but there is a rarer mixture meant for nobles in which the active ingredient is blood taken from a virgin girl of nineteen when the moon is in Virgo and the sun in Pisces. Both work, but which one to choose depends on the social position of the patient.[30]

WHAT DRUGS WERE SUPPOSED TO DO

With all of the exotic spices, minerals, strange animal products, and common or obscure herbs used in medieval medicine, their particular effects are hard to catalogue and categorize. Some are fairly simple: licorice was regarded as good against chest problems, including cough (for which it is still used). Other drugs had several applications that don't necessarily have much to do with each other. Lapis lazuli, according to *Circa instans,* was effective at purging melancholia but also against quartan fever (malaria). Absinthe, quite a versatile drug, was supposed to help disorders of the intestines and spleen, provoke menstruation, combat drunkenness, and drive out worms. While it would be easy to dismiss medieval pharmacology as entirely specious, there were rules and applications just as there are for Chinese medicine, which has a similar love of unusual ingredients and complex ideas of balancing their properties with the constitution of the individual patient. In both cultures, the role of the pharmacist is superior to that of the modern Western dispenser of doctors' decisions.

Chinese and medieval medicine share a preoccupation with what might seem, in the context of a world full of potentially fatal diseases, minor disorders. Pharmacological manuals pay more attention to hemorrhoids than smallpox, to headache than to plague. In part this reflects the implicitly acknowledged limitations of medieval prescriptions, the relative efficacy of remedies for stomach pains or sores as opposed to making great claims to cure diseases that were often fatal. At the same time the experiences of people who have annoying but not serious illnesses are in a sense more important to medical practice because these people survive as return customers. Discomfort or conditions that are humiliating or partially incapacitating are the cause of more morbid attention than the scourge of diseases about which little or nothing can be done. Even theriac, the universal cure, was deemed more effective against nonspecific fluxes and vapors than against severe diseases.

This does not mean that plague tracts and other attempts to deal with such scourges simply ignored spices and other drugs, but that they devoted more attention to prevention than to treatment. They had more suggestions for warding off the disease than for how to treat it once contracted, and given the theory that foul odors (perhaps released by an earthquake somewhere) caused the onset of epidemics, aromatic products were the obvious means of prevention.

In general, spices seem to be versatile drugs, but not very specific. There was a sense that they were powerful, but considerable variation in how to prescribe them or make them work. For the modest goal of bodily equilibrium, the hot and dry properties of spices were clearly applicable and the rules for how to use them, although complex, were codified. On the other hand, although medical experts likened their putative occult and (in terms of the science of the era) inexplicable effects to the action of a magnet in attracting iron, spices don't seem to have been as reliable, as shown by the multiplicity of often contradictory recipes. This is important, not merely to show the deficiencies of medieval pharmacology, which are now self-evident, but to get an idea of what people thought medicines could do and what they were for. It is not as obvious as saying that spices cured or prevented disease, because drugs were used not just to treat illness but to induce a more general, pleasurable atmosphere of well-being.

In connection with well-being and relieving annoying but not life-threatening ailments, enhancing sexual desire and alleviating sexual dysfunction were prominent. Humoral balance affected sexual performance just as it influenced mood and susceptibility to other ailments. Impotence might be the result of spells or other unnatural forces, but in general, indifference to sex or unfulfilled desire were thought to be caused by an insufficiency of bodily heat and a corresponding excess of the colder humors. Melancholy was especially problematic as it represented the combination of cold and dry that discouraged both lust and fertility. According to medical theories, heat physically characterized the sexual urge in a way that persists metaphorically today in the common understanding of desire as "burning," or typifying an alluring person as "hot." Also, not completely uninstinctually, moistness was associated with fecundity and the production of sperm. Spices, which tended to be hot and dry, were thought to increase sexual potency, but an ideal sexual stimulant was one that was simultaneously hot and moist. Ginger, which had this unusual combination, was probably the most important aphrodisiac spice.

In a treatise on sexual intercourse (*De coitu*), a Benedictine monk and translator from the Arabic known as Constantine the African (who died in 1087) lists eighteen pharmaceutical remedies for sexual problems and stimulants to better sexual accomplishment, most of them electuaries but also a few ointments. Constantine's unusual background as a North African Christian familiar with Arabic gave him the ability to translate what had originally been ancient Greek medical works previously unknown in the medieval West but which earlier had been rendered into Arabic. Constantine also translated original Arabic medical treatises such as Ibn al-Jazzar's compendium "Provision for the Traveler and Nourishment for the Sedentary" (ca. 900), which offers many suggestions for alleviating sexual diseases and discomforts of both men and women. It may seem odd that a monk at Monte Cassino, the first monastery established by St. Benedict, should occupy himself with a work on sexuality, but *De coitu* was, after all, part of the widespread revival of classical learning and at any rate addressed to a lay rather than a clerical audience.

All of Constantine's enhancements of potency feature spices, because their humoral properties alleviated the coldness thought to be the basic cause of impotence. Ginger, cinnamon, cloves, along with various herbs are recommended in different combinations. An electuary suitable for impotence due to an excessively humid nature (so someone with a melancholic or phlegmatic temperament) includes anise, long pepper, black pepper, ginger, cinnamon, galangal, mastic, and licorice. A simple combination of cloves and milk is also effective. The patient is advised to avoid cold foods like cucumbers, lentils, fish, and melons that restrict the generation of semen and depress sexual desire.[31]

Constantine's name and reputation did not remain confined to the relative obscurity of the world of medical expertise. In the story offered by the Merchant in the *Canterbury Tales* Chaucer mentions some typical efforts to enhance sexual energy. As with the gluttonous cleric of Eiximenis, the character taking the medication is contemptible, or at least pathetic—the elderly January, in the Merchant's Tale, who is marrying youthful May. On his wedding night, January fortifies himself with spiced wines accompanied by electuaries according to recipes set down by Constantine, who by this time has a somewhat dubious reputation:

He drinketh ipocras, claree, and vernage
Of spyces hote, t'encressen his corage;
And many a letuarie [electuary] hadde he ful fyn
Swiche as the cursed monk dan Constantyn
Hath writen in his book *De coitu*
To eten hem alle, he nas no-thing eschu.[32]

The fact that some spices might be considered sexual stimulants reflects the unstructured nature of what could at different times and places be regarded as aphrodisiacs. Spices might have the humoral properties that should encourage potency, but in fact so many different substances were credited with this power that it would be misleading to single out spices as in any sense unusual in this regard, and it would be wrong to explain the attraction of spices on the sole basis of their supposedly stimulative power.[33] The pharmaceutical handbooks don't actually say much about sexual stimulation. According to *Circa instans,* "Indian nuts" (by which is meant coconuts) are probably hot and dry, but according to some experts, hot and moist because they have the power to aid sexual intercourse and generate the good kind of blood. The author says here that substances that are hot and dry also are effective, so that by implication most spices would work, but he doesn't elaborate on this.[34]

What it means for something to "work" in this context is different from what we are familiar with. Although we live at a time when herbal medicine, "natural" remedies, and homeopathic cures have become immensely popular, most people still consider modern medicine a sign of historical progress, a reassurance that we live better than people did in the past. The renewed popularity of traditional cures says something about the perceived inadequacies of modern medicine, its impersonal methods and neglect of "holistic" ideas of individual equilibrium. Contemporary medical practice has also tended to be uninterested in well-being, in anything beyond the relief of symptoms, except insofar as it preaches an ethos of secular self-denial and prevention in the form of nutritional and other restrictions.

Paramedical fashions now fill the "well-being gap." Spas, spiritual retreats, and other wellness activities are intended as regimen (to get in shape), indulgence, and spiritual inspiration. The language of relaxation, sensory stimulus, and personal centering used to describe such experiences, along with notions of balance, equilibrium, restoration, detoxification, show how medicine and health can become more than unpleasant necessities and, rather, opportunities for expensive enjoyment. We may no longer see legitimately medical drugs as pleasurable—candy is different from medicine, perfume is different from hygienic fumigants—but some of the same sense of healing, of the beauty of natural ingredients, and above all of the power of fragrance or of aromatic products to produce beneficial effects is present in both the medieval and the modern periods. However paradoxical, the contemporary desire for expensive tranquility helps us understand why spices were regarded in the Middle Ages as both pleasurable and healthful, as drugs and as perfumes.

THREE

*The Odors of
Paradise*

Spices were used more to season food in medieval Europe than for any other purpose. The most important spice was pepper, and although it appears in drug manuals, pepper was overwhelmingly a culinary spice. Of the large quantities of all spices imported to Europe from Asia, a relatively small amount found their way into use as medicine or perfume. Yet fragrance, even more than gastronomy, explains the allure of spices because perfume (defined here to include incense, fragrance for disease prevention, enhancement of atmosphere, as well as personal adornment) joined together so many appealing effects. Fragrance was healthful and credited with crucial healing properties, yet it was also a highly sought after consumer product. Perfume heightened sexual attraction yet it was an emblem of holiness. It was condemned by moralists as a vanity and incitement to lechery, but it formed part of the ritual of church services and was associated with the scent of the terrestrial paradise of Eden and of the pleasing odor emitted by saints (both living and dead) as proof of their unusual merit. Nowhere is the versatility of spices and their costly desirability more evident than in the medieval infatuation with fragrance. What smelled wonderful had to be marvelous in its own right.

There was ample precedent for regarding perfume as sublime, both sexually and religiously. With poetic obsession, the biblical Song of Solomon details an atmosphere of love and sexual enchantment thick with scented ointments and perfumes. Myrrh, frankincense, spikenard, saffron, and cinnamon are mentioned, along with "all the chief perfumes" and "all the powders of the perfumer." To be sure, this love poem of a bride and bridegroom was taken by Christian writers to symbolize the union between Christ and the Church, but the mingling of erotic and sacred is conveyed by the constant evocation of fragrance. The longing of the bride is expressed in erotic aromatic terms: "While the king was at his repose, my spikenard sent forth the odor thereof. A bundle of myrrh is my beloved to me, he shall abide between my breasts" (1:11–12). The bridegroom echoes this fragrant eagerness: "How beautiful are thy breasts, my sister, my spouse! Thy breasts are more beautiful than wine, and the sweet smell of thy ointments above all aromatical spices" (4:10). In the Song of Solomon the bride and groom adorn themselves with perfume and ointments but they also use the notion of perfume to express desire and fulfillment: "My beloved put his hand through the key hole, and my bowels were moved at his touch. I arose up to open to my beloved: my hands dropped with myrrh, and my fingers were full of the choicest myrrh" (5:5–6).

Christian interpretations considered the constant evocation of perfumes to be a sign of divine presence. The third-century Alexandrian theologian and commentator Origen said that the bridegroom in the song was Jesus and that the bride and the maidens run after him because of his holiness, symbolized as fragrance.[1] The divine scent demonstrates something that can be tangibly felt, but not by the common senses of sight, hearing, or touch. The sacred aspect of olfactory sensation was reinforced by its unseen intensity.

Before the destruction of the Temple in Jerusalem, Jewish ritual involved sacrifices accompanied by quantities of spices burned as fragrant offerings. Spices appear throughout the Old Testament, especially in the descriptions of ceremonies. One of the Lord's commands to Moses in the book of Exodus was to build an altar covered with gold to burn incense (Exodus 30). The altar should itself be anointed with a holy oil made "after the art of the perfumer" with myrrh, cinnamon, calamus, and cassia in an olive-oil base. The incense powder to be burned on the altar is also described: "And the Lord said to Moses: Take unto thee spices, stacte [probably storax], and onycha [the shell of a Red Sea mollusk that emits a strong scent when burned], galbanum of sweet savor [the resin of an Asiatic plant, *ferula galbanitula*], and the clearest frankincense" (30:34). Exodus further instructs that these aromatics too are to be "compounded by the work of the perfumer" and "most holy shall this incense be unto you," so holy that it is forbidden to use it for personal pleasure on pain of death or banishment.

At the time of the Second Temple, according to estimates, 520 pounds of incense were burned annually in Jerusalem. The Roman conquest and the Diaspora ended such ceremonies; the use of spices in Jewish religious life diminished almost to nothing. A remnant of the fragrance of the lost Temple is the practice of handing around spices after the blessing recited at the end of the Sabbath and other festivals, a prayer known as the Havdalah. Ornate boxes used to hold spices for the Havdalah have survived, some in fanciful shapes like castles or towers, but this practice doesn't appear to be medieval and is attested to only from the sixteenth century on.[2]

The religions of classical "paganism" were very enthusiastic about incense. The odor of incense from countless sacrifices billowed forth from the precincts of the many temples. The gods received tribute from incense offered in both public ceremonies and private devotions. A third-century fresco from Roman Syria shows the proper form for solemn state occasions, as a government official places incense into a dish set on a column while smoke rises from a metal tripod with a vase-like opening.

Banquets were secular occasions to express a similar love of fragrance. Guests were even anointed with perfumed oils while the meal was served. With a typically vulgar self-satisfaction, Trimalchio, the newly rich host of the *Satyricon* by Petronius, spreads a perfume made with spikenard on his guests at the drunken end of an interminable and ostentatious meal.[3]

In reaction to the Roman passion for incense for both religious and

A Roman official making an offering of incense,
as shown in a painting from a third-century temple at
Dura-Europos in Syria. (Yale University Art Gallery,
New Haven)

pleasurable occasions, early Christianity denounced the use of aromatic
substances in connection with worship. Perfume was associated less with
cleanliness or purity than with the Roman bathhouse and brothel. Nevertheless, the idea that pleasant fragrances were healthful, even sacred, could not
easily be dispensed with, and the New Testament offered some encouragement for regarding aromatic substances as peculiarly appropriate to Christ.
The wise men of the East brought frankincense and myrrh in addition to
gold for the newborn savior. Jesus had not disdained the offering of spikenard ointment spread over his feet by Mary Magdalene. Rather it was Judas

who rebuked her for wasting money on this costly purchase, money that he said might have better been given to the poor (John 12:3–8). There was therefore a Christian tradition that incense and perfume were attributes of sanctity even apart from Roman customs.

As with so many aspects of Christian ritual and its political setting, the conversion of Emperor Constantine in the early fourth century changed the official attitude toward incense. The church accepted the practice of burning fragrant resins (eventually this would be limited to frankincense), but insisted it take place only within the church during public ceremonies, not inside the home. There were also a few other sacred applications for aromatic substances. The papal coronation included a ceremony at the Lateran basilica where the new pope received symbolic keys, a shepherd's crook, and a purse holding twelve stones and a quantity of musk. The stones symbolized the apostles and the musk evoked St. Paul's statement "for we are in the aroma of Christ" (2 Corinthians 2:15).[4] Chrism, the holy oil used to anoint clerics and kept by bishops for that purpose, was supposed to be derived from balsam, a resinous liquid from Middle Eastern plants. Fragrant oil was also used in royal unctions and anointing at coronations.

Chrism was credited with certain occult powers. A fourteenth-century document gives a formula for summoning a demon that will reveal where treasures lie buried. This complex ritual involves killing a cat that has been nourished (partially, one assumes) on chrism and holy water and using its skin to make bands to outline a circle in which the invocation to the demon is to be made.[5]

The world of Islam presents a paradox. Arabia and Persia were sources of many fragrant resins, such as frankincense and balsam. It was also via Islamic civilization that the rarest and mostly highly prized aromatics were brought to Europe, including ambergris, musk, camphor, and aloe wood, which were used as perfumes, medicines, and even food flavors. Yet alone among the great world religions, Islam has consistently rejected the use of incense in both public and private worship. It is not that aromatic substances are not regarded as at least potentially sacred. According to the Koran, the fountains of paradise will be scented with ginger, camphor, and musk.[6] But prayer is more a profession and a form of teaching and instruction than the interpenetration of this world and the next.

In Christianity the sense of perfume as sacred took many forms: the presence of incense at church services, the notion that what is holy shows itself by fragrance, and the idea that sacred places on earth, especially the Garden of Eden, are the true home of spices. Fragrance stands as a kind of beauty and denotes other-worldly holiness. It is incongruous, therefore, that Christianity tended to carry with it, at least officially, a mistrust of the erotic uses of scent and a greater focus on purity. In the material world the saints were certainly not consumers of perfume, but in death a saint's corpse exuded a wonderful aroma. Church fathers praised the magical, other-worldly spiritual fragrance of the saints while denouncing the adornment of ordinary living bodies with perfume. John Chrysostom said that nothing is more unclean for the soul than when the body is perfumed. Such a worldly fragrance is the sign of inner stench and filth.

The same paradox is present in the biographies of saints who deliberately sought mortifications that might include suppurating wounds, disgusting infections, extremes of uncleanliness, and all the resultant horrible odors. One of the most celebrated and extreme saints, Simon Stylites, who lived for decades on top of a pillar in Syria, exemplifies this duality of olfactory horror and fragrance. He cut himself with ropes, and the wounds festered. Gangrenous sores affected his legs, and they became infested with worms. Yet three days after his death, the saint's body revealed a marvelous sweet odor.[7]

The concept of olfactory purity should not be thought of as merely neutral freshness, a modern rather than medieval ideal. Medieval people were impressed by wonderful smells rather than the absence of any scent at all. The infatuation with aromatic sensations may seem surprising given that a panoply of unpleasant smells was no doubt unavoidable in everyday life, odors that those living in reasonably affluent circumstances in the developed world are spared: excrement, animals, sickness, sweat, dirt, the effects of such noxious enterprises as tanneries or smelters. It is precisely because of this inevitable familiarity with awful odors that people in premodern societies were entranced with beautiful smells. They experienced a wider spectrum of olfactory sensations than we are familiar with, both good and bad. What tended to be missing was the neutral nonsmell of modernity.

Perfume and incense were used to make the air clean and healthful. It was customary that the rooms of a comfortable house should be not merely airy and unscented but redolent of actual healthy scents from spices that might be scattered about or resins that were burned as incense. A haven from disease and decay was thus created. Too much of the outside air was hardly likely to induce good health or prevent disease. This is not a specifically Christian idea but follows Greek medical learning and domestic habits. The physician Galen warned of the danger of entering a house with an off-putting smell.[8]

The indoor climate could be refreshed by the use of aromatic substances. Humidity was regarded as unhealthful, and spices had the effect of drying out the air and overcoming unpleasant smells. Avicenna, the authoritative Arab physician whose work was known in Christian Europe by the late twelfth century, recommended that ambergris, frankincense, cloves, and even theriac be employed to dry out the air and make it smell sweet.[9] Fumigation, the systematic burning of incense, was regarded as the most effective way to combat putrefaction and ward off disease, but because the spices were consumed by the fire, this was obviously a considerably more expensive measure than just placing spices around a room.

It isn't always easy to distinguish such health-related incense burning from fumigation undertaken to create a pleasant atmosphere. A Catalan book of perfumes and sweets offers a recipe for a "marvelous perfume" meant as a fortifying house freshener. This preparation was certainly healthful, but its primary purpose was aesthetic rather than medical.

Beyond the promotion of gracious living, spiced fumigations were sometimes used to attract or invoke supernatural forces, although this was somewhat esoteric and certainly a bit unorthodox. Although Christianity discouraged the burning of incense for religious purposes at home, alternate religious tendencies gave fumigation magical dimensions. A thirteenth-century text on supernatural powers known as *Picatrix* includes directions for invoking spirits by the ritual burning of aromatics. A series of spells accompanied by invocations are organized according to an astrological timetable, so that, for example, when the moon is in the third house, the initiate should make a tiny figure in the form of a woman seated with her right hand over her head. This little sculpture, to be called "Annuncia," should be censed with a fumigation of musk, camphor, mastic, and what is described as "aromatic unguent." An invocation is recited, after which the officiant makes a wish and places the figure on a silver ring as if it were a stone in a setting. The final step is for the ring to be placed on a finger, and then exciting things will start to happen.[10]

Incense opens a door between the mundane and the supernatural. The ritual fragrance rises to permeate the other world, but it is widely agreed among many religions that heaven is already marvelously scented, indeed that a perfumed ambience is one of its chief identifying attributes. If Christianity was relatively restrained in its use of incense for sacred ceremonies, it was enthusiastic about the importance of perfume as a symbol of the supernatural manifesting itself on earth. The visits of angels or the grace of holy men and women were heralded and authenticated by fragrance.

The holy lives and gruesome deaths of those who died for the faith were an early and influential genre of Christian writing, and accounts sometimes tell of visits by angels to comfort these martyrs before their horrific ordeals. St. Vincent, a Spanish martyr during the persecutions of Diocletian (ca. 303), was supposed to have been broken on a rack, burned, flayed, and subjected to various other tortures, none of which induced him to renounce Christianity. In prison, between the inflictions of torment, he was ministered to by angels who announced their presence with a wonderful aromatic perfume. Another martyr from the same era of persecution, St. Vitus, was hectored by his pagan father who was exasperated by his son's conversion. In order to corrupt Vitus and make him renounce his self-denying doctrines, his father ordered that the young man be locked in a room with several beautiful young women. A lovely odor wafted from the room, and when the saint's father looked in, he saw his son surrounded by seven angels. As it happens, this was the last thing he saw, for he was struck blind immediately after experiencing this vision.

According to a life of St. Polycarp, whom the Romans executed in the city of Smyrna in A.D. 155, the authorities attempted in vain to burn the martyr, but rather than consuming his body the flames simply made him glow like gold or silver in a smelting furnace, and a delightful fragrance of incense (or some other "costly perfume") pervaded the scene.[11] Earlier saints' legends don't usually specify the nature of the wonderful aromatic emanations, but late-medieval legends of saints are sometimes more detailed. For example, angelic visitors to the terribly crippled and ill St. Lydwine of Schiedam, a saint of the late fourteenth and early fifteenth centuries, left behind a heavenly perfume of cinnamon and ginger.[12]

So well established was the connection between the aroma of spices and the angels that it lent itself to fakery. At Marsal in the diocese of Metz in the thirteenth century, a woman disparaged by the chronicler Richer of Saint-Denis as a "Beguine Sybil" claimed prophetic powers and attracted an enthusiastic following. She shut herself up in a cell and renounced all earthly food. That she didn't starve was due, it was claimed, to the visits of angels who appeared in her cell and brought her heavenly nourishment, even taking her up with them into the abode of bliss on occasion. Part of the evidence for the presence of angels was that, after they departed, nutmegs, cloves, and other spices were discovered lying all over the small room in which she was confined. The woman was eventually exposed as a charlatan. It turned out that normal human food had been secretly brought to her by a priest who was her confederate, and the two rogues scattered the spices as a sign authenticating the angelic emissaries.[13]

Real saints often exuded a characteristic fragrance symbolic of their un-usual holiness and the favor of the other world. The commonplace formula-tion that someone died "in the odor of sanctity" has a very literal meaning. Especially in the Eastern churches of the Byzantine world, recently deceased saints were reputed to have demonstrated their holiness by exuding myrrh.

John Climacus, a monk and eventually abbot at Mount Sinai in the late sixth and early seventh centuries, describes the miraculous transformation of the body of the holy monk Menas. Before the burial, a marvelous fragrance prompted his spiritual brethren to open the coffin and they found that streams of myrrh were flowing from his feet. The verdict was that "the sweat of his labors has been offered up as myrrh to God and has been truly accepted."[14]

That death is normally associated with quite the opposite olfactory sensations gives this phrase all the greater symbolic import, but it holds true in the medieval imagination not so much for the dying as for the bones or corpses of the saints, a perquisite of these "very special dead." The fragrant odor emitted by the bodies of long-dead saints was important as a sign of their virtue, but it was particularly meaningful in the context of how Western Europe worshipped saints and, in particular, how it acquired their bones, relics credited with tremendous and miraculous power. Once the notion that these particularly favored holy men and women exerted power from beyond the grave and could influence human fortunes, their remains came to be regarded as repositories of sacred power. One could pray to St. Thomas Becket anywhere, for example, but to pray in Canterbury, at the site of his martyrdom where he was also buried, was quite a bit more effective. Unlike St. Thomas, martyred in 1170, most saints of the church were figures like Vincent of Saragossa or St. Vitus who had lived a very long time ago and whose tombs were not at some convenient place in northern Europe. Most saints of the early church had died in what later became Muslim territories, so there were many legends about the movement, the "translation," as it was called, of their relics—how their bones had moved from Egypt to Burgundy, for example, or from North Africa to Germany.

All this movement of relics provoked understandable questions about their legitimacy. Remarkable stories developed, memorably described by the historian Patrick Geary, stories designed to explain the migration of relics. These tales of supernatural and physical adventure involve the saint instigating monks or other clerics to rescue his body from the impious. The saint might, for example, appear in a dream, lamenting the neglect or mistreatment of his tomb and ordering the monk to come and bring his remains back to those who would appropriately honor them.[15]

The monk sometimes has to be convinced by another dream or two in which the anxious saint threatens him for evading his obligation. Once the monk sets out, the story becomes an adventure in which the saint's bones are discovered in Islamic territory and taken away by stealth back to the Christian world. This pious robbery is not only sanctioned by the saint but brought about by him. The aromatic "odor of sanctity" is the key to how the saint's remains are identified. In the jumbled and neglected Christian graveyards of Egypt and North Africa, the relic hunter faced the problem of finding the saint and being assured that the bones he brought back after such a dangerous labor were genuine. Finding Mary Magdalene's grave, for example, was facilitated by an odor of indescribable sweetness that informed the "holy violator" that he had come to the right place. St. Vincent was found in Muslim Valencia, his body intact and emitting what is described as "an aromatic sweetness."[16]

The odor of the corpse as a proof of sanctity was accepted and asserted by a pious, or at least enthusiastic, public. In 1397 a Dominican named Marcolino of Forli died, and although the populace agitated for his canonization, his companions regarded him as something of a rustic and a fool. He was buried, but a crowd dug up his grave and found that a wonderful fragrance wafted from his body, demonstrating that he was indeed a saint. Anxious about succumbing to popular pressure, the church waited until 1526 before recognizing Marcolino as a saint, but his cult was well established in northern Italy from the time of his miraculous death and burial.[17]

The passage from this world to the next was marked by perfume, certainly to disguise the smell of decomposition but also to symbolize the life to come. Aromatic resins were used for embalming, so that the gift of myrrh one of the wise men of the East had brought to the baby Jesus was usually interpreted as foretelling his burial (while the gold signifies kingship and the frankincense divinity).[18] Mary Magdalene's spikenard ointment for his feet also carried this symbolic meaning. Jesus was interred with spices and fragrant oils, according to the Gospels (Luke 23:56; Mark 16:1). John the Evangelist says Nicodemus brought about a hundred pounds of myrrh and aloes to his burial and that the body was wrapped in linen strips interspersed with the spices (John 19:30–40). A secular ruler, the Eastern Roman emperor Justinian, was anointed and accompanied by more than a hundred kinds of spices and unguents. Those who paid their respects to the body of the ruler before his burial were overcome by the perfume of these aromatic preservatives.

Heaven itself was redolent of perfume. Often this atmosphere is vaguely flowery, but occasionally, as in the Latin poetic "Vision of Thurkill" written in the early thirteenth century, the fragrance is more specifically identified with the odor of spices. The Englishman Peter Idley's vision of heaven (in the fifteenth century) included "all manner of frutis and of divers spicerie." Certainly hell was a place of awful smells accompanying terrible torment. The horrible reek is the worst aspect of hell, according to a late-fourth-century text known as "St. Paul's Apocalypse," an opinion shared by Tundale, an Irish monk writing in 1149. Although Tundale gives one of the classic accounts of an underworld where souls burn in eternal fire and are skewered on pitchforks, he says that the hideous stench is even worse. Excrement, sulfur, and burning metal were among the comparisons most commonly evoked.[19]

As previously shown, fragrance signified different things in the Middle Ages, vividly conveying sensuality and gracious living, but also intimating the world beyond this physical one and diffusing a sense of holiness. The aroma of spices was effective in combating disease, but also symbolic of death. Perfume has many applications in medicine, adornment, and religious ritual. What all these have in common is the use of fragrance to evoke another, better world. Clouds of incense offered the possibility of overcoming the normal frontier separating the mundane from the divine. What the wonderful smell of spices meant fundamentally was expressed in terms of healing and purity. Dirt, corruption, illness, and sin all manifest themselves by unpleasant odors, so that the process of healing is a kind of purification and the substitution of fragrance for stench.

It is worth distinguishing between purity and healing because there are certain parallels between the medieval infatuation with spices and the contemporary vogue for "aromatherapy." Medieval and modern notions of purity are very different, and the idea that there is a vivid fragrant life beyond but occasionally in touch with this one is peculiarly medieval. What the two societies do share are concepts of fragrance and healing. By definition aromatherapy assumes that good odors produce beneficial medical effects. Few people would now try aromatherapy to cure heart disease or chicken pox, so there is a limit to the claims to be made for healing by fragrance. Aromatherapy is used to deal with stress and other mental or spiritual states, to induce a feeling of calm, well-being, and insight. But aromatherapy's supposed benefit conveys more than simple relaxation. As a "therapy" it resembles the medieval medical connections made between unhappy moods and illness, between happiness and healing, and between fragrance and health. While few modern enthusiasts for aromatherapy would analyze the body's state and afflictions in terms of humors, their ideas about balance, equilibrium, and therapeutic relaxation closely resemble medieval medical language even if this is now more likely to be expressed with a more Asian traditional medical vocabulary.

Aromatherapy is more eclectic in its choice of scents than was the case in the Middle Ages, which focused on spices and resins, but many of the same ingredients are involved: flowers, herbs, spices, various botanical substances. The animal products so admired by medieval doctors and perfumers—such as musk or ambergris—are no longer readily available although still very important in the professional perfumers' vocabulary for describing scents.

It is interesting what pleasant smells are *not* included. Even the most appealing aromas of cooking would not be considered appropriate for therapeutic uses either now or eight hundred years ago. The smell of bacon frying or of cake baking is considered pleasant (and it is notorious that house sellers use the aroma of baking cake or bread to enhance the unconscious appeal of their property), but it does not induce a religiously spiritual state in the manner of less material, more elusive and volatile scents. The scents appropriate to sexual allure or medical and spiritual healing should be substances that are found in nature ("simples" in medieval terms), not things that bear the stamp of human intervention, such as cooking. In this immateriality and natural orientation there are ideas not only of healing but of purity. We no longer believe that disease can be prevented solely by disguising unpleasant smells, but there persists a feeling that wonderful fragrances have an elevating mental and therefore to some extent physical effect, an effect related to purity and naturalness. Perfume, incense, scented candles, sachets—all these communicate an intangible sense of pleasure that the aroma of pastry turnovers or roast chicken can't match.[20]

Where modern and medieval attitudes toward fragrance differ is in the proximity of another world and the ways in which fragrance literally comes from this invisible realm or symbolizes it. In the Middle Ages, spices flourished and were harvested in a happier, blessed place. The religious meaning of incense was intense in the medieval period, and the origins of most spices were still mysterious. Spices provided a wonderful flavor and aroma, but their appeal was enhanced by their expense and their origin in a poorly understood geography of the East. Somewhere in the eastern regions of Asia was India, where spices were known to originate. The biblical lands of gold and spices, places like Ophir, Hevilath, or Sheba, also lay to the east. The Garden of Eden, the terrestrial paradise, was thought to lie at the eastern extreme of Asia. Spices came from these fragrant and distant lands. The odor of paradise and the image of purity and eternity were not just abstract metaphors but vivid concepts that permeated the geographical lore related to a tantalizing and ultimately practical question: where did spices come from?

THE SCENTS OF EDEN

The French nobleman Jean de Joinville wrote an account of the life of the saintly Louis IX, king of France from 1226 to 1270. St. Louis led two Crusades, the failure of which had the effect of deepening rather than subtracting from his aura of sanctity. The first was an attack on the delta of the Nile that resulted in the king's being captured in 1245. Joinville describes this failed Seventh Crusade and includes a brief description of Egypt. According to Joinville, the Nile brings down spices from the earthly paradise where it originates. This theory of the source of the Nile was conventional, based on Genesis 2:11–14, which says that four rivers have their source in the Garden of Eden. One of these is referred to as the "Geon," which, beginning with the biblical commentator Josephus, was identified as the Nile. According to Joinville, the people living on the southern borders of Egypt profit from the river's origins:

> Before this river enters Egypt, the people who usually do such work cast their nets of an evening into the water and let them lie outspread. When morning comes, they find in their nets such things as are sold by weight and imported into Egypt, as for instance ginger, rhubarb, aloes, and cinnamon. It is said that these things come from the earthly Paradise, for in that heavenly place the wind blows down trees just as it does the dry wood in the forests of our own land, and the dry wood from the trees in Paradise that thus falls into the river is sold to us by merchants in this country.[21]

Although this account of where spices grow is inaccurate, it is typical rather than eccentric, based on a long tradition of learning. As was the case with the odor of sanctity or the religious uses of incense, we are presented with the idea that spices evoke or symbolize another world, a world of transcendence and eternal repose. Here, however, the other world is not purely spiritual but actually physically present on earth, a real if distant and magical place. The Garden of Eden was the paradise created by God on earth for the first humans. According to St. Ephrem the Syrian (A.D. 306–73), the trees of the Garden of Eden (as well as those in the *heavenly* paradise) drip marvelously scented unguents. This fragrance supplies all the nourishment that is necessary. Adam had no need for conventional food because he was fed by this perfume. The Christian Roman poet Prudentius (A.D. 348–405) described paradise as a place of balsam, spikenard, and "rare cinnamon."[22]

When Adam and Eve were expelled from the garden, it became closed off from the rest of the earth and its inhabitants. An angel with a sword guards its entrance, or, according to some accounts, paradise is surrounded by an impenetrable wall or by flames. Additional landscape features have been set up to discourage would-be visitors. According to Honorius Augustodunensis (ca. 1080–ca. 1137), a German monastic author of a widely diffused series of encyclopedic works, the earthly paradise is surrounded by an arid no-man's-land teeming with wild beasts and snakes. Or perhaps it was placed on a mountain of inaccessible height. Johannes Witte de Hese, author of a fictitious journey to the East supposedly undertaken in 1389, claims he saw the walls of paradise high up on "Mount Edom" glinting in the setting sun like a star.[23] Or, according to Dante, it sits on top of the mountain of purgatory in the southern hemisphere.

The earthly paradise was intact but uninhabited, or it held a population of at most two, the prophets Enoch and Elijah. The Bible says these wise men never died but were brought out of this world by God. Elijah was transported in God's fiery chariot, while Enoch was said to have "walked with God and was seen no more, because God took him" (4 Kings 2:11–12; Genesis 5:24; Hebrews 11:5). They could not have gone to the celestial heaven since no living man can be there, so by a kind of process of elimination, Enoch and Elijah were thought to be long-term residents of Eden, witnesses for God's ultimate purposes of salvation.

This nearly deserted paradise was full of aromatic plants, but it was not thought of as the sole source of the terrestrial world's spices. If the entire spice trade depended on flotsam brought down by the rivers of paradise, the supply would have been even more restricted than it already was. Spices grew in other parts of Asia, in India notably, but the reason they flourished there was because of the proximity of these fortunate lands to the beneficent influence of paradise. Paradise is the archetype of a magical realm where wonderful things abound, especially objects of great rarity in Europe such as gems, gold, and spices. In examining the shape of these legends of the aromatic paradise, we are looking at the meeting point of sanctity and trade: the association of spices with ethereal goodness and beauty coupled with what were ultimately practical geographical theories that inspired the first European explorers. Where spices were *thought* to originate tells us more about medieval ideas concerning how the world was organized than knowledge of where they actually came from.

The Garden of Eden was cut off from the ordinary, fallen, earthly existence of travail, sickness, decay, and death, but there was nevertheless some contact between the two worlds via the four primary rivers of the world, all of which had their origins in paradise. The Bible says that the Tigris, the Euphrates, the Phison, and the Geon flow out of paradise. The Geon was the Nile, while the Phison was interpreted as the Ganges or the Indus. The locations of these rivers, or at least some aspects of their relative position, were known, enough so that it was realized that it was difficult to see how rivers in Mesopotamia, India, and Africa could all have a common origin. In the late fourth and early fifth centuries, St. Ephrem of Syria and St. Augustine dealt with this ingeniously by determining that the rivers ran underground for part of their course, reemerging at the point of their apparent terrestrial source (the mountains of India; Africa south of Egypt).[24] One of the best-known world maps of the Middle Ages, the Hereford Map composed in about 1300, shows the earthly paradise as an island at the extreme east of Asia. The map depicts Adam and Eve being tempted by the serpent, and also on the mainland after their expulsion watched by a disapproving angel. Paradise is walled with a closed, fortified door marked "Gates of Paradise." The four rivers issue from the island to reappear elsewhere on the map, the Nile dividing into different branches and in widely separated parts of the world.

The book of Genesis does not actually say much about the aromatic flora of paradise. The only spice mentioned is bdellium, a fragrant resin supposedly common to a land called Hevilath, which lies on the border of paradise (Genesis 2:12). Hevilath is said to be watered by the Phison and so is usually identified with India.[25] From these few hints Christian writers endowed the Garden of Eden with a specifically aromatic as opposed to merely flowery atmosphere. A fourth-century geographer claimed that there were actually inhabitants of paradise, a people known as Camarines, who live on bread that falls from the sky which they eat with honey and pepper.[26] According to the Greek church father Philostorgius of Cappadocia, writing in about 425, the clove trees growing along the River Phison are offshoots of trees originally limited to paradise.[27]

The Tigris and the Euphrates were also rivers of paradise, and territories near them, such as "Babylon" or the Caucasus Mountains, were sometimes placed near India and the Garden of Eden. The fragrance of paradise was part of a controversy over the location of Armenia. An anonymous geographer from Ravenna in the early eighth century disputed the belief that the Tigris and Euphrates have their sources in the mountains of Armenia. If that were the case, the geographer argued, then Armenia would adjoin the earthly paradise, but in fact that land is well known to be cold and infertile and besides, there is no sweet, fragrant odor there that would signal the proximity of paradise.[28]

The scent of paradise might waft over its forbidding walls, but the more substantial path of communication with this realm, cut off from the temporal world, was by means of the four rivers. Christian lore about the rivers of paradise was supplemented by a long tradition of classical antiquity about the rivers of India that bring down treasures from some remote location that are then found in the lower regions where humans dwell. The first Greek writer to describe India was Ctesias, a physician who spent many years at the court of the ruler of Persia and whose account, *Indika,* was written around 400 B.C. According to Ctesias, there is a river called the Hyparchos that carries amber in its current during thirty days of the year. The Indians say that trees growing in the mountains produce resinous "tears" during a particular season of the year, and these fall from overhanging branches into the river, hardening into amber.[29] This tale was later repeated and elaborated by Greek and Roman writers intrigued with India after the exploits of Alexander the Great, whose conquests in the late fourth century B.C. reached

The island of the earthly paradise and the expulsion of Adam and Eve,
as depicted in a detail from the Hereford Map, ca. 1300. (Cathedral of Hereford,
England, photograph copyright Hereford Mappa Mundi Trust)

as far as the Indus River, bringing the West into direct but intermittent
contact with the wealth of South Asia. Pliny the Elder (who died in the
eruption of Vesuvius in A.D. 79), an extraordinary compiler of facts, lore,
and more-or-less scientific knowledge, reported that precious stones were
taken from the rivers of India, especially the Ganges and the Acesines (the
modern river Chenab in what is now Pakistan). Pliny did know that amber
came from northern Europe and not India.[30]

In the Middle Ages, the two traditions of legends about the East, the
biblical and the classical, were often combined. According to one popular
tale that began with a Hebrew account in the twelfth century, Alexander the
Great decided to look for paradise once his army reached the banks of the
Ganges. Alexander and his companions found themselves sailing along
the wall of an immense fortified city that seemed to have no entrance. After
three days they came to a window and a man appeared there informing them
that this was the abode of the blessed, and they might not enter. He gave
Alexander a stone to take back with him that was heavier when weighed than

any amount of gold, but that once sprinkled with dust became extremely light. It was a symbol of glory and fame in the face of death, and Alexander understood its humbling message.[31]

With regard to stones of more obvious monetary value, the Orient and its rivers really were the source of the most valuable gems. In addition to being rare and beautiful, precious stones are hard and chemically stable, so that they remain unchanged when softer, more reactive material surrounding them erodes. Gold, tin, and other valuable elements or rock forming seams (such as lapis lazuli) were mined in premodern times, but gems were not. Until the discovery of gems in Brazil and South Africa in the eighteenth and nineteenth centuries, most of the world's jewels came from India.[32] Geological facts—that gems came from Indian rivers and streams—gave credence to more fanciful ideas that spices and other precious and exotic commodities floated down those same rivers out of a generalized East that included Egypt, Mesopotamia, Ethiopia, and all the lands watered by the rivers of paradise. What seems at first a bizarre supposition by Joinville, that spices like ginger or aloe wood are taken out of the river, in fact represents long-standing orthodoxies of scientific knowledge based on the model of precious stones. It is not surprising, therefore, that according to *Circa instans,* aloe wood is found in the rivers of what is referred to as Upper Babylon and that these rivers are connected to those that flow from the earthly paradise. Some say the wood falls into the river in paradise, according to the author of *Circa instans,* while others claim it comes from a desert land adjoining paradise. The harvesting of aloe wood is beautifully exemplified in Robinet Testard's illustrations to the *Livre des simples médecines* (ca. 1500). Under the heading of aloe wood he paints a turbaned man fishing out pieces of the fragrant wood with a net while a female companion arranges the pieces in boxes. The landscape looks rather temperate, but the man's turban shows that we are in exotic climes.[33]

Aloe wood was the spice most often thought to come floating down the rivers of paradise. This was because of its extremely high value and the fact that as it is undoubtedly a kind of wood, its presence in the rivers is plausible. According to John Mandeville, author of a wildly popular fictitious travelogue written in the mid-fourteenth century, aloe wood is brought from paradise by the rivers Nile and Phison. A real traveler, the Franciscan missionary John of Marignolli, last of the friars sent by the popes to convert the Mongols, visited China and India between 1339 and 1353. He claimed that gems and aloe wood come by river from paradise, which is located high on a mountain in Ceylon. The inhabitants of Ceylon (modern Sri Lanka) take these out of the lowland river fed by the mountain streams. Turning to another imaginary account, this of a voyage supposedly undertaken by the brother of the Portuguese prince Henry the Navigator, aloe wood is seen floating on the Geon/Nile in the vicinity of paradise.[34]

As Joinville's report demonstrates, other spices were scooped out of the rivers of paradise. In Wolfram von Eschenbach's grail romance *Parzival,* the mysterious and tormented custodian of the grail, the Fisher King Anfortas, suffers from a wound so severe that even spices (*würzen*) gathered from the four rivers of paradise are unavailing. The aromatic substances were fished out at points so close to paradise that their wonderful fragrance wafted over the rivers, but even such proximity did not confer sufficient strength to heal or even assuage the terrible supernatural injury.[35] The legendary Christian king of India, Prester John, a figure of the European imagination whom we'll look at later in more detail, was supposed to have tremendous wealth from precious stones that came out of the River "Idonus" whose source is in paradise. In addition to emeralds, sapphires, and topazes, the river also carries an herb called *assidios* that wards off evil demons. Pepper forests grow in the land of Prester John adjoining a spring that is just three days' journey from paradise. The spring water changes flavors constantly, and those who drink it are never ill. Although their lives are not extended, they always look and feel a healthy thirty-two years old, that being Jesus' age at crucifixion.[36]

THE LOCATION OF EDEN AND OF INDIA

Where exactly was the forbidden aromatic garden? The question had more than a merely antiquarian significance since, as the spice trade grew and demand continued to outstrip supply, the problem of the origin of spices became more intriguing in relation to possible profit. While it was unlikely that the Garden of Eden itself was going to amount to much as a direct supplier of spices, the harvest from India and other lands located near or adjacent to paradise could conceivably be found and exploited. Paradise was usually regarded as a place in Asia that exerted an influence on

Gathering aloe wood from a river that flows out of paradise;
illustration by Robinet Testard in the *Livre des simples médecines,* ca. 1490.
(National Library of Russia, St. Petersburg, MS Fr. V. VI., fol. 143)

neighboring territories, rendering them unusually rich in gold, jewels, and spices. The location of paradise and the location of India were intertwined questions with both scholarly and commercial answers and implications.

A minority opinion placed paradise west of Europe, out in the Atlantic Ocean. A fictionalized account of the life of the Irish monk St. Brendan written in the late ninth or early tenth century describes how the saint and his companions set out in small ox-hide boats from their monastery of Clonfert in County Galway to find the "Land of Promise of the Saints," an other-worldly island west of the Irish coast. After many adventures, including an island of blacksmiths who were actually demons and a mistaken landing on an island that turned out to be a whale, they reached a land of eternal happiness but were told to return home. Their travels had been inspired by another Irish holy figure, the abbot Barind, who told Brendan that he and his son Mernoc routinely visited the Atlantic island on which paradise is located. Once when they got back to Mernoc's community, they answered the monks' questions about where they had been with the words "do you not see from the fragrance of our clothes that we have been in God's paradise?" The monks acknowledged this must be true because they knew that Mernoc had previously come back from mysterious journeys, his clothes impregnated with this same delightful odor, a fragrance they had kept for more than forty days.[37]

By the seventh century, however, the scholarly consensus was that paradise was located in eastern Asia. Genesis 2:8 suggests that the Lord placed Eden in the East. In the fourth century St. Athanasius, best known as the defender of orthodoxy against the Arian heresy, argued for an oriental paradise on the basis of an analysis of Genesis, but also because everyone knows that the air becomes perfumed as one approaches India, which lies near paradise, far to the east of the Roman Mediterranean.[38] Isidore of Seville, the seventh-century author of what was for centuries the definitive encyclopedia of natural lore, placed paradise in the eastern regions of Asia, combining Christian and classical teachings about the rivers of the east, and blending Christian ideas about paradise with the Greek and Roman stories of India. For Isidore, paradise was simply a "province" of Asia, added to the usual lists of classical geographers that included India, Persia, Asia Minor, and so on.[39]

For most of the medieval period the question of where paradise was situated also affected both the image and the theoretical location of India. Both were somewhere in the easternmost realms of Asia and if India, lacking angelic guards, was more accessible, still no one from Europe ever claimed to have been there until the end of the thirteenth century, with Marco Polo. India's position on the map was crucial for the actual medieval understanding of the spice trade. Better information about where it lay in relation to other parts of Asia and ultimately to Europe would instigate the voyages of discovery and conquest at the end of the medieval period. Practical geographical information about India is therefore considered in more detail toward the end of this book, when we take up the subject of how Europeans sought routes to the places where spices originated. Here we are interested in European impressions of India apart from the question of how to find it. This land, which epitomized the exotic in both its good and bad senses, played a prominent role in the European geographical imagination and sense of wonder.[40]

Before the partial opening of Asia to Western eyes in the late thirteenth and early fourteenth centuries, the place of India was close to that of the earthly paradise. Brunetto Latini, a teacher of Dante and author of a compendium of practical knowledge, located paradise *within* India, but it was more common to situate India in the neighborhood of the enclosed Garden of Eden.[41] A popular poetic geographical treatise of the mid-thirteenth century titled *L'image du monde* places India on the far side of paradise, to the east. Usually, however, India was thought of as bordering paradise on the west. Beginning with the maps that accompanied the apocalypse commentary of Beatus of Liebana, a Spanish monk of the early ninth century, India adjoins paradise, and this tradition continues to be reflected in the Hereford Map and most of the late-medieval descriptions of the world.

India was populous, rich, and full of gold, gems, and spices as well as extraordinary animals, including elephants and unicorns. The East was, at the same time, a place of exotic danger. India was favored by its proximity to the earthly paradise, but unlike that unambiguously blessed place, it was a land of marvels both good and bad, a place of extremes and the reverse of a Europe imagined as temperate, normal, and short on the wonders of nature. In his brief description of India, Brunetto Latini says it is both fortunate in its climate and partially uninhabitable because of the heat, a land of gold and silver but also of barbaric semi-humans.[42] According to the

Dominican friar Jordan of Sévérac, one of the earliest European travelers to India (1320–28 and again from 1330 until his death in 1336), everything in India is marvelous. India is a completely different world. The Franciscan Odoric of Pordenone (who was in India during the 1320s at about the same time as Jordan) agreed: "For in the whole world there are no marvels such as in that realm."[43]

The basis for the imagery of Eastern wonders in the Middle Ages was largely classical lore accumulated in the wake of Alexander's conquests.[44] Far from discrediting the stories of India's marvels, the accounts of Alexander in India added to the stories of the wealth and strangeness of the subcontinent. Especially prominent among the tales of wonders were the fantastic semi-human peoples thought to inhabit parts of India, nations categorized into what would later be referred to as the "monstrous races."[45] The definitive codification of the monstrous races, one that would influence the European view of the far-off borders of the world into the seventeenth century, was the work of the Roman natural historian Pliny the Elder. In his thirty-six-volume *Natural History,* among the twenty thousand facts from a hundred authors he claimed to have collected Pliny listed some forty peoples, some of them based on Greek precedents, some perhaps found in versions of Greek writings now lost, and some based on more recent speculation. According to Pliny, these humanoids are prolific in India and Ethiopia. In fact, "Ethiopians" were among the races bequeathed to Pliny by his Greek predecessors, confusingly, as a black population in India. Other plausible or at least fully human groups among this catalogue were pygmies and cannibals. More fanciful were such peoples as the Cynocephali, with dogs' heads; Blemmyae, who have no heads but rather faces in their chest; "Apple Smellers" (Astomi), who have heads but no mouths and who nourish themselves by the scent of apples; and Sciopods, who have one large leg that they hop around on and use to shade themselves from the tropical sun.[46]

It is worth pausing a little on these peculiar aspects of medieval images of the East, because the monstrous races came to be intertwined with spices and the other valuable products of the East, to the degree that when Columbus was searching for the realms of these precious commodities he was encouraged by reports of dog-headed people and other well-established semi-humans.[47] Where they were to be found, he believed, so were spices.

This conjunction of the alluring with the frightening is evident in another important map of the Middle Ages, the so-called Catalan Atlas of 1375–77. The atlas, made in Majorca for the king of France, reflects the opening of Europe to the East made possible by the Mongol conquests and the discovery of China. Via citations to Marco Polo, the atlas shows some precocious awareness of the Spice Islands lying east of India. These "islands of India," numbering 7,548 according to the atlas (Marco Polo had stated the number as 7,448), are rich in gold, silver, spices, precious stones, and also strange humanoids. In the sea surrounding them there are three kinds of semi-human fish called Sirens, according to the map, but only two are actually described, one a combined woman and fish, and the other half woman, half bird. The island of "Trapobana," or Taprobane (usually identified with Ceylon, but here probably Sumatra) is rich in gold, silver, and precious stones, it says, but inhabited by black giants who eat white men. On another island, "Iana" (perhaps Java or Ceylon), wonderful spices grow, including aloe wood, camphor, galangal, nutmeg, cinnamon, and mace, but part of the island is ruled by women (the Amazons being another well-established monstrous race).

If India was seen as a territory of both riches and mystery, of fortunate yet also bizarre people or humanoids, its religious image was also ambiguous. There were evil pagans such as the cannibals but there were also supposed to be Christians in India, co-religionists of the West who might be called upon to aid in the common effort against the Muslims. The idea of a Christian India was a key inducement to finding a route to its spices, because dreams of wealth were reinforced or legitimated by dreams of a Crusade alliance.

One source of this peculiar optimism was the body of legends surrounding the apostle Thomas, who was thought to have preached in India and made many converts there. He was supposedly buried in India—at Mylapore, south of Madras (now Chennai), according to some accounts—where many miracles were performed at his tomb. According to some Western authorities, the local king and population were Christian. In fact, there really was a significant if not immense Christian population in western India, on the Malabar Coast (the modern state of Kerala), where much of the spice trade was headquartered. The Christians of these regions still refer to themselves as St. Thomas Christians, although it is more likely that their ancestors were converted by Syrian missionaries in the fourth and fifth centuries than in apostolic times.

> ### The Indian Ocean, According to the Catalan Atlas of 1375–77
>
> *Sea of the Indian islands where the spices are. In this sea sail the ships of many nations. Also here one finds three kinds of fish called* Sarenas, *of which one is half woman and half fish, and the other half woman, half bird.*
>
> #### IANA [Java or Ceylon]
> *On the island of Jana one finds many trees: aloe wood, camphor, sandalwood, fine spices, galangal, nutmeg, cinnamon trees from which the costly spices come from all of India. Also mace and "leaves" (folli).*
>
> #### ILLA TRAPOBANA [Sumatra]
> *The isle of Taprobane. It is called Magno-Caulij by the Tartars. It is the last land to the East in the Ocean. On this island are men different from all others. In certain mountains of the island are exceptionally large men that are 12 ells in height, like giants. They are very black and devoid of reason. They eat white and foreign men when they come into their power. On this island there are two summers and two winters. The flowers and grasses bloom here twice a year. It is the last of the Indian islands, rich in gold, silver, and gems.*
>
> From annotations to the Catalan Atlas, translated from *L'Atlas Català de Cresques Abraham* (Barcelona, 1975).

In the twelfth century, a new legend of a powerful Christian ruler of the East established the picture of India as fantastically wealthy and enthusiastically Christian. In about 1165 a letter began to circulate in Europe purporting to be from Prester John, who styled himself "Emperor of the Three Indias."[48] Prester John presented himself to the Western monarchs and the Byzantine emperor in particular, to whom the letter was addressed. In the letter he is rather contemptuous of the Byzantine ruler and adopts a haughty grandiloquence appropriate for one who rules over no fewer than seventy-two kings.

There had also been earlier accounts of this fabulous ruler. In 1122 a man calling himself John, bishop of India, appeared at the court of Pope Calixtus II and described the wealth of a Christian kingdom protected by the relics of St. Thomas and nourished by the River Phison, which brought jewels down from the earthly paradise. The actual monarch with the peculiar name or title of Prester John was first mentioned in the mid-twelfth century by Otto of Freising, a half-brother of Emperor Frederick Barbarossa and author of a universal history. Here Prester John is a priest and ruler (Prester from the German *Preister,* "priest") who has battled Muslim Persia and whose extraordinary wealth is symbolized by a scepter made of emerald.

The letter from 1165 elaborates on this and gives more detail about the combination of riches and strange wonders in the land of this potential ally. His vast territory is located near the earthly paradise and abounds in jewels, exotic animals (centaurs, the phoenix), and strange humanoids including giants, Amazons, pygmies, and dog-headed people. A magical mirror allows him to see what goes on everywhere in his realms. Only one meal is consumed during the day, but thirty thousand people are served in his grandiose palace. Most of his subordinate kings are pagan, and so his land is by no means uniformly Christian, but everyone is just and there is no lying, adultery, or theft. Nature is not merely generous but profligate: "Our magnificence is overflowing and resplendent with all the riches of the world." Spices are less obsessively described than jewels, but there is a great pepper forest and the palace burns balsam exclusively in its lamps.

What the original purpose of this letter was may have to do more with papal-imperial propaganda than with raising the hopes of an Eastern ally to help the Crusades. John is a Christian but does not seem to recognize the pope, nor does his kingdom appear to have a clerical class at all. The letter expresses the desire of Western Christians for a great ally. Whatever its immediate context, the letter launched a long career. In 1177 Pope Alexander III sent an emissary to Prester John, but nothing further was heard from him. Over the course of the next three centuries, Prester John's location shifted between India and Ethiopia and his realm became identified with the search for spices. Departing in 1497, Vasco da Gama carried letters from the king of Portugal addressed to Prester John.

In spite of the persistently fantastic image of India, the period between the letter of Prester John and the arrival of da Gama's ships in Calicut saw a tremendous increase in European knowledge of the East and witnessed the first European visitors to India since the end of the Roman Empire. The allure of fragrance and aromatic products influenced the seemingly changeless association of paradise, India, and the East in general. Demand for spices would also drive innovations that ultimately made it possible to arrive at the source of these intoxicating perfumes.

THE SPICE ROUTES

We have seen that the demand for spices in the medieval West was based primarily on food preferences but also encompassed health, medicine, and fragrance. The delight in spices and their mysteriously distant origins provoked speculation about geography based first on classical and Christian lore, then supplemented by relations with Islam that provided indirect contact with India and the rest of Asia. Muslim societies introduced many luxury products to Europe and served as the trendsetters for fashion, even though Islam and Christianity were mortal religious enemies.

Desire for spices produced a fluctuating but consistently high series of prices. Information about the market in spices comes from merchants' records, household account books that record expenditures on various purchases, and some less expected documents such as inventories of property made after death to value an estate. In this latter case the stock of a retail spice business received a detailed estimate of value that included the current prices. Merchants' records include accounts from retail stores, such as apothecaries or others who sold spices, and also the wholesale costs at markets in the eastern Mediterranean, at such ports as Alexandria, Beirut, Acre (in what is now Israel), or Famagusta (Cyprus) where spices were bought in large quantities by import and export merchants for distribution to Europe. Usually there was no shortage of supply, but the demand was sufficient for spices to be considered rare. We will explore what "rare" might actually imply for the hopes of Europeans to find a direct route to the spices, bypassing Muslim lands and middlemen, in order to reap the entire profit of this lucrative trade. We discuss the spice trade, therefore, not only in terms of the real economic networks of Asia and Europe but also as a mental outlook, a European perception of economic forces that might be fanciful but whose very fantasies fueled the search for the Indies.

The spices that arrived in the eastern Mediterranean to supply the European market were a small part of the global trade in these commodities. The importance of aromatic substances in the cuisine, medicine, and affluent manner of life of India, China, and the Islamic regions meant that the bulk of the world trade and consumption of spices took place considerably east of the Mediterranean. Europe was a peripheral player and India was the center of a trade that reached eastward to China for sales and to Indonesia and Indochina for supply, and westward toward Persia, the Persian Gulf, the Red Sea, and Egypt for distribution to both the Islamic Middle East and ultimately Europe. The Indian subcontinent was, in the words of the economic historian Janet Abu-Lughod, "on the way to everywhere," not, as the European intellectuals imagined, at the edge of the world.[1] The Coromandel Coast of southeast India maintained a substantial trade with Ceylon and the East Indies, importing nutmeg, mace, and cloves that grew only in the Molucca Islands of what is now eastern Indonesia. These spices were brought to intermediate ports, notably Malacca (in modern Malaysia), by Javanese and Malay traders and thence carried to India largely by Indian vessels. The Coromandel region also traded with China, supplying it with Indian spices (pepper notably), Indonesian spices, and jewels in return for silk and porcelain.

The western edge of India included two prominent trading zones, the Malabar Coast to the south and Gujarat farther north, near what is now Pakistan. Gujarat had been in direct contact with the Roman Empire and was the entrepôt for the export trade in pepper, which grew in Malabar. In the Middle Ages much of the trade based in Gujarat supplied Persia and Iraq with spices, and also with cotton, metal utensils, textiles, dried food, and other bulk commodities. Some of the spices that reached Europe were brought by merchants of such cities as Baghdad who had made their purchases in Gujarat, or by Gujarati traders who brought spices as far west as the Persian Gulf. Malabar and its ports, including Quilon, Cochin, and Calicut, welcomed ships from China, the Persian Gulf, and the Red Sea. India's large pepper crop was shipped out of Malabar in all directions.

The direct trade with the West was largely in the hands of Arab entrepreneurs. A Venetian map from 1450 designed by Fra Mauro has an annotation about the port of Ormuz on the Persian Gulf, where ships come from India with pearls, pepper, ginger, and other spices. These are then transported by land to Baghdad and Asia Minor.[2] When the Portuguese commander Pedro Álvares Cabral confiscated two Muslim ships at Calicut in 1500, there were perhaps as many as fifteen thousand Muslim merchants resident in that city.

Two pictures from a French compendium of marvels based on the real and fictitious travels of Marco Polo, John Mandeville, and Odoric of Pordenone demonstrate European conceptions of the spice trade in India. One, accompanying Marco Polo's account of "Cail" (Quilon), shows small black-skinned men bringing pepper to a Muslim merchant who is tasting or sniffing a sample. In the same manuscript, illustrating Mandeville's travels, pepper is harvested near the city of "Polomb" (again Quilon) and brought by a Muslim-looking merchant to a rather European-looking ruler.

European merchants did not have direct access to this trade except in unusual instances. In the era of Mongol hegemony, from about 1260 to 1350, Western merchants reached China and even established some small settlements there. They were also active in western Central Asia in places such as Tabriz and Sultaniyeh (in modern Iran), and Urgenj (a town in modern Turkestan, whence the term for the fabric organdy). A group of Venetian merchants belonging to the Loredano family visited Delhi by way of Urgenj in 1338, but before da Gama most visitors to India from the

Harvesting and selling pepper in India, an illustration of Marco Polo's travels from the *Livre des merveilles,* fourteenth century. (Bibliothèque nationale de France, Paris, MS fr. 2810, fol. 84v; photograph, Bridgeman Art Library)

West were missionaries, and there were very few trade ventures.[3] Of course this impression may be due to what kinds of texts were written and what survives. A chance encounter shows that there were Europeans on the coast of India at the time of da Gama. The third Portuguese expedition to India, led by João de Nova, in 1502 brought back two Europeans living on the Malabar Coast: a Venetian named Benvenuto d'Albano (elderly and poor), who had been in India for twenty-five years, and a Valencian referred to as Antão Lopes, who had lived there for fifteen years.[4]

Whatever hidden contacts there might have been, there was certainly nothing resembling a commercial infrastructure. No one from Malabar, let alone farther east, made a commercial voyage to Europe, and no one in medieval Europe before Marco Polo near the end of the thirteenth century can be shown to have visited India, a country whose very location was obscure to European geographers. Only toward the end of our period was it realized (again beginning with Marco Polo) that there were Far Eastern islands that produced spices.

We are dealing, therefore, with Europeans whose desire for spices was

Workers gathering pepper (at right) in India and a merchant presenting sacks
of it to a ruler, an illustration of Mandeville's travels from the *Livre des merveilles,*
fourteenth century. (Bibliothèque nationale de France, Paris, MS fr. 2810,
fol. 186; photograph, Bridgeman Art Library)

so strong as to draw them across an unknown world. The producers and
most of the middlemen had no idea of the end user, while the European
consumers thought that these treasures came from a magical far-off realm,
perhaps the lands of the monstrous races, or the domain of Prester John,
or an imagined India.

The major commercial intermediaries between Europe and the real India
were the Arabs, and it was Arab traders and travelers who had the experience
and knowledge to understand nearly the entire sequence of the spice trade.
An unusual manuscript painting now in Modena (Italy) shows a distinctly
foreign cinnamon merchant, probably a Muslim trader, selling to a European at one of the Arab trade emporia on or near the Mediterranean.

The knowledge of Arab geographers and travelers such as Ibn Battutah
or Ibn Khaldun did not quite extend to the Moluccas, which are first mentioned in Arab writings only around 1460, but Java, Sumatra, and Ceylon
were known in Islam as sources of spices at a time when Europe still thought

A cinnamon merchant, shown in a painting from *Tractatus de herbis,* fifteenth century. (Biblioteca Estense, Modena, MS lat. 993, fol. 36v; photograph, Bridgeman Art Library)

of India as their sole country of origin. This does not mean that the Indian Ocean trade was in any sense an Arab monopoly. There were several different stages of off-loading, division, and consolidation from Indonesia to Egypt, but the bulk of the Arab trade drew spices from India to the Persian Gulf (the port of Siraf, for example), the Red Sea (where Aden was the most important transfer point), and Alexandria.

There were other routes and possibilities of at least indirect contact with the sources of spices. When Europeans held territory in Syria and Palestine that the Crusaders had wrested out of Muslim hands (from 1099 to 1291), spices and other Eastern luxuries were marketed in Acre and other ports. One of the lavishly illustrated poems in honor of the miracles of the Virgin Mary, the *Cantigas de Santa María,* produced and supposedly composed by King Alfonso X "the Wise" of Castile in the mid-thirteenth century, shows a commercial voyage to Acre and depicts merchants looking over spices along with oriental carpets, gold, jewels, and other luxuries. Spices picked up in this manner in Christian outposts came overland via Persia or through the Red Sea. The intermediaries here were Muslim, but the actual entrepôts where Western merchants bought spices were under Christian control.

Before this, from the ninth to the twelfth centuries, Constantinople had been the great supplier of Asian products. Liutprand of Cremona, a Western imperial emissary to the court of the Byzantine emperor in 949 and 968, complained bitterly in his account of his second mission that the purple-dyed silk he had purchased was confiscated by the Byzantine authorities upon his departure because silk of that color was reserved for the "real" emperor of Rome in Constantinople, not for upstarts in the West.[5]

With the eclipse of Byzantium, the Black Sea became an important place for trade and for organizing trips to Central Asia and China during the period of the Mongol hegemony. Trebizond on the northern coast of Asia Minor and various ports on the Crimean Peninsula connected Constantinople and Western Europe with Tabriz in Persia and with Bokhara, Samarkand, and Kashgar on the famed Silk Road, in what is now Uzbekistan and western China. The Genoese had obtained privileges in Constantinople as early as 1155 and in the fourteenth century established a strong presence in the Crimea from their base at Caffa, trading with Silk Road merchants and with the Mongol rulers of Persia. Venice, Genoa's archrival, controlled Constantinople commercially during much of the thirteenth century, but Venetian enterprises farther east were less sustained than those of the Genoese.

The period of the Mongol empire, from the early thirteenth to the mid-fourteenth century, was a crucial moment in the history of commerce, not so much because of permanent changes—in the fourteenth century the opening of Asia would be reversed by the resurgence of Islam and the self-imposed isolation of China—as in its impact on the European sense of the layout and wealth of Asia, topics to be explored further in subsequent chapters.

The voyage of a merchant to Acre in the Holy Land, as depicted in
the *Cantigas de Santa María* from the mid-thirteenth century.
In the center panel at right, the merchant is buying exotic goods,
including an oriental rug. (Biblioteca Monasterio del Escorial,
MS T.I.1, fol. 229; photograph, Bridgeman Art Library)

Traders from Venice, Genoa, Barcelona, Marseilles, and a few other commercial cities of Mediterranean Europe traded regularly with Muslim ports in the eastern and southern Mediterranean despite prohibitions of the church enacted after the fall of Acre, the last mainland Crusader fortress in 1291. The papacy itself, author of the prohibition, granted exceptions as did kings and other rulers, so by the mid-fourteenth century at the latest the embargo on trade with Islam became simply a way of extorting money from merchants.

In addition to the costs, there were dangers in dealing with a different religious and political culture, and no one could ensure against surprises, such as a brief Christian conquest and plundering of Alexandria launched from Cyprus in 1365, but there was a long-term stability and familiarity with the Egyptians and with the spice market that meant substantial and reasonably reliable profits for those with experience and connections. The great European commercial centers were able to negotiate treaties with Muslim ports that governed crucial issues of customs payments, safety, self-regulation, and resolution of disputes. Merchants from Mediterranean cities were afforded a degree of immunity, autonomy, and corporate identity. They and their goods resided in the *fonduq* (plural *fanādiq,* Italianized as *fondaco*), a commercial facility not so different from free-trade zones in modern ports or the kind of recognized foreigners' neighborhoods characteristic of all premodern ports. Venice itself and other European commercial centers had *fondaci,* such as that of the Germans, the Fondaco dei Tedeschi, which is still an identifiable place near the Rialto.[6]

The fondaco began as an inn where foreigners were housed. Their segregation from the local population was partly for their own safety, but it also allowed the local ruler to regulate and tax them. Separation promoted a sense of community far from home, allowed intense commercial networking, and assured fairness by centralizing transactions in one location. As long as regulation was not too intrusive or limiting, the fondaco was a mutually advantageous institution and it expanded to encompass warehouses, social and charitable activities, and customs houses. The fondaco had something like the extraterritorial status of a modern embassy building, and efforts were made to isolate it from the nonmercantile local population. Usually no one could enter or leave the fondaco at night or on Fridays, the Muslim sabbath. While the fondaco might welcome foreign Christian merchants if it had space going unused by its citizens, Jews and Muslims were not allowed to reside in it.

A consul represented the individual foreign community before the local authorities and was empowered usually by his government (Venice, Aragon-Catalonia) to negotiate and regulate commercial and political relationships. The Catalan consul in Alexandria, for example, was appointed by the municipality of Barcelona for a three-year term. He was supposed to be present when commodities were being weighed in case of disputes. This official resolved contention within the Catalan commercial enclave while representing the traders as de facto ambassador before the sultan and his officials. This was sometimes a dangerous job as, for example, in about 1415 when the Catalan consul was severely beaten by the sultan's men not only because of an attack by Catalan pirates, but because he advised merchants to flee in anticipation of the sultan's reprisals. A Catalan consul in Damascus lost a considerable amount of property seized by an emir in 1405, but the emir himself was fleeing the armies of the resurgent Mongols under Tamerlane.[7]

The fondaci in Alexandria were large buildings of two stories surrounding a courtyard. Each merchant community had a separate facility, the Catalans from Barcelona, Valencia, and Majorca; the Provençaux from Marseilles; the Venetians; and the Genoese. They were built with a single well-guarded entrance for protection in case of riots or other disturbances, but so were all important buildings holding valuable property, whether belonging to Muslims, Jews, or Christians. The ground floor was used for stables and for storing goods purchased and awaiting the arrival of ships to transport them to Europe. The upper stories served as places of lodging. Spices and other Eastern goods were piled in the storerooms in different kinds of containers depending on their value. Relatively inexpensive spices like pepper, ginger, and sugar were shipped in large sacks weighing a hundred pounds or so. Rarer spices were wholesaled by the pound and came in boxes of about fifty pounds wrapped with canvas (typically cinnamon), or in jars (cloves, which were more perishable and expensive). The volatile and extremely valuable perfumed substances (musk, ambergris) were packed in small metal boxes where they were kept once they had been purchased until ready for shipment.

European merchants at the markets in Alexandria, Beirut, Damascus, or other Near Eastern cities had to know how to judge the freshness, aromatic properties, and possible adulteration of spices. A Venetian mercantile handbook known as the *Zibaldone da Canal* includes tips on how to distinguish good-quality spices. Here the concern is not so much deliberate dishonesty as deterioration. Few of the aromatic products sold in the eastern Mediterranean could be described as fresh from the tree. Great emphasis was placed on the units being "big," which seems to have meant full and not shriveled or in bits. Cassia reeds (a laxative related to cinnamon) ought to feel "whole, big and heavy," and when shaken they should not make a sound. Gum arabic must be big, white, and bright. Ginger needs to appear long, firm, and big. It should be cut open to make sure it is white and not dark. Nutmegs are to be bought only when they are big and firm, and no more than one-fourth of a measure should be unripe. When the shell of a nutmeg is pierced with a needle, it should yield a small amount of water, "and any other way is not worth anything."[8]

The merchants' handbooks also devote considerable attention to different weights and measures, which varied among different cities and commodities, as did the monetary units. It took skill to compare prices per unit of weight given the immense number of possible permutations. Even when there was a reasonably standard language of measurement, local fluctuations were substantial. According to the *Zibaldone da Canal,* pepper was sold in Alexandria by a unit of weight called a *carica,* equal to 715 "light pounds" of Venice, but ginger, sugar, and frankincense were sold by the *canter forbore,* equivalent to 142 light pounds. The gold dinars of Alexandria (known in Venice as *bezants*) bore a fluctuating relationship to silver dirhams, and to make matters more complex, there were periods when the Venetian coinage (gold ducats) was standard in Alexandrian transactions.[9]

The merchant also had to cope with volatility in the prices charged for spices at the eastern Mediterranean entrepôts. Prices were affected by many external factors ranging from the harvest conditions in Asia to transport problems created by warfare, political instability, shipwrecks, or piracy. Fluctuations in demand worldwide might also influence prices. Marco Polo claimed that for every shipload of pepper taken by European merchants from Alexandria, one hundred were off-loaded in the southern Chinese port of Zaiton (modern Quanzhou).[10] This is very likely an exaggeration, but it does show the global nature of the desire for spices and the many factors that might affect the relatively small European sector of the spice trade.

There is considerable information about spot prices in Alexandria and other ports and enough consistency in weights and units of currency to demonstrate considerable price variations. In 1355, for example, an Alexandrian *sporta* of pepper (about five hundred pounds) cost 163 gold dinars, a very high price for the period. Eleven years later pepper cost less than half that amount—between 75 and 86 dinars. It declined to a quite inexpensive 60 dinars per sporta in 1386, but in 1392 (for reasons we don't know) it was already 88 dinars in April and soared to 129 by August of that same year. It hovered between 60 and 100 for the remainder of the 1390s, but reached a breathtaking 200 dinars in 1412 before beginning a long decline.[11]

All of these challenges notwithstanding, the spice trade was sufficiently profitable to attract merchants who benefited from a considerable markup. It is very hard to compare the price where the spices were grown with what was eventually charged in the wholesale markets of Europe. For cloves in 1496–98, it has been estimated that the Venetian price was about one hundred times what traders paid for them in the Moluccas, which provides a rough picture of the tremendous transport and transfer costs, but also of the profits.[12] The price in Venice, it should be kept in mind, was itself greatly increased when the goods were then brought to northern Europe and sold at retail shops. It is easier to understand the profits of transporting spices from the eastern Mediterranean to Christian Europe. In 1343, Barcelona merchants bought spices in Cyprus and sold them in Barcelona at a 25 percent profit for pepper, 41 percent for cinnamon, and 20 percent for cloves. In the early fifteenth century Venetians were able to sell cloves for 72 percent more than they had paid for them in the Levant and nutmegs for as much as 400 percent profit.[13]

These revenues were garnered from a substantial trade, not just from a few small boxes of exotic miscellany. In an average year during the fifteenth century, Venetian merchants obtained at least 400 tons of pepper from Alexandria and another 104 tons from Beirut. There were occasional opportunities to acquire even greater quantities. In November 1496, on the eve of the Portuguese discovery of the sea route to India, four galleys arrived in Venice from Alexandria carrying, according to one estimate, what might have been four *million* pounds of spices, mostly but not exclusively pepper. Another convoy arrived in the same year, reportedly with another two million pounds, of which about half was pepper.[14] The scenes upon arrival might have resembled an admittedly much later account by Samuel Pepys in his diary for 1665. His duties as a customs officer in London included examining incoming spice cargoes, and he describes going through the hold of a captured Dutch vessel from the East Indies filled with "pepper scatter[ed] through every chink, you trod on it; and in cloves and nutmegs, I walked above the knees—whole rooms Full." The Dutch ship would have been larger and deeper than a medieval Venetian galley, but the cargo quantities are comparable even if perhaps the Venetians organized their containers better.[15]

THE RETAIL TRADE

The Venetians, Genoese, Catalans, and Provençaux distributed to the rest of Europe the spices they acquired in Alexandria and other eastern Mediterranean ports. Intermediate markets, such as Montpellier, served as regional suppliers, so that spice merchants from all over southern France would obtain their spices from what functioned as both a wholesale and retail market. Montpellier was known for special preparations made with the spices it acquired from international merchants. Among complex medical compounds, the theriac of Montpellier was particularly prized. Medieval gingerbread and preserved ginger from Montpellier were sold throughout France and beyond its borders, commanding prices twice as high as comparable confections made anywhere else.[16] Nuremberg was another center for the distribution of spices, in this case for central Europe. To this day the town is famous for its spiced Christmas cakes and gingerbread.

Retail merchants were not classified simply as sellers of spices and nothing more. The fundamental ambiguity of spices as condiments and spices as drugs carried over into consumer choices and retail outlets. The spice merchant (called a spicer in medieval England) could also function as an apothecary, a more-or-less licensed dispenser of medicine. There was also a change in the word "grocer," which had originated in English to mean a spice merchant who handled larger or wholesale quantities (thus dealing in "gross" amounts), before later becoming extended to someone handling all manner of edible products. The same semantic transformation occurred in French, wherein "épicier" went from meaning a spice merchant to the owner of a small food shop ("épicerie").

An apothecary's shop, from a fresco at the Castello di Issogne, Val d'Aosta (Italy), ca. 1500. (Photograph, Bridgeman Art Library)

In London spice merchants organized into guilds, initially as "pepperers" (first mentioned in 1180), slightly later as "spicers" and "apothecaries." These were not fixed, well-defined categories, and the same person could appear in the various records sometimes as apothecary, sometimes as spicer, sometimes as pepperer. A certain Simon Gut was denoted in London records by all three occupational titles. He was also called a grocer.[17] By 1400 the Grocers' Company of London had taken over the trades related to spices, drugs, and other exotic goods, until the apothecaries split off definitively in 1617, by which time the culinary and medical attributes of spices were conceptually separate. Among the mayors of London in the period between 1231 and 1341 were nine pepperers. Seventy spicers are mentioned in thirteenth- and fourteenth-century sources.[18] In late-fourteenth-century Barcelona there were 115 *especiers*.[19]

Merchants who supplied medicines also furnished spices to be used for various other purposes, just as spice merchants supplying cooking needs also dispensed drugs. A medieval French political treatise contains a miniature

Mary Magdalene buying spices to anoint the body of Jesus with,
in Pseudo-Bonaventure, *Meditationes Vitae Christii,* produced in Italy
in the mid-fourteenth century. (Library of Corpus Christi College,
Oxford, MS. 410, fol. 147, courtesy of the President and
Fellows of Corpus Christi College, Oxford)

painting of an urban street where wares are displayed outside shop entrances. The spice merchant has posted a sign advertising "good hippocras," and he also offers sugar and various pharmaceutical remedies stored in apothecary jars. A mural in the entryway to the castle of Issogne in the Val d'Aosta, painted in about 1500, depicts the interior of a lavishly appointed apothecary's shop. To the right a ragged assistant grinds the spices in a mortar. Another illustration of a pharmacy transaction is from a series of meditations on the life of Jesus that went under the name of the great thirteenth-century philosopher and spiritual writer St. Bonaventure. This Pseudo-Bonaventure manuscript from the mid-fourteenth century was composed in Italy, and one of its pictures shows Mary Magdalene's purchase of spices for anointing the body of Christ (Matthew 27:61 and Luke 23:55–56). She stands outside the shop as the apothecary offers her the mixture in a typical jar, with the scales, mortar, and pestles indicating his trade.

The medieval spice merchant or apothecary seems to have handled several kinds of products whose relation to each other is not all that clear: edible spices, medicine, sweets (including medicinal preparations but also candied fruit, sugar-coated nuts and spices, nougats, confectionary of all kinds), cordials (spiced and fortified wines), wax (candles and sealing wax), paper, and ink. Such establishments might even sell pasta or gunpowder.[20] From Constantinople the regulations for the guild of perfumers show the overlap between fragrance and dyestuffs. The members of the guild were instructed to have a standing supply of exotics that included edible spices, incense substances, and dye-coloring agents in addition to perfume ingredients.

We can get an idea of what sorts of medical remedies and other things apothecaries or spice merchants had on hand through property inventories made after a merchant's death by his executors. A spice merchant in Perugia who died in 1431 left a relatively modest stock of goods that included edible spices, such as pepper and ginger, but also dragon's blood, aloe wood, mastic oil, and coral, which were primarily used as medicines (although dragon's blood was also used as a red dye, aloe wood was important in devising perfume, and mastic oil was probably used more for cosmetic than medical purposes). This merchant also dealt in "myrobolans," a type of small dried plum imported in several varieties from India and used as a laxative, to purge an excess of bile or phlegm, and to warm "cold" stomachs.

At about the same time, in 1439, a Dijon pharmacist had twenty-four separate "spices" in his shop when he died, along with many other ingredients and compounds. The spices included exotic items on the order of pearls, coral, aloe wood, myrobolans, camphor, ambergris, frankincense. The inventory gives prices, showing that pepper and myrobolans were relatively inexpensive while camphor was three times costlier than pepper, ambergris five times, and musk an astronomical twenty-five times more.[21] A similar list (drawn up in 1353) for a Barcelona shop mentions more than a hundred different herbs, spices, scented waters, oils, and other preparations. Among the spices are gum arabic, galangal, cinnamon, cubeb, mastic, dragon's blood, and nutmeg.[22] Postmortem surveys of London grocers' shops from the reign of Richard II (1377–99) show that besides spices and drugs they might sell soap, honey, alum, lamp oil, seeds, pitch, and tar. These merchants diversified and carried on both a distributive trade (importing spices to be sold to provincial merchants) and an export trade in wool, for many years England's major international commodity.[23]

A more detailed picture of what apothecaries and spicers actually sold to clients is available from an account book kept by the Barcelona merchant Francesc ses Canes for 1378 to 1381, the last years of his life. Among his best customers was the count of Empúries, who ordered, among other things, medicines for his pet lion, including sugared bread and rose oil.[24] Francesc dealt in medicinal products and edible spices, but also in spiced wines, sauces (mostly involving pepper combined with other spices), scented waters, sealing wax, ink, and paper. He sold medicines in many forms: unguents, syrups, oils, washes, plasters, preserved in sugar (electuaries), and as clysters (suppositories or anal injections). Particularly conspicuous among the accounts of ses Canes are sugared luxuries, such as glazed or candied quince, anise, almonds, ginger, even small birds (larks, for example). These seem to have been ordered frequently by the count of Empúries when entertaining distinguished guests, like the king's eldest son, the bishop of Valencia, or a papal ambassador.[25] It is hard to distinguish medicines from luxurious sweets in the spice orders made by the agents of the count of Empúries. This same indeterminacy was present at the Grail Castle in *Perceval* where the banquet guests were served fruit, candies, electuaries, and medicinal cordials. Francesc ses Canes sold more than two hundred different products and at least one hundred aromatics confected in diverse forms for various uses.

A similar mix of products was purveyed by an apothecary in mid-fifteenth-century Arles (Provence). Raymond de Tarascon dealt in medicine all year round, but his sales of edible spices were concentrated in the fall (winter requiring hotter and drier foods, according to humoral theories). Like his Barcelona counterpart Francesc ses Canes, Raymond also supplied a certain number of ready-made spiced wines, powders, and sauces (to accompany lampreys, for example).[26] Even apothecaries in the provinces might have a surprising number of remedies on hand. A pharmacist from the town of Manresa, northwest of Barcelona, died in 1348 (presumably from the Black Death), and his shop contained 133 different medicines.[27]

Not all spices were sold through apothecaries or other authorized guild outlets. Ordinary people, especially in rural areas, might not have frequent access to such expensive commodities, but the taste for spices, especially as medicines, extended well below the level of the most affluent. Traveling peddlers carried medicinal herbs along with spices among their wares. An anonymous thirteenth-century French poem called the "Dit du Mercier" (The Peddler's Poem) gives an amusing and not completely inauthentic version of a salesman's patter to an audience of unsophisticated yokels. He sells all manner of trinkets, including gloves, purses, cloaks, thimbles, and relics, but also ginger, galangal, saffron, pepper, and cumin. Another work in the same genre by the well-known comic poet Rutebeuf alternates verse and prose self-advertising for a traveling quack specializing in medical cures. In this "Dit de l'Herberie" (The Herbalist's Poem), the self-described "doctor" has herbs that purport to be from Sicily and southern Italy (including the medical center Salerno), but also exotic plants "from the Indian deserts and the isle of Lincorinde." This somewhat mysterious country is said, confusingly, to border "on the water on all four parts of the world," leading some commentators to identify it as Ceylon, and others as a kind of floating island, but in either event a place of fantasy.[28]

The line between wandering charlatans and authorized apothecaries and spicers was not always absolutely fixed. Guild regulations might protect and limit certain trades, such as spicers, but other merchants too sold spices. In John Langland's allegorical *Piers Plowman,* "Glutton" thinks he will go to church to cleanse himself of his sins, but on his way he is accosted by all manner of tradesmen, including a woman who brews ale. She asks him if he'd like to try some and invites him to join the company in her establishment. Glutton asks if she has "hot spices" to flavor the ale and, in response to her affirmative reply that she has pepper, peony, and fennel seeds, he changes his mind about church and reverts to his old customs.[29]

As this example shows, we shouldn't imagine that storekeepers quietly waited for customers to come through their doors. The narrow urban streets resembled a bazaar more than a shopping mall. Retailers hawked their wares in the street, hoping to attract passersby, and we have some account of their sales pitches from the poem "London Lickpenny" in which the impoverished narrator stumbles through London, colliding with all kinds of merchandise and services that he cannot afford. The refrain for every stanza is a pathetic "For lacke of money, I may not speed." The poem comically juxtaposes urban wealth with individual poverty. Passing from the courts of Westminster to Cheapside in the City of London, the narrator is accosted by a spice seller urging him to buy pepper, saffron, cloves, "grains" (of paradise), and also rice flour, but he has money for none of these.[30]

The image of spice sellers was affected by their role as apothecaries and their often tense relationship with doctors. From the point of view of physicians, apothecaries were little better than itinerant merchants, whatever their guild status might be. Doctors accused them of carelessness in com- pounding medicines and a propensity to do their own prescribing. Then as now, the sale of drugs was quite lucrative, and doctors tried to wrest control of this trade from the hands of the apothecaries, alleging their lack of medical expertise and the danger of giving them the power to recommend such powerful substances. The medical faculty of the University of Paris, for example, in about 1271, forbade both spicers and peddlers from selling botanical drugs.[31]

Whoever was doing the selling, the problem of fraud in the retailing of spices was immense. The mercer and the herb peddler in the French poems are obvious charlatans who virtually announce this to their gullible audiences. But even if the consumer were spared the fake silver goblets or animal-bone relics, the purchase of spices was tricky. There was, in the first place, the problem of freshness. Spices are durable, and their aromatic virtue can be released by crushing them even when they have been dried out, but they are not immortal. After a series of voyages in stages from India or Indonesia to Europe that might have consumed several years, the condition of the spice cargoes was not ideal. The pharmaceutical guide *Circa instans* and its French translation, the *Livre des simples médecines,* offer advice about the durability of different drugs. That nutmeg lasts seven years is certainly credible, but the claim that pepper keeps for forty years will seem optimistic to anyone who has cleaned out their spice rack recently. Freshness and intrinsic quality were already issues at the wholesale stage in the markets of Alexandria and Beirut, and these deficiencies would hardly have been helped by a further sea voyage and overland transport.

The real challenge for retailers, which they passed along to their clients, was adulteration, which was practiced both to "stretch" good ingredients and artificially to enhance those of poor quality. Few commodities lend themselves as readily to adulteration as do spices. Jewels might be faked, but not so as to fool experts, and as objects sold and examined individually, they can't readily be watered down: one buys diamonds singly rather than, as with cloves, by the five- or fifty-pound sack. The very aromatic haze that made spices attractive allowed the unscrupulous to disguise substandard or fake ingredients among genuine nutmegs, peppercorns, or other aromatics. Some foreign material in spice shipments was expected and priced into retail tariffs. Spices required sorting and cleansing to get rid of impurities, a process called "garbling." The guild of Pepperers of Sopers Lane, the spice street in the City of London, appointed garblers to inspect and certify purity before spices were weighed.[32] Spices were sufficiently valuable so that even the inferior residue, what the Italian merchants called the *garbellatura,* was not simply discarded but sold as a cheaper, lower-quality version of an intrinsically precious product. Francesco Pegolotti's commercial handbook lists the spices that are normally garbled and compares the price of the inferior siftings with the pure aromatics. Thus mastic garbellatura is worth one-fifth the price of first-quality mastic. The ratio for pepper is one-third; for ginger one-half; for nutmeg one-third as long as there was no dust in the garbellatura.[33]

In *Piers Plowman,* the character "Liar" decides to become a spice merchant. This is appropriate not only because he is said to know a lot about aromatic "gums" but also because he knows how to extend them fraudulently.[34] Mixing fake with authentic spices is enshrined in a small corner of American historical lore. Legend has it that sharp Connecticut traders perfected the manufacture of imitation wooden nutmegs that were added to real ones, the fakery covered by the cunning artifice of their making and the powerful aroma of the real nutmegs. The popularizer of this story was Thomas Chandler Halliburton (1796–1865), a Canadian judge from Nova Scotia, who wrote folkloric stories about Sam Slick, a Yankee peddler who sold nutmegs liberally laced with wooden fakes. The tale was so appealing that the state adopted the unusual sobriquet "the Nutmeg State," which says something about the admiration of business success over mere ethics.[35]

Medieval adulteration was not always so ingenious. One easy fraud was dousing spices with water to increase their weight. In 1316, the London pepperers prohibited any moistening of saffron, ginger, or cloves.[36] *Circa instans* and its French translation note some common ploys and recommend tests to combat them: fake ambergris can be broken into pieces, but genuine ambergris can't. Poor-quality cloves are artificially enhanced by being wrapped with a little powder made from good cloves to which perfumed wine and vinegar have been added. To detect this more painstaking fraud, the cloves need to be tasted to see if the flavor comes from inside the spice (in which case they are genuine) or if they exude their fragrance from the outside (the mark of adulteration).[37]

The temptation to profit from adulteration was great. Saffron was especially vulnerable because of its extremely high price, which explains the corresponding value of even a small addition to its weight or diminution of its purity. Catalan regulations of the fifteenth century describe three ways of adulterating saffron: mixing in foreign but not readily visible ingredients such as (apparently) eggs, must, and lard; not cutting the stigmas of the flower closely so that some of what is called the "style" (the stem) is included (this still goes on); and adding to the weight by moistening the saffron with olive oil.[38]

By the fifteenth century, Catalonia was a leading exporter of the spice and Spain as a whole was thought to produce the best-quality saffron. Rulers and merchant associations were careful to safeguard the reputation of such a valuable commodity, but fraud at the point of sale remained a significant problem. Records for Nuremberg and Cologne in the fifteenth century show many instances of punishment for selling illegitimate saffron. Quantities of false and adulterated saffron were publicly burned in Nuremberg in 1441, 1447, and 1449. A falsifier was himself condemned to death by burning in 1444.[39] A particularly detailed case of saffron adulteration comes from Montpellier, where in the mid-fourteenth century, twelve pounds of suspicious saffron were seized by the municipal government from the merchant Johannes Andree. He claimed immunity from the town's jurisdiction on the grounds that he was an official coiner of money for the king and so answerable only to royal courts. The case dragged on for a few years until Johannes Andree finally gave up his claims of immunity. He was found guilty and deprived of the right to sell spices. Interestingly enough, he readily admitted that he moistened the saffron, but denied that he had introduced any sort of foreign substance. The impression one gets is that dishonest weight was a less serious matter than adulteration. At any rate, experts who inspected the confiscated sacks suspected that honey, oats, powder, or liquor had been added. The witnesses, including pepperers, apothecaries, and others with practice in weighing material for sale, all agreed that the saffron in question had been heavily adulterated.[40]

THE COST OF SPICES

Finally we reach the important but tricky question of what spices actually cost when they were bought by the person who was going to consume them. Information about prices survives, but what it means in terms of purchasing power or in comparison with expenses familiar to us is not easy to determine. Part of this problem is the incredible variety of medieval weights and measures, both in their terminology and in how such seemingly standard units as pounds or pence varied in different towns and kingdoms. Part of it also has to do with what people wanted to spend money on. Clothes, weapons, retainers, and spices were all considerably more important expenses than they are now. Obviously it is possible to spend lots of money today on things that didn't exist in the Middle Ages—unusual automobiles, wildly expensive art objects, school tuition, for example—but retainers ("service professionals"), charity, and jewels have a greater degree of continuous significance for wealthy households. Clothes and food, however, do not now constitute a very substantial expense on a percentage basis in the way that they did in the Middle Ages. It's not just that spices cost a lot in the past—in some sense they still do. A pound of nutmeg now requires an outlay of about one hundred dollars, but how many affluent people in the Western world buy nutmeg by the pound? The fact that nutmeg was used in large quantities in both medieval cuisine and medicine means that its value as a percentage of household expenditure was vastly greater than in modern times. Historians who have studied the day-to-day expenses of royal households have shown that the purchase of spices consumed a substantial portion of the money paid out to furnish the king and his large entourage with victuals while they traveled the kingdom or were in their palaces. Spices were bought in fairly small quantities, but very frequently and at great cost. The kings of Aragon-Catalonia seem to have served and consumed a lot of spiced wine, while the vehicle for spices in the English court was more likely to be sauces.[41]

The importance of spices in aristocratic and royal expenditures is related to their unit cost and to the fact that they were bought and consumed in large quantities. An idea of the value of spices can be obtained by comparing their prices to the overall cost of living and average wage. John Munro, an economic historian at the University of Toronto, has calculated the price of spices in England in the year 1439 using a skilled London craftsman's average daily wage as a yardstick for comparison. The craftsman could earn eight pence per day. For one penny he could buy a gallon of milk, a pint of butter or lard, or a quarter bushel of coal. Seven yards of good-quality wool cloth cost about ten days' wages, seven shillings (eighty-four pence), but the same quantity of velvet, a luxury fabric, would have a stratospheric price equivalent to between two and three hundred days' earnings. A pound of sugar cost sixteen pence, so about two days' labor. Pepper cost slightly more, ginger somewhat less in 1439. A pound of cloves would cost four and a half days' work, while a similar quantity of cinnamon would require three days' wages. To purchase a pound of saffron, however, required at least fifteen shillings, the equivalent of a month's work.[42]

The small kingdom of Navarre in the western Pyrenees on either side of the modern French-Spanish border provides an example of relative prices in a less cosmopolitan setting than London. The kings of Navarre were important princes with connections throughout northern Spain and southern France. Between 1408 and 1412, royal household accounts show that the price of pepper doubled from eight to sixteen *sueldos carlines* to the pound.

A pound of ginger, somewhat more expensive than pepper, remained steady at an average of three and one-half times a carpenter's daily wages, while cloves rose from five to six times those wages.

Commercial accounts and inventories of retail spice businesses made by estate executors also show something about the pricing structure. The accounts of Francesc ses Canes in Barcelona for the years 1378 to 1381 show what retail customers actually were charged. Pepper seems to have cost five *sous* per pound. Saffron was eighty sous for the same weight, and cloves were nearly as expensive. Ginger in its various grades ranged from an economical four sous, four pence per pound for "Mecca" ginger, to seven sous, ten pence for the whiter "Belledi" variety. The price of camphor, as always, was extremely high, here 176 sous (shillings) per pound. If these prices are compared with a valuation made in 1348 of another pharmacist's estate nearby, in the Catalan town of Manresa, it's clear that some prices were steady (the price of pepper was the same at Manresa in 1348 and Barcelona between 1378 and 1381), and others fluctuated greatly (saffron was only ten sous per pound in Manresa in 1348, compared with eighty in Barcelona thirty years later).[43]

From the detailed but not-always-conclusive or easy-to-evaluate records, we certainly have evidence of the variety of spices available and of the large volume of traffic. The price was high, but neither uniform among spices nor consistent over time given all the factors affecting particularly the supply. Spices fall into four medieval price categories. First were the basic spices, which made up the bulk of the spice trade and were expensive but relatively affordable: pepper, ginger, and sugar. A second category comprises common but more highly prized and costly spices, such as cinnamon, long pepper, and galangal. An even more expensive and greatly desirable group of edible spices were those from the Moluccas, especially cloves and nutmeg. The most extravagantly priced spices were a fourth category consisting of precious medical substances like ambergris, camphor, and musk, but also saffron, which in certain respects occupies a place of its own since it was both extremely expensive and widely used. Saffron was both a European and Asian product and so crossed certain conceptual boundaries in classifying spices.

There arises at this point the fundamental question that underlies this entire book: why were spices so valuable? Earlier chapters described how they were used in cooking and medicine and their intangible mystique—the fact that they came from far away, their association with exotic lands, even with the earthly paradise, the combined allure of expense, healthfulness, flavor, and prestige. In the next chapter we look at their economic value and rarity, not in terms of price or availability as such, but in terms of the *idea* of rarity and contemporary explanations for why spices cost what they did. This will help us not only to understand the basis of the demand for spices (what it meant to say that they were valuable because they were rare), but to determine why Europeans ventured out into unknown waters, at considerable peril, to find something already available through the safer, routine trade with the eastern Mediterranean. If spices in reasonably large quantities were being picked up in Alexandria by the Venetians and Genoese, why run the terrible risks of disease, shipwreck, and almost every other kind of danger to sail to the Indies? The answer has to do with perceived opportunity and a belief in staggering profits way beyond the respectable markup achieved by the Italian merchants.

FIVE
Scarcity, Abundance, and Profit

Supply and demand is the simple but not completely sufficient answer to the question of why spices were so expensive in medieval Europe. Here we want to know how contemporaries explained the high prices. Although they lacked mathematical economic models, medieval observers were aware that cost had something to do with demand. Europeans loved spices and this infatuation enriched distant infidels, a fact that sometimes provoked outrage over what was denounced as a frivolous if long-lasting fad. Yet the elevated prices commanded by spices were also understood to be the result of distance and scarcity—in other words, related to the supply. Supply was limited by the remoteness of Asia from Europe, and by the irreplaceable nature of particular commodities (there were no European substitutes for pepper and ginger). Since few spices flourished in Europe, the fact that these aromatic products came from far away made it logical that they should cost a lot.

But supply is a complicated matter. There are different kinds of rarity, depending on whether something is naturally scarce or in some sense artificially restricted through human intervention. Monopolies tend to make things that are not necessarily or intrinsically expensive cost more, because of the hold a cartel has on the gathering or distribution of a commodity. Medieval people understood the effects of hoarding, speculating, and withholding goods from the market. They knew all too vividly how prices could be manipulated by fear, especially the cost of necessities like wheat in times of famine. There were stringent laws and plenty of moral censure against speculation and profiting from panic and dearth, but these were not always (or even usually) effective.

Spices were hardly in the same category as basic foodstuffs, and interruptions in their supply caused only limited perturbation compared with the threat of starvation. Yet, because spices came to Europe through Muslim intermediaries and because their ultimate origins were mysterious, it was not surprising to Europeans that prices might be manipulated by middlemen who were already considered religious enemies.

There were three possible kinds of rarity: intrinsic, circumstantial, and artificial. Intrinsic rarity would be something resembling the current status of Italian white truffles: nature just doesn't produce many of them and it has so far proved impossible to cultivate them. As with the truffles, there might not be very much spice in the world because it only grew in certain places under special conditions or climates.

Circumstantial rarity is natural in the sense that nature rather than human intervention limits the supply, but here the limitation is imposed not by climate, soil, or other intrinsic obstacles but rather by the difficulty of acquiring the product desired. Saffron is today extremely expensive, just as it was in the Middle Ages, not because it is a rare plant—in fact it can grow in many climates—but because the usable part is tedious to harvest and requires an immense amount of labor. Each flower has only three orange-red stigmas, so that seventy thousand flowers are needed to obtain a single pound of saffron.

A third kind of rarity is that imposed by human action, usually through deliberate restriction of the supply in order to increase the price. The product may then not be as rare as its price might lead one to believe. Diamonds, for example, are more common in the modern world than the prices they command would seem to indicate. When monopoly control by the De Beers Company of South Africa was effective, the price of diamonds was more than twice what it has become since the end of the cartel in the 1990s. Thus until recently a moderately rare product was monopolized and so rendered artificially even rarer.

Of course not everything that is rare is necessarily valuable. Mastic, a resin derived from a plant in the acacia family, grows only in Chios (an Aegean island), and was highly valued and expensive in the Middle Ages. As earlier discussed, it was used in medicine, as both a fumigant and an oral drug, and to a lesser extent in cooking. So valuable was it that Columbus mentioned it in his first exultant letter to Ferdinand and Isabella along with such things as gold and silver, as precious commodities he was (wrongly) sure he had found. Unlike other important medieval aromatics, mastic has never been transplanted and it still grows only in Chios (and only in southern Chios at that), so its supply remains quite limited. Nevertheless, today it has only marginal value as a flavoring in some Greek and Turkish sweets and liqueurs. The price of mastic is merely a fraction of what was obtained in the Middle Ages when it was credited with great curative powers.[1]

Natural and artificially imposed scarcity interacted with demand, so that rare substances might not be particularly valuable, or things not especially rare might nevertheless be credited with great value. Crucial decisions depended on how merchants and entrepreneurs interpreted the reason for the high price and perceived rarity of spices. If spices were intrinsically rare, then even if one made the perilous voyage to India one would find them still set at a high price. Such a trip would not be worth the extraordinary effort and danger. To quantify and exemplify the risk, we might consider the fact that less than half of Vasco da Gama's crew returned from his first voyage to India in 1497–99. The first circumnavigation of the globe by Magellan's ships set out with something on the order of 260 men, but only 18 made it back to Lisbon.[2] Even well after these pioneering voyages, when the journey to the Indies might seem to have become routine, the chances of survival were not good. Between 1500 and 1634, 28 percent of all ships that set out from Portugal bound for India were lost at sea, and this doesn't even take into account the deaths from disease and malnutrition of sailors whose ships survived the voyage.[3] Who would gamble with life on such frightening odds for a mere 20 percent profit?

Those who ventured as far as India and Indonesia must clearly have assumed that spices were abundant, not in fact rare at all, in their native habitat. Their high price in Europe might be explained partially by distance, but even more by the monopolistic hold Muslim intermediaries were attempting to protect. They had to believe that circumventing the Mediterranean entrepôts controlled by the Muslims in order to find the direct path to the Indies would lead to exorbitant profits, because the price of spices in East Asia must be so low that even the length and difficulty of the voyage would make it economically worthwhile. In fact this generally proved to be the case. Da Gama's second voyage to India in 1502–3 resulted in the acquisition of 1,700 tons of spices, equivalent to what Venice obtained in an average year, and the profit realized was something on the order of 400 percent.[4] The purpose of this chapter is to explore the late-medieval European confidence in the abundance of spices in Asia and how this replaced earlier beliefs in their intrinsic or circumstantial scarcity.

CIRCUMSTANTIAL RARITY AND THE DIFFICULT PEPPER HARVEST

In the seventh century, the learned polymath Isidore of Seville, author of an etymologically based encyclopedia, wrote that pepper comes from India where there are forests of pepper trees. The trees are "guarded" by poisonous snakes, so that it is impossible to harvest the valuable berries in a normal fashion. Instead, the natives set fires among the trees to drive away the snakes, and incidentally turn the white peppercorns black, which is why what is commonly sold is black and shriveled. Here is a classic, if inaccurate, example of circumstantial rarity. There are whole forests of pepper trees, so even though pepper grows only in India, it isn't really rare in the way that, for example, truffles or rubies are. What makes pepper de facto rare, hence legitimately expensive, is the difficulty of gathering it, because of the snakes.

Later writers noted that if the trees had to be burned for the pepper to be gathered, the entire pepper grove would have to be entirely replanted, presumably at great additional effort, time, and cost. The author of the pharmacological manual *Circa instans* says flatly that this is reason enough to doubt the entire story, but there were many later commentators and experts who repeated, elaborated, and debated the serpents' infestation of the pepper groves, a surprisingly durable legend whose origins lie centuries before Isidore himself.[5] There is a long-standing association of precious substances with dangerous creatures, an aspect of the same pairing of the alluring and the perilous exotic found in accounts of the earthly paradise surrounded by deserts or monstrous races, the same relation between images of India as wealthy yet replete with frightening animals, humanoids, and bizarre customs.

As far back as Herodotus, writing in the fifth century B.C., snakes and other dangers made it difficult to acquire spices. Frankincense, according to Herodotus, is guarded by snakes, while cassia is patrolled by dangerous batlike creatures. Cinnamon does not have perilous guardians, but it grows in inaccessible mountains in Arabia. The only way to obtain the cinnamon is to trick birds of the region who build their nests out of cinnamon sticks and twigs. The natives of Arabia leave out pieces of meat, tempting the birds, who drag the pieces back to their nests. The weight of the meat is sufficient to break the nests, which fall to the ground where the valuable spice twigs can be collected.[6] Writing about three centuries later, Pausanias, author of a kind of tour guide of the religious, artistic, and historic sites of Greece, remarks that in Arabia the precious aromatic resin balsam grows surrounded by vipers. Pausanias is unusual because he actually tells the reader why the snakes are so fond of this aromatic plant. Apparently they nourish themselves on balsam and become so happily docile under its influence that their bite is no longer poisonous.[7] So balsam is in fact easy to collect, compared with the spices mentioned in Herodotus.

Tales of snakes and how they are thwarted were useful to merchants as explanations or justifications for the high cost of spices. Retailers often emphasize or exaggerate the difficulty of obtaining exotic (or putatively exotic) or high-quality ingredients—"rare" botanicals for perfumes, "hand selected" or "belting" leather for car seats, "diver" scallops. When it isn't really known where a valued commodity comes from, this mystification is all the more plausible, tempting, and attractive. Hellenistic and Roman writers, such as the naturalist Pliny and the botanist Theophrastus, ridiculed Herodotus' "fables" and his credulity for believing stories spread in order to elevate prices by the people of Arabia and other regions where spices grew. Yet Pliny (not someone normally known for his skepticism about wonders) and Theophrastus elsewhere describe aromatic plants as being guarded by snakes, or discuss without derisive comment the alleged habit of the immortal phoenix in building its nest out of cinnamon sticks.[8]

Yet the attractiveness of these stories cannot be attributed solely to commercial exaggeration. Consider a variant on Herodotus' account of using slabs of meat to acquire, in this case, not spices but jewels. Epiphanius, a fifth-century bishop of Constantia in Cyprus (modern Famagusta), wrote a treatise on the gems mentioned in the Bible. He had no commercial investments or interests. Epiphanius commented on the book of Exodus, where the complicated instructions for furnishing the Temple in Jerusalem include a list of gems that must ornament the breastplate of the priests' garments (Exodus 28:15–20, 39:8–13). The importance of these gems is reinforced by their reappearance in the book of Revelation, which describes the walls of the New Jerusalem decorated with topaz, emeralds, pearls, and other precious and semiprecious stones (Revelation 21:18–21). Writing in his lapidary about the biblical jewel known as hyacinth or jacinth (probably to be identified with the zircon), Epiphanius reports that this stone is gotten out of inaccessible Scythian gorges by throwing pieces of meat down into the ravines. The gems adhere to the meat, trained birds fetch the meat, and the inhabitants retrieve the stones.[9]

Epiphanius reflects the basic appeal of exotic products associated with difficult and peculiar circumstances in gathering them. His account may be related to merchants' tales, but it has clearly taken on a life of its own. No one can say that scholars of the medieval period lacked imagination. What is more significant than this odd bit of lore in itself is how persistent, how attractive it would be across cultures and centuries. Later reworking of Epiphanius and other versions of the meat and gorge phenomenon added snakes, making the ravines all the more inaccessible. The tale traveled east, to be found in the Sinbad story of the Arabian Nights as one of the wonders of India and in Chinese and Byzantine lore as well. A medieval treatise on gems falsely attributed to Aristotle says it is the glance, not the bite, of the serpents that is fatal. Alexander the Great put up mirrors so that the snakes stared at themselves and so died. Just to be on the safe side, however, he retrieved the gems by using sheep carcasses and birds according to the pattern established by Epiphanius.[10] The snake-infested gorges also appear in Marco Polo's description of how diamonds are obtained in India: Diamonds are found only in deep crevasses in one part of India. The gorges are infested with poisonous snakes, and so white eagles are trained to lift out the meat, along with the diamonds. The diamonds are retrieved by either scaring the birds or collecting the gems they leave behind.[11]

The difficulties of gathering spices and jewels were curiosities that might be doubted or even refuted, but the attraction of these accounts was so great that they appear in travel literature, books of strange facts, geographical treatises and notes that accompany maps, and encyclopedias.[12] The story flourished because it meant something to consumers of spices and gems. An already exotic commodity was further enhanced by being thought of as strangely difficult to acquire.

Such legends, imaginative as they are, have economic implications. As was already pointed out, the scarcity of pepper in Isidore's classic formulation is not absolute because, after all, there are entire forests of pepper trees. The rarity of pepper is circumstantial because its acquisition involves danger and requires both labor and skill. The price of pepper, even in India, must therefore be substantial to reward all that effort, not to mention compensation for the very long intervals between harvests if the trees have to be burned. If there really are snakes and the pepper trees are burned, this is going to limit the profits to be made from cutting out the middleman and buying from the producer, which in turn will discourage plans to make such direct contacts given the risk and difficulty involved.

The period leading up to the voyages of discovery, commerce, and colonialism at the end of the Middle Ages saw the triumph of different, more optimistic though not necessarily more accurate ideas about the supply of spices and other precious commodities. These new accounts emphasized either naturalistic availability of precious commodities (pepper grows and is harvested more or less like other plants), or abundance and an almost absurd ease and lack of expense in acquiring goods that are valuable in Europe (the El Dorado myths of cities paved with gold). Both the unexotic accounts that made spices appear a more normal commodity and the fantasies of absurd plentitude were important in spurring the desire of Europeans to find the lands where spices grew, but the latter were more important even if wildly inaccurate, because it was only the expectation of magical abundance, not a merely adequate supply, that drew men like da Gama and Columbus and that sufficiently excited their patrons to put up the money for these ventures.

"NORMAL" SUPPLIES AND HARVESTS

It stands to reason that valuable commodities impossible to grow or mine in Europe should be less expensive and so less spectacularly desirable in the distant lands where they originate. How much less expensive is, of course, the issue. Medieval observers noted that what is deemed wonderfully rare in one place might be ordinary and unremarkable elsewhere. There is a rhetorical trope of "parallelism" in travel writing, a relativistic observation that foreigners seem strange to us, but we in turn seem strange to them.[13] One aspect of this phenomenon is that what seems exotic and rare in Europe might be commonplace in Asia. An example of this appears in the previously quoted passage from Joinville about how the Nile brings down from paradise pieces of aloe wood and cinnamon that fall into it just as regular trees drop unexciting branches into European rivers. One of the early European visitors to India, the Franciscan Odoric of Pordenone, says in the Italian version of his account that on the Malabar Coast of India, pepper is as plentiful as grain is in Europe. Marco Polo, the first European to describe Japan, claimed (without having visited it) that gold was so common there that the imperial palace was roofed with the precious metal in the same way that lead is used for church roofs in Europe.[14]

Conversely one might imagine that everyday items in Europe could be regarded as rare and valuable far away. According to St. Jerome (and as repeated by Isidore of Seville in his *Etymologies*), the ordinary European herb pennyroyal costs more in India than pepper does. In a poem about gardens, the ninth-century monk Walafrid Strabo varied this slightly to say that the price of pennyroyal in India is the same as the price of pepper in Europe.[15] It was also believed that in China olive oil was rare, costly, and treasured as a sovereign medical remedy.[16]

Such relativism tends to render foreign customs less bizarre and makes it possible to imagine life in places like India as understandable, even unexotic. The first Europeans to recount their visits to India did not completely discredit the story of the snakes and the pepper trees, but they offered more naturalistic accounts. Marco Polo, avoiding saying anything about snakes or fire, simply reported that pepper is a domesticated crop that grows in Malabar and is harvested from May through July. His account of the diamonds of India, however, makes use of the inaccessible gorges and poisonous snakes. Odoric of Pordenone, writing over twenty years later, depicts pepper realistically (and accurately) in terms of plants familiar to a European audience. Pepper grows on vines, not on trees. The vine leaves resemble ivy. Pepper is planted between trees in the manner of grape vines, which need something to grow around. Odoric has seen that pepper is dried not by fire but by being laid out in the sun.

According to Odoric, the supply of pepper is restricted in that it grows nowhere else in the world except Malabar. On the other hand, the unique pepper forest extends as far as a man can travel in eighteen days, so the supply is in fact immense. Dangerous animals haunt the pepper groves: crocodiles (which Odoric considered a kind of serpent) infest the rivers. In one Odoric manuscript, the crocodiles have to be driven away by fire, so we are not yet completely out of the fog of legend, but the reptiles are timid and scared off by what seem to be smoldering campfires rather than a great conflagration.[17]

Writing at about the same time, the Dominican friar Jordan of Sévérac likened the pepper vine to the European wild grape. The fruit is green when unripe, but eventually it turns black and wrinkled. Jordan was very fond of marvels (indeed his travelogue is entitled *Mirabilia descripta*), but here he is contemptuous of the idea that pepper is burned or cooked by fires set to drive away snakes, saying it is simply a lie. John Mandeville, whose supposed travels from 1322 to 1356 were invented (as was his name), also uses the description of the pepper harvest to show off how careful he is about accuracy (in a narrative that is more or less one marvel after another). The trees don't really have to be burned, as that would mean no harvest could take place for years. There are indeed infestations of poisonous snakes, according to Mandeville, but it is easy to protect against them. The serpents flee from a repellent made of lemon juice, snails, and unspecified other ingredients.[18]

The Franciscan missionary John of Marignolli returned to Europe in 1353 after a long stay in first China and then India. John tended to favor sober, nonmiraculous explanations for seemingly strange phenomena. So, for example, stories invented about Sciopods, the one-footed monstrous humanoids who use their oversize foot to shade themselves from the sun, are a misunderstanding of the umbrellas people in India carry against both sun and rain. With regard to pepper, John is the most naturalistic observer. He repeats what Jordan and Odoric said about the pepper plant being a creeper that resembles European grapevines. Pepper grows in regular orchards, not in the middle of the desert as some believe. It is harvested in a prosaic way, without burning or special tools. John says he himself has seen pepper being harvested. So unexotic is the process that his account portrays the natives themselves as familiar rather than different—they are even Christian! Like Odoric, John claims that the entire world's supply of pepper comes from India and adds that it is exported through the Indian port of Quilon on the Malabar Coast.[19]

All of these naturalistic accounts of a plentiful pepper supply by visitors to India did not completely displace the venerable legends of scarcity. Cardinal Pierre d'Ailly (1350–1420), author of many important works of theology, philosophy, and the political theory of the church, was also an influential geographer. His findings, in a work titled *Imago mundi,* encouraged Columbus in his belief that only a small expanse of ocean separated western Africa from eastern Asia. D'Ailly reports the story of the serpents guarding the pepper trees without comment. The same is true of the erudite Aeneas Sylvius Piccolomini (1405–64), who took the name Pius II when he was elected pope in 1458. In his geographical work, known as the *Cosmographia,* gems and other valuable products abound in India. There was no work that Columbus read more closely than the *Cosmographia,* and it contributed to the admiral's expectation of immense Asian wealth, but still the snakes surround the pepper trees, a lingering example of marvelous scarcity.[20]

The Venetian merchant Niccolò de' Conti, who traveled to India and as far east as Java, returned to Europe around 1440 after having been away for twenty-five years. He was debriefed by the papal secretary, the humanist Poggio Bracciolini, who also obtained absolution for Conti's forced apostasy and conversion to Islam while in Egypt. Conti confirmed Marco Polo's narrative about the wealth and extent of China and the importance of the islands east of India. He also repeated Marco Polo's account of how diamonds in India are taken out of snake-infested gorges. He was more accurate about the geography of India, identifying the region within the southern kingdom of Vijayanagar ("Bezengalia") where diamonds come from. Regarding pepper, however, Conti was aware that it grows in "Taprobane" (here meaning Sumatra) as well as in India. The serpents in Malabar (where along with pepper, ginger, brazil nut, and cinnamon also flourish) are not very formidable in comparison with those in the diamond valleys. They are inoffensive unless provoked and can be caught and tamed by enchantments known to the natives.[21]

The survival of the belief that snakes impede the gathering of pepper or diamonds did not mean that the consensus on the eve of the European explorations was still that such valuable imports were scarce. By this time the blame for the high cost of spices tended to be focused on economic rather than marvelous interference, on avoidable human agency rather than on fixed natural conditions. Obstacles to acquiring and profiting from spices, according to this view, have nothing to do with either intrinsic or circumstantial rarity restricting supply, but rather with commercial exploitation of a long and fragmented import route.

An unusually clear and detailed explanation for the cost of spices in Europe comes from the annotations to the oldest surviving globe, created in 1492 by Martin Behaim, a cartographer who worked in Nuremberg.[22] Behaim's depiction of the world is often taken as the most up-to-date understanding of global geography on the eve of the great voyages of discovery. Although there is no proof that Columbus was familiar with Behaim's scheme, it is widely assumed that his view of the layout of oceans and continents follows this model closely.

Behaim preserves some of the marvels associated with valuable products and the difficulty of gathering them. Diamonds and gems abound in India, for example, but they are watched over by snakes. Most of Behaim's annotations about spices, however, describe a purely man-made reason for their high cost: the monopolistic practices of intermediaries. The many points of transfer in the shipment of spices from their origins in Asia to the consumer in Europe offer opportunities for governments and traders to profit, elevating the price at each step of the route.

Behaim was aware that spices grew in other places besides India, although his list is somewhat eccentric. He included Java, Indochina, and Sumatra, which do produce spices, but also Japan and the Nicobar Islands in the Indian Ocean, which do not. The reason why spices are expensive, according to Behaim, is not rarity but rather the transaction costs involved in their transport. There are no fewer than twelve stages that spices have to pass through before arriving in Behaim's native Germany. First the inhabitants of the island he calls "Java Major" (Java or perhaps Borneo), collect spices from other islands and sell them to merchants coming from Ceylon. Brought to Ceylon, the spices are then sold to traders from the legendary "Golden Khersonese," which may be a dim reflection of the Malay Peninsula (Kherson, an ancient name for the Crimea, serving as a general term for any peninsula). The spices are then transferred again, to merchants from Taprobane (probably Sumatra). Thus far we have a sophisticated, if inaccurate, description of a meandering progress of spices around East Asia. Behaim becomes more accurate as the spices are brought westward by the "heathen Mohammedans" via Aden and Cairo. The remaining steps involve the distribution of spices by way of Venice, Frankfurt, Bruges, and finally to retailers in Germany.

All these points of transfer involve taxation by public authorities and opportunities for private profit. The customs levies alone, Behaim claims, account for a substantial share of what is ultimately a quite astronomical markup. His conclusion is succinct: "One must know that the spices from the islands in East India must pass through many hands before they come here to our land. . . . No wonder spices for us cost their weight in gold."

Growing understanding of the economic situation certainly represented progress over an obsessively miraculous worldview. By offering a human rather than marvelous explanation for the cost of spices, observers like Behaim contributed to the optimistic expectation of profits that was a necessary motivation for European attempts to find spices in their place of origin. In themselves, however, such theories could not have overcome the risks and expense of undertaking dangerous and distant voyages. The profits of middlemen had to be linked to an abundant, even spectacularly plentiful supply, not just moderate quantities of a restricted commodity. In order to be tempted to find unknown lands and exploit their wealth, entrepreneurs had to be confident that on arrival they would find an inexhaustible and easily acquired supply. Spices had to be not just a bit cheaper and easier to find than in Europe: they had to be available in East Asia for virtually nothing.

Accurate information and better technology are important in promoting discovery, but so are excessively optimistic, unrealistic, even flat-out false anticipations. The marvelous is more important than the scientific in the initial and most risky stages of innovation. Business histories tend to emphasize technological or conceptual, "paradigm-shifting" breakthroughs, but it is the crazes, fads, and marvels that seize the imagination, including that of investors and those who undertake physical and financial risks. The gold rush, the Internet craze, tulip mania, the South Sea Bubble—some of these were exaggerations, others were swindles, but they have a prominent, if unappealingly irrational, place in the history of innovation.

Marco Polo's golden roofs of Japan are a classic example of overpromising. Polo himself did not devote very much time to elaborating on this image of plenitude, but it had a long life as a popular idea and was featured in recruitment for the first voyage of Columbus. When Martín Alonso Pinzón, the captain of the *Pinta,* addressed prospective sailors, he contrasted their current miserable poverty with the allure of the lands they were about to explore, "where the roofs are made of gold."[23] Myths of abundance were built into the medieval European imagination. India in the Alexander legends was full of marvels but also of inexhaustible riches. The wealth of King Solomon in the Bible came from gold mines in the land of "Ophir." All the Bible says is that Ophir is a three-year sea voyage from Israel, and medieval commentators and geographers attempted to identify its location in various distant corners of the world. The king of "the Three Indias," Prester John, epitomized medieval faith in the riches of the East and confidence, or at least hope, that these could be mobilized to rescue Christendom.

On a more applied level, enchantment with the riches of Asia is evident in the annotations Columbus made to the works of geographers and travelers, such as Marco Polo, Pierre d'Ailly, and Pius II. In his book about Marco Polo, the historian John Larner likens these marginal comments about exotic products to "some miser's bright recollections of an Aladdin's cave." In Asia, according to Columbus' notes, there are "great treasures," "much incense," "pepper, cinnamon, nuts." It is not only that aromatics and precious metals happen to be found in far-off lands, but that they exist "in abundance" or "in great abundance." Japan has "gold in the greatest abundance" along with red pearls. The islands south of China (the East Indies) have "infinite spices," "whitest pepper," and "perfumes in abundance." The port of Aden teems with "many ships carrying aromatics."[24]

By the time of Columbus, the astonishing wealth of Asia was accepted, entrancing, and widely mulled over. The frightening marvels of Asia were also still important and associated with exotic products, so that insofar as Columbus heard rumors of dog-headed humanoids or other "monstrous races," he believed he was close to the spices and gold of his dreams, but the classic marvels—monsters, snakes, rivers of sand, a land of perpetual darkness—tended to yield to stories that concentrated on the continent's riches. The strangeness of the East became more a surrounding atmosphere for its wealth rather than the main narrative.

The image of the Great Khan and of China exemplifies this emphasis on wildly alluring tales of wealth, but here without a supernatural basis. Part of what Marco Polo accomplished (and one reason why he was not at first widely believed) was that his marvels were not the expected ones. Marco

Polo wrote almost nothing on the monstrous races, relegates Prester John to near irrelevance, doubts the existence of the fireproof salamander, and identifies the unicorn with the rhinoceros. What he emphasizes is the new marvel of the endless and populous cities in China, all unknown to classical and biblical commentators. The wealth of China according to Marco Polo is the result of human effort, not of profligate nature. Japan and the Indies abound in gold and spices, but China is depicted as productive on a gargantuan scale. It imports all that pepper into Zaiton, a hundred times as much as Alexandria receives. Quinsay is one hundred miles in circumference and has twelve thousand bridges. The magnificent life of Kublai Khan, the size of his court, the splendor of his hunting parties, coaches, and banquets, are based not on magical elements of the Prester John type but on the diligent work of his subjects.

In summary, the wealth of Asia could be conceived according to different but not completely incompatible patterns. Asia might be naturally rich because of climate, proximity to the earthly paradise, or simply nature. Or perhaps Asia was just better governed and more industrious than Europe and this was why it was so wealthy and populous. These images of widely distributed, nearly infinite quantities of precious substances replaced the earlier emphasis on the exotic and adverse creatures or phenomena (snakes, griffins, terrible heat) that limited the ability to exploit or create wealth. The snakes still haunt the pepper groves in the letter of Prester John and in Marco Polo's Indian diamond mines, but by the crucial fifteenth century they no longer substantially interfere with a picture of vast opportunities for profit.

What if the inhabitants of these far-off regions didn't want to help Europeans enrich themselves? This seems not to have bothered anyone involved in the speculation and planning leading up to the voyages at the end of the fifteenth century. It is not that Europeans assumed the people in Asia were primitive and so easily quelled. In fact the first explorers preferred to deal with politically and economically well-organized states where the pepper orchards and gold mines were already functioning rather than to try enlisting the services of "primitive" people. Columbus was increasingly annoyed at finding only those he regarded as savages instead of the cultivated and efficient representatives of the Great Khan he expected.[25] The ease of taking things from unsophisticated indigenous people was not going to compensate for the difficulty of setting up from scratch an infrastructure of exploitation, or so it seemed.

Whether civilized or uncivilized, the inhabitants of the realms of gold and spices were thought to share, in European eyes, a usefully underdeveloped appreciation of how valuable their possessions were in a global context. Competitors who *did* understand the comparative price structure were those (considered to be largely Muslim) who profited inordinately from the status quo. If the bottom line was an immense, preferably fantastic supply of such valuable products as aromatics, then distance and danger were not discouraging.

All of these El Dorado myths, the exaggerated sense of riches lying over the horizon, may seem typically medieval and typically fanciful. But not only were they necessary to put into effect the very real colonial ventures that carried European power to Africa, Asia, and the Americas—in a curious sense the fanciful expectations of profit were fulfilled, if not quite in the ways anticipated. The gleaming gold roofs of Japan didn't exist, but the gold and silver of Peru and Mexico were extensive enough to satisfy the most extravagant avarice. It turned out that the Portuguese and later the Dutch did make immense profits on the spices of India and the East Indies. That such good fortune was temporary, or dissipated, or even ended up weakening once great powers like Spain is no more significant in terms of the imagination of riches than is the misdistribution of oil revenue or profits from West African diamonds today. Wealth may be temporary or go to the wrong people, but it is quite real nonetheless. European colonial profits and their consequences have moved much of world history for the past five centuries. How those profits were imagined and realized comes from the peculiar medieval ideas of rarity and plenitude.

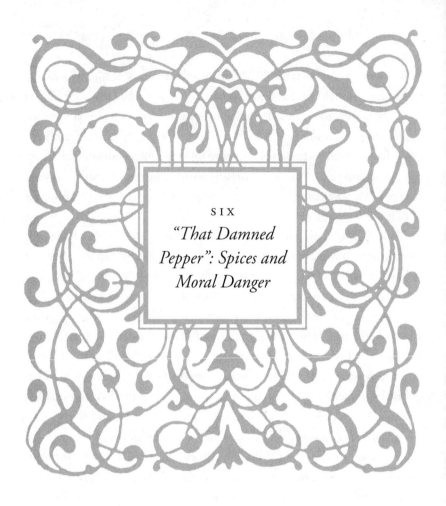

SIX

*"That Damned
Pepper": Spices and
Moral Danger*

So far it should be clear that the medieval infatuation with spices embraced many sectors of society and diverse activities, from noble feasts to the relics of saints, and from medical treatments to ostentatious display. The very popularity of spices along with their expense and the ephemeral nature of the pleasure they evoked could hardly escape the notice of moralists for whom spices were, above all, a symbol of the ridiculous human preference for transitory pleasures as opposed to the frugal righteousness that would earn eternal life. Spices might be associated with the earthly paradise and the odor of sanctity, but they resembled gold in instigating human wickedness rather than being evil in themselves.

In the eyes of social critics, the wickedness caused by spices was not so much the consequence of greed (in the manner of gold) as a ludicrous self-indulgence that sapped both individual moral fiber and the economy of lands that sent their treasure abroad in return for unnecessary and instantly consumed luxuries. At the time of the Protestant Reformation, the German satirist Ulrich von Hutten condemned how his countrymen had been seduced by foreign merchants into spending their money on such fripperies as "that damned pepper, ginger, cinnamon, saffron, cloves," and other spices.[1]

It's remarkable how much of his era's moral decay von Hutten attributed to the baleful influence of spices. As is often the case in denunciations of contemporary bad habits, an idealized past was evoked, an era of virtue, happiness, and simplicity before corruption set in. At one time, von Hutten observed, Germans nourished themselves in a manner both simple and wholesome. He seems almost to anticipate the "Slow Food" movement in extolling locally grown produce. In those golden, distant days, food was enlivened by the good, "honest" herbs of the Fatherland, but now everyone has become addicted to luxury. The taste for imported spices enriches rapacious merchants, specifically the grand commercial house of Fugger, bankers to the emperor and stalwart Catholics, and so the object of von Hutten's particular hostility.

The deleterious impact of spices, according to this tirade, affects physical and spiritual health. Food no longer sustains but pampers the body, thereby undermining its strength and leaving it susceptible to illness. Von Hutten elaborates on this in a dialogue titled *Fever,* in which the allegorical figure of the title is looking for victims and von Hutten is quizzing him on his likely targets. Fever initially comes to attack von Hutten, but as he is such a careful and healthy person, he is able to direct Fever's attention to more vulnerable potential victims who don't observe such virtuous abstemiousness. In keeping with his anti-Catholic intentions, von Hutten makes the clergy particularly tempting for Fever's wrath. The priests and cardinals of Rome are sunk in gastronomic depravity (one of the vices associated with the clergy even by Catholic moralists, as with the gluttonous cleric portrayed by Eiximenis). The degeneracy of the Roman priests is evident in the fact that they drink wine, eat pheasants, and season everything with pepper, cinnamon, ginger, and cloves. Fever agrees that spices are unhealthful. The fact that they harm the bodies of those who indulge themselves makes such people all the more attractive to Fever, as part of his work is already accomplished before he attacks. Far from the usual image of spices as healthful humoral balances to food and as wonder drugs in their own right, von Hutten considered spices addictive, almost the sixteenth-century equivalent of cigarettes.

The danger posed by spices is not just to health but to both morals and the economy. The consumption of spices encourages arrogance and ostentation. Moreover, it transfers money out of the German territories into the hands of foreigners. Apart from the Fuggers as treacherous German intermediaries, von Hutten denounces the king of Portugal, the master of the spice trade in the early fifteenth century. The insatiable appetite for spices beggars Germany's economy while enriching the Portuguese monarch. Martin Luther himself, the force behind the Reformation, echoed this condemnation of Portugal and the deleterious effect of exotic luxuries on German moral fiber and wealth. "Foreign commerce," he wrote, "brings goods from Calicut and India and such places, goods such as expensive silk and articles of gold and spices, which have no purpose other than magnificent display, and which suck out money from the land."[2]

Denunciations of moral laxity often involved spices as emblems of a kind of greed even more pointless than the pursuit of gold (which is at least durable). Spices were particularly frivolous because their long journey from virtually unknown lands to the European consumer ended with their being enjoyed in a few minutes. Gold and gems were dangerous temptations, but even if avarice was a deadly and pervasive sin, the pursuit of gain was at least understandable in terms of worldly advantage.

Delight in food always seems absurd, at least to those who are not attracted by culinary novelties, because the momentary pleasure it affords is disproportionate to the effort and expense involved in procuring it. The expenditure of thousands of dollars on a better car has a wider appeal and is at least excusable by some medium-term benefit (display, smooth ride), but wildly expensive meals are all the more scandalous because the valuable ingredients are immediately digested. Spices were symbols of gluttony and stimulants to this particular sinful self-indulgence, but they were also associated with sexual immorality, another form of transient pleasure. It is not just that gourmandise leads to and encourages lechery, but that both represent, according to the Christian moralists of the Middle Ages, the human propensity for immediate and ephemeral gratification.

Spices represented folly, a fondness for feeding pride and the senses in order to acquire a merely temporary pleasure—at best a poor investment and at worst a demonstration of profound immorality. The use of spices reflected the increasing wealth of a substantial segment of society that could pursue luxuries during a period of sustained and rapid economic growth. From about 1000 to 1300 there was a dramatic expansion of European population, of cities, and of agricultural and commercial sectors of the economy. The range of imported products increased exponentially and all sorts of clothing, furnishings, decorations, crafts, and commodities became available, so that the pleasure to be derived from connoisseurship, enjoyment, and what we would consider high-end marketing expanded to the point of provoking moral anxiety and eventually outrage.

Much of this anger was directed at the rich, whose manner of life always can be portrayed as both enviable and silly, as magnificent and laughable. Are Imelda Marcos' shoes, Elvis Presley's gold Cadillac, or Dennis Kozlowski's six-thousand-dollar shower curtain splendid or absurd? But credulous ordinary people were also fooled and made ridiculous by luxuries such as spices. As already described, itinerant peddlers and self-described herbalists glibly hawked tales of miracle cures to prey on those with only a small amount of discretionary spending.

SPICES AND IMMORALITY

Fueled by consumers' desire for aromatic products, the spice trade lent itself to all sorts of business transgressions, especially, as discussed earlier, adulteration. The itinerant merchants described by comic poets like Rutebeuf have credulous hence contemptible clients. But the folly of spices extends beyond mere commercial fraud to embrace gluttony and other sins that aren't limited to simple people. Spices stimulated the appetite or at least offered a sufficient variety of tastes to encourage eating not because of hunger but out of an insatiable desire for culinary pleasure. Delight in food was more than merely gross appetite: it embraced even more dangerous self-regarding vices of good taste, gourmandise, and selectivity. Sophisticated enjoyment is worse than just guzzling food and drink indiscriminately because it reflects the characteristic arrogance of the upper classes, and because the waste of money is so much greater (truffles being more expensive than potato chips; spices more costly than salt).

"That Damned Pepper"

The first large public controversy over what was regarded as indecent affection for fine food took place in the monastic world. On one level this might seem surprising, since the great occasions for excesses in spice consumption were most obviously the banquets of the nobility, but the aristocracy was expected to live in a certain style, and their vices, which included all sorts of violent acts, were unsurprising. Monks, who were supposed to have renounced the world and whose diets were in theory restricted to simple and basic ingredients, might indulge themselves more easily in the realm of varied and even elegant food than in logistically difficult and very risky sexual offenses.

Confrontations arose particularly between the French monasteries of Cluny and Clairvaux in the twelfth century over the proper form of monastic common life. Cluny had been a model for the tenth and eleventh centuries because of its beautifully organized prayers, which were regarded as efficacious not just for the community but for noble patrons and donors eager to ingratiate themselves with a God that their military and materialistic way of life habitually offended. Cluny's magnificence grew as it became the head of a large family of monasteries offering liturgical splendor backed up by large establishments with many of the accoutrements of palaces. The abbey of Cluny in the twelfth century included among its monastic buildings the largest of all European churches. Such grandeur was on one level appropriate, for pious donors wanted the prayers of monks to be sung and recited in dignified surroundings, but generosity threatened to interfere with the austerity that was supposed to characterize monastic life and that made those prayers powerful.

St. Bernard, abbot of Clairvaux and head of the relatively new Cistercian order, criticized Cluny's wealth and magnificence, calling into question its dedication to the original ideals of the founder of Western monasticism, St. Benedict. The lavish decor, elaborate sculpture, and fine clothes of the monks at Cluny were offensive to Bernard, whose Cistercian churches were large but simple, even stark. Cluny's high standards of cuisine and the monks' indulgence in multicourse, complicated, and highly spiced meals were scandalous, in Bernard's opinion. Indeed Cluny was a pioneer in the development of medieval cooking, in part because of its size, wealth, and the presence of a certain degree of interest in cooking. The historian of medieval cuisine Johanna Maria van Winter observed that Cluny taught

Europe how to cook, and to the extent this is indeed the case such innovation merited considerable opprobrium in St. Bernard's opinion.[3] The fact that Cluny officially shunned meat except for medicinal fortification of the infirm meant that all the more ingenuity went into preparing fish in succulent and complex ways that met the letter of the law but mocked its intended maintenance of austerity.

In his *Apology*, written in 1125 to counter accusations that he had slandered Cluny, Bernard elaborated on the monastery's culinary excess, indignantly pointing to multicourse meals whose quantity of dishes and exquisite manner of preparation are scandalous.[4] The monks' appetites are spurred on by the variety of the skillfully prepared dishes and the effect of the piquant spices that encourage and revive voracity:

> Course after course is served and in the place of a single one of meat, which is abstained, there are two great courses of fish. And when you have been sated by the first, if you touch the second, it will seem that you have not even tasted fish yet. The reason is that they are all prepared with such care and skill by the cooks that, four or five courses having been devoured, the first does not impede the last and satiety does not impede the appetite. For the palate, as long as it is enticed by the novel seasonings, gradually loses its attractions to the familiar and is hungrily restored in its desire by foreign spices as if it had fasted until now.[5]

The Cluniac monks eat beyond what should be an appropriate sufficiency to test the stomach's capacity for pleasure, Bernard says. He condemns spices as a kind of gastronomic stimulant resembling an aphrodisiac, encouraging gluttony by offering new sensations and rekindling desire. They are particularly wicked inducements because they are foreign (presumably, domestic herbs would not have this effect). Bernard is especially indignant about this passion for spices insofar as it encourages drinking sweetened and spiced wines when the monks of Cluny assemble to mark major holidays. How can they be so heedlessly self-indulgent? Surely they are not sick (the only justification for imbibing such tonics).

The monastic manner of life was supposed to challenge and tame sensuality, but once a path around fasting was discovered, the way was open additionally to illicit sexual pleasure. In an earlier letter of remonstrance to a cousin who had chosen Cluny in preference to the Cistercians, Bernard denounced the rival order's taste for spices in broader terms than mere gluttony. Pepper, ginger, cumin, and "a thousand seasonings of this sort" not only stimulate the appetite in an unseemly way, but increase sexual desire. There was an imputed aphrodisiac property accorded to spices, but in Bernard's conception, the problem was really that one form of self-indulgence, gluttony, inevitably encourages another, lust.[6]

The role of spices in connecting gluttony with sexual desire appears in the work of another Cistercian, Alain de Lille (ca. 1130–1203). In his *Plaint of Nature,* Alain made the allegorical figure of Nature denounce all forms of sensuality that interfere with her duty to increase the earth's population. In this elaborate praise of procreative sex and condemnation of sterile sexual pleasure, Alain's major target was homosexuality, which he regarded as a vice furthered by gluttony. The clergy's susceptibility to homosexuality was due not solely to rules against consorting with women but to the pervasive fondness for fine dining. Alain attacked clerics who had their cooks "torture" pike and salmon along with meat and fowl, preparing them with spices: "On the same table the land animal is submerged beneath a flood of pepper, the fish swims in pepper, the fowl is held fast in the same sticky substance."[7] Whether or not priests and monks really paid more attention to the pleasures of the table than laymen, it was common to satirize them for their gourmandise, and even the Cistercians themselves were not immune from criticism. They responded with rules against the enjoyment of spices in particular. A Cistercian statute dating from between 1133 and 1147 prohibited monks from consuming pepper or cinnamon. In place of these decadent imports, the common herbs "that our land produces" were supposed to suffice.[8]

A final example of the monastic love of spices and the bond between gluttony and lust comes from the *Libro de buen amor* (The Book of Good Love), a fourteenth-century comic poetical masterpiece from Castile. In one of its episodes, a dubious character named Trotaconventos (Convent-trotter) tells the poet about his years living in a nuns' convent where he and other illicit male friends obtained digestives, cordials, electuaries, and other medical delicacies from the sisters. The passage is an accurate list of compound medicines and preparations, especially those used to calm the results of gluttony. Nine digestives appear, including rose syrup with honey, *garriofilata* (a compound electuary based on cloves), and *estomacón* (another compound designed for stomach relief, as its name implies). There is also one classic aphrodisiac, *disanturión,* a venerable recipe composed of more than twenty-five ingredients, including many spices.[9]

The taste for luxurious food was thus more than a petty form of monastic self-indulgence, but rather a prologue to worse sins. According to the fourteenth-century English reformer John Wycliffe, spices and other culinary luxuries symbolized a literally apocalyptic level of evil. Wycliffe's denial of transubstantiation in the eucharist and exaltation of secular power over the church later earned him posthumous condemnation for heresy. Wycliffe agreed with Bernard in denouncing monks who comforted themselves with spiced wines. In a tract on the Antichrist and his entourage, Wycliffe asserted that the Antichrist had already arrived and succeeded in turning men away from the truth. This is proven by the greed, hypocrisy, and love of luxury flaunted by his many followers, who are marked by their fondness for delicate meats, hot spices, sauces, and syrups.[10]

Although the clergy were preeminent targets for denunciation, the sin of gluttony was well known outside the stocked refectories of the richer monasteries and churches. For laymen it was not so much hypocrisy that was at issue, since laymen were not living according to a strict ascetic rule. Rather it was the propensity to an excessive and foolish self-indulgence that turns one away from the important things in life in order to wallow in passing distractions. As with lust for wealth or the stirring of sexual longing, it is not the object of desire that is evil but the perverse chasing after lesser, ephemeral goods that is wrong, a tendency that ensnares Christians of all social conditions. The expense of spices, the trouble necessary to acquire and use them, and the rapidity with which they are consumed made them ideal targets for secular moralists.

Spices were often regarded as decadent, as signs of the erosion of an original manliness by pleasure and excess. In the course of a largely imaginary history of the early Danes written between 1186 and 1218, Saxo Grammaticus condemned the "extravagant riotousness" and "effeminate lasciviousness" of Denmark, where German tastes for fine cooking and "dainty spices" were undermining virtue.[11]

The wicked combination of sensual pleasure and the desire for social distinction is shown by Dante in canto 29 of the *Inferno,* where alchemists are punished. Cappochio, who had been a citizen of Siena, is covered with leprous sores that exude a horrible stench that Dante likens to that of a hospital, a contrast with the delicate spices Cappochio and his friends had enthusiastically consumed as members of a group of spendthrift connoisseurs who were especially fond of cloves. There really was a circle of Sienese food enthusiasts who may collectively have been responsible for one of the earliest medieval cookbooks, a work known as the *Treatise of the Twelve Gourmands.*[12] A certain Niccolò was responsible for bringing the extravagant fashion of seasoning food with cloves to Siena. That this offhand dismissal of the foolish pleasure afforded by spices appears not, as one might expect, in the circle of gluttons, but rather among the falsifiers (alchemists and counterfeiters) may reflect the practice of adulterating spices. These sensualists were perhaps duped by their passion for spices into becoming victims of the common sorts of consumer fraud that some of them, such as the alchemist Cappochio, attempted to perpetrate on others. At any rate, the gluttons are punished elsewhere in hell by being torn apart and eaten over and over again by the ravenous dog Cerberus. In the *Inferno,* the earthly sins are recalled and mocked by inversion (*contrapasso*), so that the spice lovers exude an awful stench and the gluttons are themselves devoured. In *Purgatorio,* however (canto 24), the gluttonous Pope Martin IV, who had a particular fondness for eels from Lake Bolsena and white Vernaccia wine, is not tortured but merely thin and emaciated.

Geoffrey Chaucer also used spices as symbols of foolish, ephemeral pleasure, but with more frequency than Dante and with some complexity. On the most basic level, Chaucer regarded spices as part of the mad chase after luxuries characteristic of his time as opposed to an idealized golden age of simplicity, when humanity was content with what nature provided. In his short poetic diatribe titled *The Former Age*, Chaucer lamented the passing of the happy time when people lived without the need for trade, work, and cheating: "A blissful lyf, a paisible and a swete / Ledden the peples in the former age" (lines 1–2).

At some fateful moment in the past, men "first dide hir swety bysinesse," going to the effort of digging precious metals out of the ground and seeking gems in the rivers. Now we live, as Chaucer inimitably puts it, "forpampred with outrage," torturing nature to extract pleasure. In those happy days of old, people gathered food from trees and meadows and did not think to exert themselves by pounding spices to make exquisite sauces or spiced wines: "No man yit in the morter spyces grond / To clarre, ne to sause of galantyne" (15–16).

Laments for the passing of a simpler, happier time are commonplace, in fact so much so that Chaucer may not have been completely serious here about the advantages of the past and is actually mocking clichés about the end of virtue.[13] In this poem he affects to disdain all human effort and ingenuity. Moreover, the food provided by nature's bounty in the good old days is not very appealing—"They eten mast, hawes, and swich pounage"—in other words acorns, beechnuts, and the fruit of hawthorns. The word "pounage" is telling, as it was generally used for animal feed, particularly that provided for pigs. The people of the former age slept in caves, on grass and leaves, or in woods "softe and swete," which also seems primitive, not just simple. This is not to deny Chaucer's dislike of covetousness and the soul-destroying passion for luxury, but he seems aware of some of the ludicrous implications of excessive praise of a simpler past, a perennial topic of moralists as can be seen in Ulrich von Hutten's denunciation of spices.

In his *Canterbury Tales* (written in the last decades of the fourteenth century), Chaucer accepts many of the circumstances of the world as it now stands. Spices are not uniformly signs of frivolous waste but occupy a place in the life and habits of important people. A cook is one of the pilgrims, and he is portrayed as a capable artificer. He knows how to prepare meat and pies and is also familiar with galangal and the tart spice combination known as *poudre-marchant* (Prologue, lines 379–84). Spices are also appropriate (within the terms of a pre-Christian aristocratic world) for use in the cremation of the noble Arcite, whose pyre is scattered with "spycerye" and myrrh (Knight's Tale, 2935–38). There is a certain ambiguity about the Franklin, a prosperous man of property and local prominence. Described in the prologue as "Epicurus owne sone," the Franklin enjoys the pleasures of the table: it fairly "snewed [snowed] in his hous of mete and drinke." Some of this love of food merely expresses an open-handed country-squire hospitality, but his fondness for "sharp" (spiced) sauces and fat partridges indicates at least borderline gluttony (Prologue, 331–54).

Spices are also both good and bad in the abortive "Tale of Sir Thopas," the comically tedious story started by the character of Chaucer himself. After only a few stanzas the Host interrupts Chaucer, begging to be spared the poem's chivalric clichés and long-windedness, and so Sir Thopas remains but a fragment. Even in this short space, the atmosphere is saturated with fragrance. Sir Thopas rides through a magical forested landscape where such exotic plants as zedoary ("cetewale"), cloves, and nutmeg proliferate. In town he is served spiced wine and gingerbread. Clearly Chaucer is mocking the artificiality and fatiguing luxury of a mannered sort of chivalric romance, but spices are apparently necessary ornaments of such adventures, so conventional as to be comical (Sir Thopas, 50–52, 140–45).

Even if he himself is hardly a figure to be admired, the Pardoner expresses a serious (if still conventional) condemnation of spices as encouragements to gluttony with overtones of lust (Pardoner's Tale, 536–46). Spices and other luxurious foods require extraordinary effort and expense to obtain. These go sweetly down the gullet, but, as the Pardoner observes, all the work and cost of cooks to stamp, strain, and grind produces in the end only disgusting excrement while feeding the "likerous [lecherous] talent" of the stomach. "Spicerye of leaf and bark" goes into sauces that just rekindle the jaded appetite. Spiritually the gourmet is dead as long as his vices animate him: "But certes he that haunteth swiche delyces / is deed, whyl that he liveth in tho vyces" (547–48).

The Merchant's Tale exemplifies how spices indicate conventional ideas of luxury and health and at the same time serve as symbols of foolishness. In this story, the elderly January weds young May, and his inappropriate infatuation is punished as he unwittingly aids his wife's deception. On the wedding day the besotted January orders spices to be strewn around the house. That night January bolsters his sexual performance by consuming electuaries and wines flavored with "hot spices" (Merchant's Tale, 526, 561–66). These measures work to the extent of aiding January's pleasure, but do nothing to prevent his later being made a cuckold. Conventional wisdom is borne out (spices have stimulative properties); at the same time, however, spices are also the active ingredients in promoting a kind of folly that joins gluttony and lust. The old man's desire for May is more a kind of visceral greed than the rekindling of youthful sexual desire. He is described as having a "newere appetit" for young flesh or tender veal. Chaucer frequently uses "delit" or "delicacye" to refer to pleasures that are greedy and voluptuous, at once gastronomic and sexual.

The metaphoric association of spice, sweetness, lust, and error are epitomized by the Miller's Tale, where we have another elderly man, John the carpenter, who has married Alisoun, a girl of eighteen, in violation of the well-known rule that men should keep to the same demographic in choosing a wife ("men sholde wedden after hir estaat"), since youth and old age are not compatible (The Miller's Tale, 43–44). The clerical student Nicholas, who boards in the house, is more appealing than the carpenter. Not only is he reasonably young, but he is also careful about grooming and personal appearance, as sweet as licorice root or zedoary (20–21). In the complicated and farcical conclusion, Nicholas and Alisoun enjoy each other's company while the credulous carpenter has been fooled into anticipating another occurrence of Noah's flood. The parish clerk Absalon, also enamored of the carpenter's wife, calls out to her from beneath her window: "What do ye, hony-comb, sweete Alisoun / My faire byrd, my sweete cynamome?" (512–13). Poor Absalon! He is a comical figure even if his yearning imitates serious love poetry, as in the English poem "Annot and John" (written in about 1340), wherein the young lady Annot is likened to nutmeg, cubeb, sugar, cinnamon, and other spices and medicines.[14] In the Miller's Tale, Absalon has already prepared himself for a night of love by combing his hair and chewing grains of paradise and licorice to freshen his breath (504–5). His hopes are, of course, sorely deceived as he is tricked into kissing Alisoun's posterior through the window. The tale ends with the carpenter having broken his arm and being regarded by his neighbors as irremediably mad,

Nicholas branded in his rear, and Absalon humiliated as well. One can't claim that spices are the center of the narrative, but they function at least as hints and symbols of folly.[15]

In Chaucer, as with many other literary and didactic writers of the later Middle Ages, spices provoke anxiety more than admiration. The growth of what can start to be called a consumer society meant that human greed took on more varied and specific forms. As the ability to display wealth expanded both in the number of people possessing sufficient means and in the variety of objects to denote affluence, finery on the order of silks, furs, or jewels became more vivid symbols of arrogant selfishness than the merely generic gold and silver.

Spices represent pleasure, but of a foolish and wasteful sort. Yet how can all of this high-minded denunciation of the viciousness of spices be reconciled with what we've seen regarding their aura of sacredness and association with the saints and the earthly paradise? The answer has to do with appropriate use. Things created by God, who is completely good, are in themselves beneficial. Otherwise God would be the deliberate creator of evil, which would make him not wholly benevolent, a heretical notion that had been refuted and worried over for a thousand years before the time of Dante and Chaucer. Gold, gems, and spices are good things and the value attributed to them is not simply arbitrary. The biblical gold and bdellium of Hevilath or the stories of gems and spices that wash down the rivers of paradise are appropriate glories of blessed places. It is fitting that Jesus was anointed with scented ointment and buried with fragrant spices. Saints' bones should be kept in bejeweled reliquaries rather than plain boxes. It is certainly right for incense to be burned in church, expensive though it is.

The unreasonable use of spices is to satisfy carnal appetites and to impress others. In some measure, the spectacle that newly rich people are inclined to make of their wealth is always seen as unpleasant, but it is not just the ostentation of the vulgar that is at issue. Even the well-born are seduced by the really significant danger of luxuries: the effort and cost they eat up, the moral and financial expense that wastes time and treasure, divert Christians from a proper concern with the eternal and real, as opposed to ephemeral and unimportant worldly luxuries. The need to seek salvation and to heed the will of God should outweigh the pursuit of pleasure, not only because the church so commands, but because it is shortsighted to prefer momentary satisfactions over eternal bliss, and to run the risk of eternal torment for heedlessly seeking out those momentary satisfactions. St. Augustine had distinguished between *use* and *enjoyment,* between possessions like clothes, food, beauty, intellect, all delights of this world that should be used for a higher purpose, and things that are good purposes in themselves: faith, modesty, prayer, the way of God.[16] Living for sexual or culinary gratification, taking excessive thought to achieve wealth and the trappings of worldly success, these divert us from the way our life should be taking. But they are not only distractions—they are a kind of idolatry in which transitory goods are worshipped as if they were everlasting.

This theological background is significant because of the work involved in obtaining spices and the expense required to enjoy them. Spices are not spontaneous or easy-to-obtain pleasures like delight in a sunset or quenching one's thirst. All the difficulties of long-distance transport and distribution served as emblems of the skewed priorities involved in the distinction between mere use of passing objects and the appropriate enjoyment of eternal virtues. If spices were readily available, hence inexpensive, they would not be occasions of sinful temptation. Eating too much cabbage may be a form of gluttony, but it doesn't carry much moral opprobrium or significance beyond that. The desire for spices is not in itself perverse, but what is out of proportion to the pleasure they confer is the effort and concentration that has to go into their exploitation.

Even after the spices have finally arrived, they must be ground in mortars and made into sauces or infused into wines, processes that are also difficult. Hence Chaucer's complaint about the effort of grinding spices and concocting new dishes in *The Former Age,* which is stylized and perhaps even comical but nevertheless conventional. True, those of sufficient affluence regularly employ others to do tedious work: in this case a cook, or more likely one of his minions, performs the task of pounding the spices. In *Piers Plowman,* temperance is contrasted with excess in dress and food: "No ne mete in his mouth / That Maister Johan spicede."[17] The cook, "Master John," surely delegates this work, but this just means more people are involved in the ceaseless task of producing objects for others' enjoyment. The toil of so many anonymous servants to further the pleasure of the rich is in some sense scandalous, or at least a reversal of priorities, and it is often morally offensive to sensitive observers within and also outside the Christian tradition.

Fashion gives employment to millions (a current way of rating effort and economic benefit), but it is by definition an enterprise focused on transitory rather than durable value.

In the Garden of Eden there is an effortless quality to the way spices flourish, so before the Fall they would have been appreciated with minimal fuss, picked ripe from the trees, as it were. In their native Asian environment, with paradise nearby, aromatic products abound and the very breezes are filled with their scent. To bring them from these faraway origins, from the European point of view, requires real exertion, risk, and expense that elevate their price, prestige, and ultimately moral danger. If cloves were as cheap as leeks or ale, their excessive use would be mere basic gluttony. Given that spices were extravagantly expensive, however, the disjunction between such effort and the trivial ways in which spices are ultimately consumed seemed scandalous to medieval moralists.

The moral argument, concentrated on individual priorities, is accompanied by what to us is a more familiar economic argument about waste and the deleterious impact of imported luxuries on the community and state. The king of Portugal (or before him the Muslims, or the natives of the farthest East) should not be enriched by spendthrift desires, as Luther and von Hutten observed. Echoing the latter's complaint about the perverse neglect of the flavorful herbs of the Fatherland, King Ferdinand of Aragon, a contemporary of these German critics, observed that there was really nothing wrong with good old domestic garlic.[18] Of course this was not an opinion widely shared by members of the upper classes, and it is unlikely that balance-of-payments concerns led to pepper and cloves being scrapped from the king's meals in favor of garlic and herbs.

Medieval understanding of economic theory and anxiety about the lust for exotic imports are particularly evident in *The Libelle of Englyshe Polycye*, a late-fifteenth-century poem about naval and commercial power that is a monument to strategic thinking about England's strengths and weaknesses.[19] For the most part the *Libelle* (that is, "small book" or pamphlet) energetically celebrates trade. The products of France and the Low Countries, as well as England's own exports of wool, tin, and cloth, are praised. Goods brought by the Prussians, for example, are clearly useful: beer, bacon, pitch, copper, wax, and fur pelts. The Portuguese are "oure ffrends," and their olive oil, wine, figs, raisins, dates, and hides are undoubtedly worthwhile even if the dried fruits are not strictly speaking basic necessities. Traditional commercial rivals are suspect. The author remarks on the Flemings' monopolistic practices and ridicules their gross fondness for beer. Some of his hostility may be because the Flemish competed with England in the manufacture of woolen cloth. Yet whatever the vicissitudes of commercial or political relations, there is no question about the importance of trade with Flanders: "For Fflaunders is staple [center of the market], as men tell me / To alle nacons of Chrytianté."

The real villains are the Italians. They are singled out as suppliers of unnecessary yet expensive goods whose popularity drains England of treasure without sustaining real productive needs. The poet regards finery and spices brought by the Italians with mistrust, even disdain. The Genoese furnish silk, cloth of gold, and pepper—what might be considered basic luxuries—and the poet is suspicious but not downright hostile to them. He reserves his real contempt, however, for the "nifles and trifles" that the Venetians, Lombards, and Florentines sell to England. These merchants are denounced for providing "thynges of complacence" loaded off their great galleons, including all manner of spices ("alle spicerye"), sweet wines, and exotic animals including "apes, japes, and marmusettes tayled," picturesque but sinister. Foolish luxuries confuse normally stouthearted Englishmen, tricking them into buying things that are expensive and not needed.

In this discussion of the Venetian trade, the contrast between reliable if unglamorous domestic products as opposed to exotic imports arises once again. Why do we need all these fancy overseas laxatives, such as turbit or rhubarb, to void the humors when there are all sorts of plants that grow in England that are equally effective? Sugar is the only exception—otherwise there is no reason to import medicines. To the extent that spices are bought for pleasure, they are mere fripperies; as drugs, they are unnecessary. That the English are willing to trade their fine and useful commodities for expensive junk shows a flaw of character that the author attributes particularly to the upper classes:

> And wolde Jhesu that oure lordis wolde
> Considre this wel, both yonge and olde;
> Namelye olde, that have experience,
> That myghte the yonge exorten to prudence.

Hortatory and alarmist recommendations in favor of virtuous simplicity were not particularly effective, for silks and spices continued to be in vogue. A logical way to have met at least the economic anxieties of importing luxuries would have been to figure out how to cultivate spices at home. Sugar was the only medieval spice successfully transplanted from its original Asian habitat. Sugarcane needs a certain degree of consistent warmth to grow, so it could not be produced on most of the mainland of Europe except for southern Spain, but sugar plantations were established on Mediterranean islands including Cyprus and Sicily by the end of the Middle Ages. The Canary Islands and Madeira, discovered in the fourteenth century, were covered with sugar cultivation in the course of the fifteenth century, a foretaste of the fate of the West Indies, which were adapted to growing sugar through colonization and transatlantic slavery, thereby transforming the world.

Saffron was much more adaptable than any other spice and grew in many parts of Europe. Tuscany had a certain fame for its saffron, with San Gimignano as its commercial center. Saffron was grown in the Pyrenees, not at first glance a promising territory. A judicial process in 1491 against the rebellious Count Hug Roger III of Pallars (in northwestern Catalonia) mentions his destruction of the saffron harvest at Salàs.[20] By this time the Iberian Peninsula was famous for its saffron, and considerable quantities were exported from its Mediterranean ports, especially Valencia.[21]

Most spices, however, proved impossible to transplant. Attempts had been made as far back as the Hellenistic era and the Roman Empire, but the climate was deemed too temperate. The Roman naturalist Pliny acknowledged regretfully that even if spice plants could be grown in Mediterranean lands, they would not produce a commercially viable crop. Where would enough sunshine be obtained to "suck the juices of these plants, or ripen the drops of resin that they shed"?[22] In any event, little to nothing was known in Europe about the actual spice plants except for their seeds, bark, or other aromatic parts.

For medieval moralists and economists, the solution to the high price of spices was to turn away from them, to resist the fad that encouraged their popularity. The result of rejecting spices would be an enhancement of both personal virtue and national finance. Assuming, however, that such nagging and hectoring did not slacken demand, there was another plan to overcome scarcity and cost. In the later Middle Ages traders and explorers embarked on an intermittent, often poorly researched, but nevertheless inexorable campaign to discover the lands where spices proliferated and find a way to bring them back directly to Europe for glory and for profit.

The great expeditions at the end of the fifteenth century, journeys that marked the beginning of Europe's global reach, were launched by the desire for spices. In 1497, King Manuel of Portugal authorized Vasco da Gama to undertake a sea voyage around the southern end of Africa to India "in search of spices." The Portuguese had been familiar with the African coast for decades, going farther down its length and deeper into the continent's interior as they developed techniques for overcoming adverse and unfamiliar winds, currents, and climates. They had already established profitable enterprises, notably the enslavement of Africans, but the commercial possibilities of spices and the effort to use Africa as a pathway to India emerged as their most attractive prospect.

When the three Portuguese ships made it to Calicut in July 1498 (almost exactly a year after setting out from Lisbon), da Gama's first messenger on shore was accosted by merchants from Tunis, and they were able to converse together in Spanish. "The devil take you, what brought you here?" the Muslim traders asked. The succinct reply was, "We came to look for Christians and spices." Despite what might seem like a confrontational opening, the conversation was actually friendly and good humored in the manner of familiar business competitors. The merchants of Tunis praised the riches and opportunities of Calicut and wished their Portuguese colleagues good fortune.[1] The story shows the Portuguese desire for spices and also points to the long-established presence in India of Muslim merchants from the Middle East, accustomed to trade by way of Egypt and the Red Sea, routes closed off to Christian Europe. The arrival of the Portuguese was hardly a "discovery" of how to get to India but rather of how to get to India bypassing the points of traditional access.

The accounts by Columbus of his four transatlantic trips return again and again to the quest for spices and his over-optimistic belief that he had found them. This was not just a private obsession of his, however, but represented what others too imagined to be the purpose of any attempt to find eastern Asia. The Florentine doctor and geographer Paolo Toscanelli (1397–1482) was the leading advocate for a westward route to "the Indies," radically underestimating, as it turned out, the size of the globe and not realizing, of course, the existence of an entire hemisphere between Europe and Asia. Toscanelli is thought to have responded to a letter from Columbus about his theories by praising the explorer's desire to seek the lands "where the spices are." In an earlier letter (of 1474) to the Portuguese cleric Fernão Martins, Toscanelli wrote about the western way "to the lands that are exceedingly rich in spices and gems."[2]

We have previously discussed how Europeans thought of the earth and its potential riches, how progress toward making direct contact with India and other fabled lands of Asia was spurred by inaccurate stories of abundance that replaced inaccurate legends of scarcity, and how spices were the goal of European study and expansionist ambition. Having considered India in the European imagination, we need to see how the expectations of profit and wealth were made into practical, realizable schemes. The quest for spices required answers about geography, and progress in this regard was possible because, paradoxically, of the unparalleled power of the thirteenth-century Mongols, who built the largest empire the world has ever seen. Destroyers of cities and civilizations, the Mongols subsequently governed their vast territories effectively and peacefully, allowing an unprecedented opportunity for European travel and the accretion of knowledge of peoples beyond the lands of Islam. During the period of Mongol power, from about 1240 to 1360, Western travelers for the first time in centuries visited India and for the first time ever became familiar with China and other realms east of India. From this new knowledge arose the desire for large-scale ventures to exploit the wealth of Asia.

A crucial advance in European understanding about the geography of Asian territories took place a bit less than 250 years before da Gama sailed, with the journey of the Franciscan envoy William of Rubruck across Central Asia in 1253–55. William was chosen by King Louis IX of France at a time of optimism about the Mongols, who were thought to be ready for conversion to Christianity and an alliance against Islam. Indeed it was rumored that Sartaq, son of the western Mongol ruler, had already chosen Christianity. William traveled about four thousand miles from Constantinople to the Mongol capital at Karakorum across the steppes, returning via a more southerly route involving Persia, Armenia, and southern Turkey.

Of the one hundred or so intrepid Europeans who can be shown to have traveled to eastern Asia from 1240 to 1360, William may well have been the most perceptive and thoughtful observer. Marco Polo traveled much more widely and was the first to describe the extent and wealth of China, but William displays a more careful intelligence and a surprising adaptability. He attentively observed the customs and material culture of the Mongols and thought their national beverage of fermented mare's milk, *comos*, was delightful and potent. He was the first European to describe Buddhism and to realize that Chinese characters are ideograms rather than letters. On the basis of experience and local informants he contradicted ancient authorities, such as Isidore of Seville, who had asserted that the Caspian Sea drained into the ocean. William was dubious about the monstrous races.

For the future of the spice quest, William's most important observation had to do with the geographical position of India. He was the first European to understand that India was not at the farthest eastern reaches of the world but rather that it lay to the west of the Mongol capital and considerably west of China. At the court of the great khan Möngke, where he held an extraordinary debate with representatives of Islam and Buddhism, William met envoys from India who were bringing gifts of leopards and greyhounds. William asked the envoys where India was in relation to Karakorum and noted in his report to King Louis that they pointed to the west. He made his return trip accompanied for part of the way by these envoys, journeying westward for three weeks before their paths diverged.[3]

William has nothing to say about spices, because he was not primarily interested in blazing a trail for commercial enterprise, but also because the overwhelming impression he received from his arduous trip was of the desolation of the Mongol realm, its empty and almost uninhabitable spaces. At this point, in the mid-thirteenth century, the possibility of exploring a vastly expanded world opened up by the Mongol conquests was first realized and tested, but it took some time for the wealthy parts of Asia to be found and for the spices to be located.

THE "PAX MONGOLICA"

When the Mongols first imposed themselves on European consciousness, in the second and third decades of the thirteenth century, they appeared as frightening savages whose depredations suggested that the apocalyptic disasters foretold by the book of Revelation had truly arrived.[4] Matthew Paris, an English chronicler, likened the Mongols to locusts, monsters rather than men who enjoyed sucking the blood of their victims and devouring their flesh.

The first indication that the Mongols were to amount to threatening significance came in 1206, when they were forcibly united with the Tartars, Keraits, and Naimans by a charismatic leader born with the name Temujin (1167–1227). At the age of about forty, Temujin began a series of conquests with his now formidable army, taking the name Genghis Khan, or universal ruler. The Mongols seized northern China between 1211 and 1215. Between 1219 and 1227, the Mongols turned westward, invading what is now Uzbekistan and Afghanistan and for the first time attacking Muslim states. Genghis Khan's successors, Ögedei and Möngke, extended these conquests to the heart of the Islamic world, utterly destroying Baghdad in 1258 before finally being checked in 1260 by the Mamluk (Egyptian) army in Syria.

The successors of Genghis Khan expanded their sway both eastward, destroying the remnants of the Chinese Empire by 1230, and to the west, devastating Russia beginning in 1237 and arriving in Poland and Hungary by 1241. For the first decades of the Mongol expansion, Europe was first apprehensive and then terrified, but never sufficiently united to organize any effective resistance even at a time of real emergency. The Mongols inflicted a crushing defeat on a hastily gathered Christian (largely Hungarian and Polish) army at the Battle of Leignitz in Silesia, and Europe was open to what would have been a catastrophic invasion. Indeed, during the later months of 1241, Hungary fell and the Mongols, pursuing the king of Hungary, arrived on the shores of the Adriatic Sea. But in one of those contingent and coincidental events that deflect the apparently inevitable course of history, the Mongols suddenly and voluntarily departed Europe at the beginning of 1242. Their withdrawal was in response to news of the death of the great khan Ögedei and the forthcoming election of a successor at Karakorum. The Mongols continued to control Russia, but they never again came so close to seizing the rest of Europe.

Within a few years of the near catastrophe of 1241, the European attitude toward the Mongols shifted. The Mongols still inspired a healthy degree of fear, but also curiosity and even hope as they were increasingly regarded as enemies of the Muslims rather than sworn opponents of Christianity. The epic destruction of Baghdad, capital of the Islamic caliphate, in 1258, combined with the European impression that the Mongols didn't really have a religious doctrine, made it feasible to conceive of a common alliance against Islam or even a Mongol conversion that would fulfill the Prester John legend at least obliquely. The Mongols at various times proposed alliances with Western rulers, as did Hülegü, ruler of the western Mongol kingdom of greater Persia, in 1262. In a message to King Louis IX of France he suggested a shared sea and land attack on Egypt. Negotiation to put schemes of this sort into effect gained greater urgency in the West as the beleaguered Crusader territory in the Holy Land continued to weaken, but nothing came of it. The cultural divide was enormous, the military problems insurmountable (the days of large-scale international Western crusades were nearly over), and internal quarrels and self-interest made such grand alliances of Europeans and Mongols unlikely at best.

The inability to put specific aggressive plans for alliance into effect is secondary, however, to the indirect opportunities the Mongols afforded to the Europeans. The central irony of Mongol hegemony, from the European perspective, is that once the undoubtedly brutal wars of expansion had subsided, the Mongols imposed what has been called the Mongol Peace, a "pax Mongolica" reminiscent of the pax Romana of an earlier empire. Relative stability and freedom of travel extended from the Black Sea to the Pacific Ocean, from the borders of Hungary and Poland to China, from the Persian Gulf to the Arctic Sea.[5] Certainly the Mongols remained frightening in European eyes. John of Plano Carpini, a Franciscan who completed a journey to the court of the khan eight years before that of William of Rubruck, describes the desolation of Kiev and its surroundings six years after it had been sacked and its inhabitants massacred. Nevertheless, for about a century after the journey of William of Rubruck, Central Asia was open to travel, commerce, and ideas. The Mongols were perceived in the West as violent and primitive, yet also as deliverers from the Islamic threat. Gradually the horrific stories of the era of Genghis Khan gave way to the image of Kublai Khan (who ruled from 1260 to 1294) as a magnificent, wise, and just autocrat.

The Mongol Empire reached its limits and established its vast shape in the mid-thirteenth century, although its rulers began to divide and quarrel. The late thirteenth and early fourteenth centuries provided a degree of stability across an immense territory. Travel across Central Asia was hardly unprecedented. It had been traversed by merchants for centuries along the famous Silk Road that reached from China to Persia. What was different in the Mongol era was the easy connection to the West, in effect the extension of the Silk Road as far as the Black Sea, where the Genoese established themselves in the Crimea. Western merchants could also trade in Mongol-controlled territory, in cities like Persian Tabriz or farther east in Urgenj, places that had previously been controlled by Islamic rulers who feuded among themselves while maintaining their enmity toward the Christian states. Eventually the Mongol hegemony offered Western Europe its first glimpse of China, and of the islands of the Indies where many of the spices so highly prized in Europe actually originated.

The routes from the eastern Mediterranean or the Crimea to China have usually been perilous and remain so at the present time—especially now, in fact. Contrast the danger of an overland journey today through Turkey,

Iraq, Iran, Afghanistan, and so forth with the easy (if certainly slow) progress depicted by the Florentine merchant Pegolotti in the early fourteenth century.[6] Pegolotti said the journey overland from Tana on the Crimean Peninsula to Beijing should take about nine months, passing through Saray (Uzbekistan), Urgenj, Otrar, and Almalik (all in Turkmenistan), into western China. Pegolotti assured his reader that "the road leading from Tana to Cathay [China] is quite safe both by day and by night." The only problem was that if the merchant died en route, or in China, his goods would be confiscated.[7]

This route was never quite as easy as Pegolotti depicts, and it was certainly long, but during the Mongol era a significant number of mostly Italian merchants made the journey, and some took up long-term residence in China and in cities along the Asian routes protected by the Mongols. The Venetian travelers to Delhi mentioned earlier (in Chapter 4), for example, set out from Urgenj. In the early fourteenth century there were two Catholic bishops in China (at Zaiton/Quanzhou and Cambalac/Beijing), and colonies of Genoese and Venetian merchants settled in small but significant numbers in Quinsay and Zaiton.[8]

Apart from a few adventurers like the Loredano merchants in Delhi and individuals, mostly missionaries, there were few direct commercial ties between Europe and India, even on the modest scale of Italian contacts with China. Jordan of Sévérac claimed he occasionally met Italian merchants in Quilon on the Malabar Coast, but it was silk and porcelain acquired in China more than spices bought directly in India that European traders in Asia handled during the Mongol period.[9]

At this point, however, Europeans still had the sense that they were acquiring spices, if not from their producers in India, at least from European bases in Asia. The establishment of Crusader kingdoms in the Holy Land meant that throughout the twelfth and thirteenth centuries, eastern Mediterranean entrepôts in Christian hands, such as Acre, received spice shipments that came from East Asia via the Persian Gulf, or overland through Persia and Arabia. The fall of Acre in 1291, the last Crusader outpost in the Holy Land, was to some extent offset by the diversity of new routes opened up by the Mongol peace. We know that in the fourteenth century spices came to European traders overland to the Crimea on the northern side of the Black Sea and to Trebizond on the south side, the Turkish coast. They

Francesco Pegolotti's Advice on Traveling to China

First from Tana to Astrakhan it is twenty-five days by ox wagon, and from ten to twelve days by horse wagon. Along the road you meet many Mongolians, that is armed men.

And from Astrakhan to Sarai it is one day by water on a river, and from Sarai to Saraichuk it is eight days by water on a river. . . .

And from Saraichuk to Urgench it is twenty days by camel wagon—and for those who are carrying wares it is convenient to go through Urgench, because that is a good market for wares—and from Urgench to Utrar it is from thirty-five to forty days by camel wagon. . . .

And from Utrar to Almaligh it is forty-five days by pack asses. And you meet Mongolians every day.

And from Almaligh to Kan-chow [now Ganzhou] it is seventy days by asses.

And from Kan-chow to a river called [Yangtze?] it is forty-five days by horses.

And from the river you can travel to Quinsay [now Hangzhou] and sell there any silver somni *[coins] you have, because that is a good market for wares. And from Quinsay on you travel with the money you got for the silver somnii you have sold there, that is, with paper money . . .*

And from Quinsay to Khanbaligh [Beijing], which is the master city in the country of Cathay, it is thirty days. . . .

It is advisable for [the merchant journeying to China] to let his beard grow long and not to shave. And at Tana he should furnish himself with dragomans [translators], and he should not try to save by hiring a poor one instead of a good one. . . . And from Tana to Astrakhan he ought to furnish himself with food for twenty-five days—that is with flour and salt fish, for you find meat in sufficiency in every locality along the road. . . .

The road leading from Tana to Cathay is quite safe both by day and by night, according to what the merchants who have used it report.

From Francesco Balducci Pegolotti, *La pratica della mercatura,* written between 1310 and 1340, translated in Robert S. Lopez and Irving W. Raymond, *Medieval Trade in the Mediterranean World: Illustrative Documents* (New York, 1955), pp. 355–56, 358.

also were gathered by merchants operating in countries formerly under Muslim domination but now controlled by Mongol dynasties, notably what was known as the Ilkhanate (*il-khan* meaning lesser or subordinate khan), corresponding roughly to the territories of greater Persia.

The hegemony of the Mongols affected the silk trade more directly than commerce in spices, but the indirect impact of the pax Mongolica was to allow Europeans extensive trade and travel opportunities. They were able to extend their geographical knowledge of Asia far beyond that of classical antiquity and quasi-biblical assumptions to assimilate three basic facts: the size, wealth, and contours of China (which had been no more than a vague realm of silk to the Greeks and Romans); the relative position of India and China; and the realization that many spices came from islands and part of the Asiatic mainland east of India and south of China.

The gradual disintegration of Mongol unity and the reassertion of China under the Ming Dynasty in the 1350s and 1360s stopped almost all travel from Europe to Central Asia and China, and ended almost all direct contact between Europe and the non-Islamic eastern kingdoms. The Mongol Yuan Dynasty was replaced by the Ming, who closed China to Western trade. The rulers of the Ilkhanate of Persia, after wavering about their religious orientation, definitively converted to Islam and allied with their former enemies, the Mamluk rulers of Egypt in 1322, shortly before the Mongol dynasty collapsed in 1335. Although a Christian archbishopric was established at Sultaniyeh in Persia in 1318 and lasted until almost the end of the fourteenth century, hopes for a grand alliance against Islam and in particular Egypt and Syria faded.

The retreat of the Mongols and the resurgence of Islamic rule meant a gradual end of European missionary efforts and, by the late fourteenth century, of the network of European merchants in Asia. In the fifteenth century, most of the spices consumed in Europe were acquired by Mediterranean traders in Islamic Alexandria, Beirut, or Damascus. Christian territories of the eastern Mediterranean, such as Cyprus, were also important entrepôts, but Martin Behaim, the Nuremberg cartographer, was right in the annotations to his globe: the entire European spice trade was dependent on a relatively small number of routes controlled by Muslim states and traders.

In the fifteenth century there was virtually no direct contact between Europe on the one hand and China or India on the other. The Red Sea was held by the Egyptians, who prohibited the entrance of any Western commerce. There was no longer an overland trade from the Mediterranean through Inner Asia, at least none that involved Europeans as principals. Fra Mauro in his map drawn in about 1450 said that spices used to come to ports on the Black Sea, but now they no longer reached that far. He blamed this change on the deteriorated condition of the roads rather than on political shifts, but he expressed nostalgia for an earlier and better economic and logistical climate.[10] There was in general a persistent memory of a time when the court of the khans beckoned and could be approached by a significant number of admittedly hardy but not necessarily heroic travelers. In what seems to be his bizarrely out-of-touch belief that he would find the domains of the khans, Columbus was no more than a product of this recollection of the pax Mongolica. The khans, described as so formidable in their power by Marco Polo, Odoric of Pordenone, and John Mandeville, must still be in charge, it seemed, although the last remnant of their power in China had in fact been destroyed in 1368.

The trade in Eastern luxuries, including especially spices, reverted to Muslim control, and Alexandria resumed its place of dominance in the wholesale provision of spices and was able to prevent realization of various schemes of European entrepreneurs for getting access to what were now understood to be connections among the Red Sea, India, the Indian Ocean, and the rest of East Asia. This arrangement satisfied the Italian merchants, especially the Venetians and the Genoese, who were able to profit from their control of the traffic with Alexandria and other eastern Mediterranean centers for the spice trade, but for others, such as the Portuguese patrons of da Gama or the Spanish patrons of Columbus, the revelation of the East from 1250 to 1350 remained tantalizing, and a direct sea route to the Indies offered the promise of going around Venetians, Turks, and all other middlemen to find for their own benefit where the spices grew.

MAPS, TRAVELERS, AND THE GROWTH OF KNOWLEDGE

The Hereford Map, composed in about 1300, is a comprehensive summary of traditional knowledge of the world based on biblical and classical lore. It depicts the earthly paradise and India with its pepper forest at the eastern edge of the world. Jerusalem lies at the center of the map. The Red Sea is situated in eastern Asia, toward the south. Monstrous hominoids inhabit the farther reaches of Asia and southern Africa. Although when it was composed there had been about fifty years of information accumulated by travel to the Mongols, the Hereford Map does not reflect the new information about Asia. Assimilation of recently acquired knowledge by mapmakers came slowly. Although Marco Polo's account was written and diffused shortly after 1300, the first map to show his description of a previously unknown world was the Catalan Atlas of 1375–77.[11]

Despite the delayed reception of the expanding picture of Asia on the part of mapmakers, there was energetic speculation among leaders and intellectuals about where spices really came from, where India was in relation to the rest of the world, and how to wrest trade away from the Muslims and in so doing revive the moribund Crusades and increase the profits of merchants. Here we are interested in the interaction of such strategies with the accounts of travelers who exploited the opportunities afforded by the pax Mongolica.

Some aspects of the voyages of Marco Polo and those who followed him to eastern Asia have already been described, especially in relation to European ideas about India. The European discovery of China meant that the parched, desolate Asia of the Mongols depicted by William of Rubruck and other pioneers of the mid-thirteenth century was dramatically reconfigured by awareness of the wealth farther south and east. There are many things that Marco Polo, whose trip occupied the last decades of the thirteenth century, was the first to report: the extent of China and its many cities, the existence of Japan, Burma, Indochina, and Indonesia. He was the first European known to have visited India since the ancient era and the first to describe China beyond the vague fables of the peaceful silk weavers far to the east. For purposes of understanding the spice trade, Marco Polo's significance is especially the identification of lands other than India that produce spices, particularly the 7,448 islands (according to his reckoning) of what is now Indonesia, south of China and east of India. These islands of the Indies are the greatest and most varied producers of spices, according to Polo. He described the island of Java (which he heard accounts of but probably did not visit) as the source of the world's spices, more important even than India. In particular Polo specifies pepper, nutmeg, spikenard, galangal, cubeb, and cloves. This is not quite right, as Indonesian pepper production was concentrated on Sumatra, and a few small Moluccan islands produced all of the world's nutmeg and cloves, but the identification of Java and the Indonesian archipelago was an immense step forward for the Europeans.

Marco Polo's return to the West in 1295 came shortly after the disastrous fall of Acre in 1291 and at a time when hopes of a military alliance with the Mongols were waning. Even before the travels of Marco Polo were published and regarded as reliable, groups of strategic thinkers devised plans to combat Muslim commerce. The papacy prohibited all trade with Islamic powers in response to the end of the Crusader kingdoms, and although this edict was breached frequently by the Venetians, Genoese, and others (indeed, it was typical of medieval public finance that the papacy later sold licenses to evade the prohibition), the embargo stimulated visionary plans to go around the regions controlled by Islam to find the realms of spices, plans that would take two hundred years to be realized.

Despite the tendency of maps, such as the Hereford example, to place the Red Sea in East Asia, there was some practical realization that this narrow body of water led from the Mediterranean to the Indian Ocean and that it was conceivable to block it to the south. Merchants and crusaders realized that India could be reached relatively easily from Egypt by water, and that most spices came into Europe along this route. Over a century before the fall of Acre, as early as 1182, the notoriously violent crusader Reynald of Châtillon tried to implement a plan to control the Red Sea by fortifying the port of Eilat on the Gulf of Aqaba, an arm of the Red Sea, presently in Israel and an important strategic naval base. Reynald built five ships and began attacking Muslim merchants and pilgrims traveling between Egypt, Arabia, and India. Had this effort succeeded, Reynald might have substantially interfered with the spice trade and undermined Egyptian military and commercial power. The enterprise came to naught, however, as the Muslim leader Saladin took care to launch a campaign against Eilat and destroyed it in 1183. Reynald was among those captured by Saladin after the crucial Battle of Hattin in 1187, and he was executed.

In 1291 there is at least a hint, for the first time, of an alternative plan to combat Egyptian control of the spice trade by circumventing it. A mysterious expedition was launched from Genoa led by the brothers Ugolino and Guido Vivaldi. Their two galleys went beyond the Straits of Gibraltar into

Marco Polo's Description of Java

From Chamba [Indochina] a traveler who sails south-south-east for 1,500 miles comes to a very large island called Java. According to the testimony of good seamen who know it well, this is the biggest island in the world, having a circumference of more than 3,000 miles. The people are idolaters ruled by a powerful monarch and paying no tribute to anyone on earth. It is a very rich island, producing pepper, nutmegs, spikenard, galingale [galangal], cubebs, and cloves, and all the precious spices that can be found in the world. It is visited by great numbers of ships and merchants who buy a great range of merchandise, reaping handsome profits and rich returns. The quantity of treasure in the island is beyond all computation. . . . It is from this island that the merchants of Zaitoun and of Manzi in general [in southern China] have derived and continue to derive a great part of their wealth, and this is the source of most of the spice that comes into the world's markets.

From Marco Polo, *The Travels*, written ca. 1300, translated by Ronald Latham (Harmondsworth, 1958), p. 251.

the Atlantic, probably with the intent of going around Africa, or at least of seeing how far southward Africa extended. Although they may have gotten as far south as the Canary Islands (known to the ancient world but forgotten in Europe in the intervening centuries), nothing was ever heard from them again. This failure and the obscurity surrounding the purpose of the expedition gave it a subsequent notoriety. Dante's portrait of the recklessly adventurous Ulysses in canto 26 of the *Inferno* is sometimes thought to have been inspired by the Vivaldi episode as Ulysses and his men, bored after many adventures and still reckless and greedy, sail through the Pillars of Hercules at Gibraltar and are eventually wrecked on the island of Purgatory in the southern hemisphere.

During the fourteenth century there are some traces of both plans: getting ships into the Red Sea and the Indian Ocean to disrupt Egypt's trade with India, or circumnavigating Africa and so avoiding direct engagement with the Muslim Near East altogether. In 1318 William of Aden, a Dominican friar and later archbishop of Persian Sultaniyeh, proposed plan one: a Christian blockade of the Red Sea and the Gulf of Aden using Genoese galleys (because, he said, the Genoese were both skilled and avaricious). William emphasized both the commercial and military advantages of his plan:

> Everything that is sold in Egypt like pepper, ginger and other spices, gold, and precious stones, silks, and those rich textiles dyed with Indian colors, all the other valuables, to buy which merchants from these [European] countries go to Alexandria and expose themselves to the snare of excommunication [because of the papal interdiction of trade with Muslims], all those are brought to Egypt from India.

William also believed it was at least possible to go around Africa and enter the Indian Ocean, but he preferred the Red Sea as a closer and more direct strategic site for the contest with Islam.[12]

The blockade plan had another advocate in Jordan of Sévérac, the Franciscan missionary who had spent many years in India and dismissed the tales of using fire to drive snakes away from pepper as lies. Jordan wrote directly to the pope in 1329 to recommend that galleys be stationed in the Indian Ocean to harass and damage Egypt and Islam generally.[13] A more extended treatment of the same idea was put forward by Marino Sanudo the Elder, the Venetian author of a treatise on reviving the Crusades presented to two popes in different versions. A third version, written between 1321 and 1333, was circulated to several European princes along with a map probably drawn by Pietro Vesconte, one of the first professional cartographers.[14] The Vesconte Map reflects some of the new information about Asia and the empire of Kublai Khan, showing the realm of Cathay and mentioning the Mongols ("Tartars"). The Caspian Sea is no longer open to the northern ocean but rather, as William of Rubruck had asserted, an enclosed lake. There are a few Southeast Asian islands (if not Marco Polo's full complement of thousands), and one of them is described as "the island of pepper." Ginger and nutmeg, however, on this map grow along the coast of eastern Africa.

Vesconte's map also reflects Sanudo's preoccupation with Egypt. As opposed to the tradition represented by the Hereford Map, the Red Sea is here correctly oriented to Egypt, and the strategic position of the Sinai Peninsula, controlling access from the Mediterranean to the Red Sea and ultimately to India, is noted. Sanudo's earlier version of his treatise reflects a more commercial view of the situation faced by Christian Europe. There he emphasized the importance of the two Indian ports that handle most of the world's spice trade, "Mahabar" (Ma'abar) on the Coromandel Coast (the eastern side of south India), and "Cambeth" (Cambay) in Gujarat, on the northwest coast. The wealth, honor, and "exaltation" of the sultan of Egypt comes from the spices he receives from India, so that to strike at the spice trade in the Indian Ocean and the Red Sea would be to cripple Egypt without the need to attack it directly, an effort whose futility (or at least great cost) had been demonstrated during the previous century. Sanudo proposed a blockade of Egypt's trade with India and the diversion of India's spice trade with the West to other channels (presumably northern land routes). In later versions Sanudo became more fixated on the Crusade and less on its mercantile context, advocating in a more conventional fashion an all-out assault on Egypt to be coordinated and financed by the papacy and supported by the Venetian navy.[15]

None of this was going to happen. The papacy now had its seat in Avignon rather than Rome and so was regarded as a tool of French political interests, no longer the independent arbiter of Christian affairs as in the thirteenth century. As the fourteenth century progressed, the divisions of Christendom, the weakening of the Mongols, and the rise of a new Islamic power, the Turks, closed off the various windows to Asia. The end of the pax Mongolica meant that China was no longer accessible, and as the Turks took control of Asia Minor and then the Balkans, Constantinople became terminally weak, and the Black Sea became less favorably situated for the enterprises of the Genoese who had pioneered its use in the spice and silk trades. There were a few temporary successes, from the European point of view, such as the plundering of Alexandria by an expedition launched from Cyprus in 1365, but Egypt was now becoming eclipsed by the power of the Turks, whose hold on the Balkans and the northeastern Mediterranean was sealed by the crushing defeat of Crusader armies led by the French and Burgundians in 1396 at Nicopolis on the Danube. By the beginning of the fifteenth century, the Crusade to the Holy Land on the traditional model was a chimera, and everywhere, it seemed, the realms of Christian Europe were hemmed in.

The only region of Christian victories over Islam was the Iberian Peninsula, where the Spanish kingdoms and Portugal had reduced Islamic control to a small remnant, the kingdom of Granada. Ventures launched from these territories of the far west of Europe would eventually fulfill some of the plans put forward by visionaries over previous centuries.

The frustrations of the fourteenth century hardly diminished the allure of spices, nor did they mean an end to all progress in knowledge and technique. The coincidence or reconciliation of old and new images of Europe, Asia, and the world can be seen in the development of new maps showing what had been learned during the era of the pax Mongolica. Between 1375 and 1377, a Jewish convert to Christianity in Majorca named Abraham Cresques made an immense and splendid map of the world for the king of France, probably as a gift from the king of Aragon. The map was divided and placed on panels to accommodate its vast size, so it forms a series of maps known as the Catalan Atlas. Its accuracy, of course, diminishes the farther away one gets from the Mediterranean. In Asia the Catalan Atlas depicts and discusses sirens, giants, cannibals, and other paraphernalia of a long imaginative tradition along with gems and spices of India and the East. It includes a number of innovations in Asia, however: the earthly paradise is gone, and the map presents the first surviving cartographic record to cite Marco Polo and the still relatively new information he had furnished. Cambalac (Beijing), the Mongol capital of China, is described in an extensive annotation. India is clearly a peninsula west and south of China and east of Arabia. To the east of India and south of China are the islands first identified for Europeans by Marco Polo. The atlas states that this "sea of the Indian islands" is "where the spices are."

Maps in the fifteenth century radically altered the established picture of the earth provided by the Hereford Map and other world maps of the high Middle Ages. Two factors influenced this shift: the rediscovery of the ancient Greek cartographers Ptolemy and Strabo, and the continuing reception of knowledge about Asia as well as Africa. Ptolemy's *Geography*, a work of the first century A.D., was brought from beleaguered Constantinople to Italy by Manuel Chrysolares, a refugee scholar, and translated into Latin in 1406. Strabo's works first appeared in the West shortly after Constantinople finally fell to the Turks in 1453. The reverence for the classical past that was characteristic of both the scholastic culture of the Middle Ages and the secular culture of the Italian Renaissance explains some of the popularity of

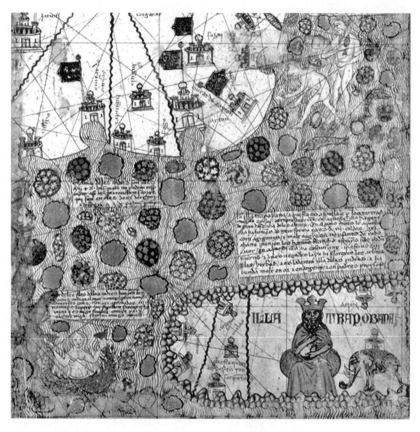

The jewel-like islands of the Indies, home of spices and
strange peoples, as depicted in the Catalan Atlas of 1375–77.
(Bibliothèque nationale de France, Paris, MS esp. 30)

Ptolemy and Strabo among the intellectual classes, but in practical terms,
their ideas about the oceans and continents of the world fit both experience
and theories of mariners and their patrons, whose plans for finding the lands
"where the spices are" were encouraged by the more accessible view of global
interconnectedness afforded by the ancient cartographers.

A critical shift was that now, under the influence of Ptolemy and Strabo,
the world was thought to have more ocean in relation to landmass than in
the traditional world maps. In the Hereford Map and in every other world
map before it, even in the Catalan Atlas, the ocean is only on the fringes of
a gigantic supercontinent. The land is broken up by a narrow Mediterranean

and a few largely enclosed bodies of water such as the Red Sea, but there is no sense of continents separated by water. Up to this point, the Bible was interpreted as suggesting that almost all of the earth consisted of land rather than bodies of water. In the Apocrypha, the second book of Esdras says that God created the earth so that land occupied six-sevenths of its surface: "On the third day Thou didst command the waters to be gathered together in the seventh part of the earth; six parts Thou didst dry up and keep so that some of them might be planted and cultivated and be of service before Thee" (2 Esdras 6:42). This wasn't absolutely authoritative, since Esdras was not part of the canonical Bible, but nevertheless, it was sufficiently credible so as to be widely assumed to be true. Before 1400, medieval maps reflect this disproportionate ratio of land and sea.

The discovery of China and other parts of Asia simply increased the already immense size of the continent on maps in order to accommodate old and new territories, both real and legendary. Maps created before the knowledge of the Mongols and China was received in the West were already fairly crowded. Just for a start, they had to include paradise, the land of the Dry Tree (Ezekiel 17:24), the gold mines of Ophir, the Ten Lost Tribes of Israel (2 Kings 17:6), St. Thomas in India, the kingdom of the Magi, and the apocalyptic savage nations of Gog and Magog whose release would signal the end of time (Genesis 10:2; Ezekiel 38:15; Revelation 20:8). To all this biblical and medieval lore, the opening up of Asia to the West added Cathay, Prester John, the Monstrous Races, the Mongols, and the Indies.[16]

Ptolemy gave a scientific basis to geographical positioning by dividing the earth's circumference into degrees and sectioning it off by latitude and longitude. The newly received view of the world presented a more open system of communication by sea than what was possible overland. Ptolemy still underestimated the extent of the ocean in relation to the land, notably by including a southern landmass connecting Africa with Asia, but a large landlocked sea (corresponding to the Indian Ocean, more or less) showed how Arabia, India, and an oversized Ceylon (which he identified as Taprobane) were connected by water. Ptolemy's enclosed Indian Ocean made it impossible to arrive at India from Europe by means of circumnavigating Africa. Strabo reinforced this relatively open Ptolemaic picture of the interconnected oceans and added considerable detail to the list and descriptions of places. Ptolemy also has extensive Asian territory east of India, although he identifies neither

China nor the islands of the East Indies. Ptolemy and Strabo's Asia had to be reconciled with the information about Cathay, Tartary, Tibet, and Southeast Asia provided by Marco Polo and the missionaries, merchants, and travelers who followed him, or, as was increasingly realized in the course of the fifteenth century, some of Ptolemy's picture had to be discarded.

Ptolemy placed a considerable part of Africa and at least some Asiatic islands below the equator, encouraging the increasing skepticism of the late Middle Ages about legends that the "torrid zones" near the equator couldn't be inhabited or even traversed. Ptolemy calculated that the earth's circumference was 180,000 stadia, rejecting the larger and more accurate estimate of Eratosthenes (259,000 stadia). This would encourage the plans of those like Columbus who believed the western ocean separating the eastern side of Asia from Europe could be easily traversed.

In addition to the revival of classical geography, the fifteenth century also saw a few additions to the store of information about Asia, even though the days of frequent overland travel were finished. Not a single European can be shown to have visited China over the course of the entire fifteenth century, but the voyage of Niccolò de' Conti to India and east to the Indonesian islands, which lasted from 1415 to 1440, represents an important intermediary between the knowledge accumulated during the Mongol era and the grand voyages of the late fifteenth century. Niccolò's findings were made known to the world of scholarship through the work of the Florentine humanist Poggio Bracciolini. Poggio's treatise on the varieties of fortune, published in 1447, includes (as book 4) his account of Niccolò's journeys. For the purpose of understanding the layout of the spice trade, the major significance of Niccolò de' Conti was his identification of the Spice Islands east of Java. We have already seen that Marco Polo was the first to suggest that a substantial quantity of the spices circulating in world trade come not from India but from islands farther east. Niccolò claimed that Java was the entrepôt or gathering point of the Southeast Asian spice trade, but he noted that nutmeg and cloves don't actually grow in Java (contradicting Marco Polo), but rather on two small islands, "Sondai" and "Banda." Sondai produces nutmeg and mace, and Banda is the sole place that produces cloves. In fact Niccolò mixed things up a bit: the small Banda archipelago at this time produced all the world's nutmeg and mace, while cloves were limited to a few islands of the northern Moluccas (notably Ternate and Tidore).

"Sondai" has been identified with many possible islands (there isn't one with that name), but what is significant here is the separation of the Spice Islands, where the most valued edible spices originate, from the rest of Indonesia.[17]

A map that reflects Ptolemy, Marco Polo, and Niccolò de' Conti's influence was produced by Fra Mauro of Venice and finished by his collaborators shortly after his death in 1459. Here land still occupies most of the earth, but the ocean separates Europe from Asia. Fra Mauro was willing to contradict ancient authority by following Niccolò in identifying the legendary island of Taprobane with Sumatra rather than Ceylon (as in Ptolemy). According to Fra Mauro, Ptolemy erroneously confused the two. Fra Mauro also followed Niccolò's description of Indonesia, accurately identifying the Banda archipelago as a source of spices, but mixing up its monopoly on nutmeg with the cloves that grew farther north. Spices proliferate in "Java Minor" and on the numerous islands of the Indian Ocean, "very fertile in precious spices and many other new things." "Bandan" is a little island close to the shadows (a realm of darkness) where a lot of cloves grow. "Sondai," an island near Bandan, produces nutmeg.[18]

Fra Mauro was innovative in another important respect: he showed Africa surrounded by ocean and argued explicitly, once more against Ptolemy, that the Indian Ocean was open and not enclosed as a glorified lake. On one hand his authority for this statement was the classical author Solinus, a notorious spinner of marvelous stories, so this would appear to represent something less daring than a break with classical tradition, but Fra Mauro also cited Pliny, who said spices came from Arabia to Spain around Africa, and a certain Fazio degli Uberti, author of a geographic treatise written around 1360, who said much the same. Fra Mauro remarks that the possibility of circumnavigating Africa is confirmed by prudent men who have taken this route.[19]

With regard to the map of southern Africa, Fra Mauro mentioned another recent backer of this opinion, the king of Portugal, whose ships, he says, have explored the coast of Africa and discovered harbors, rivers, gulfs, and capes, all of which they have named. He claimed to have a copy of the Portuguese charts of Africa, but his actual account is confused, and his only firm argument that someone actually made this circumnavigation is taken from an ancient Roman writer, Pomponius Mela, who claimed that a man named Eudossus fled from Alexandria to Cadiz in Spain by going around Africa and into the Mediterranean through the Straits of Gibraltar.[20] Fra

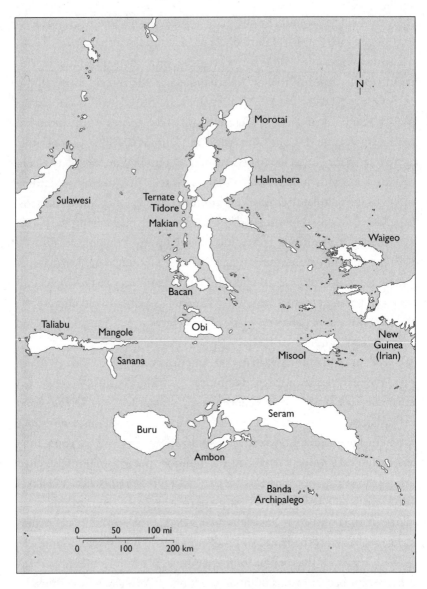

The Molucca Islands, east of Borneo and south of the Philippines,
including the two archipelagos that until the modern era were the world's only
source of cloves (Ternate and Tidore) and nutmeg and mace
(the Banda archipelago in the south). (Map by William L. Nelson)

A detail from the Fra Mauro Map, ca. 1459, showing the
"small island of Banda, near the shadows," identified as the source of cloves.
(Biblioteca Marciana, Venice)

Mauro wasn't the first mapmaker to show an open Indian Ocean connected
to the Atlantic, and as he demonstrated in quoting Fazio degli Uberti, the
idea had circulated for quite some time. Yet his invocation of the experience
of recent sailors and of the Portuguese explorations does indicate a degree
of vigor and enthusiasm beyond the level of abstract speculation.

Here then was a strong argument for the possibility of evading Islamic
control of the spice trade by way of an eastern route around Africa, a project the Portuguese were in fact pursuing at least intermittently, and which
would reach fruition forty years after Fra Mauro's death. A map without
annotations, composed in 1489, showed the possibility of two ways of circumventing the Islamic control of the spice trade. Henricus Martellus,
a German cartographer working in Florence, depicted the southeastern
islands first reported by Marco Polo. His also is the first surviving map to
show Japan ("Zipangu"), a large island quite some distance east of Cathay,
whose position, along with the Ptolemaic scale of the ocean, encouraged

the hope of arriving at Asia by the westward route. At the same time, India is accessible (if just barely) by going around Africa. Africa extends very far to the south, but there is a kind of channel of water around it. A long peninsula also extends south from the eastern extreme of Asia and then curves back west in a shape some have described as a "tiger leg," so that the Indian Ocean is surrounded on three sides. Nevertheless, according to this map, the Indies could be reached by two alternative sea routes, via southern Africa and by the western Atlantic.

Finally in considering the implicit and explicit theories of late-medieval maps, we return to Martin Behaim of Nuremberg whose annotated globe of 1492, as we have seen, presented an economic explanation for the cost of spices. His globe is generally Ptolemaic in its arrangement of continents and oceans, but as with Martellus, Behaim contradicts Ptolemy's enclosed Indian Ocean. According to this map it is at least feasible to contemplate going by sea from Europe to India either by the African (eastward) route, or by sailing west into the Atlantic. Behaim's emphasis on the spice trade may be more detailed than what is contained in the annotations of other mapmakers, but the location of the spice lands, what spices they produce, and how they are placed in relation to the rest of the world were by now long-term preoccupations and speculations provoked by Europe's difficult commercial situation and by the opening up of information about Asia and its most prized products beginning in the thirteenth century.

EUROPE, ISLAM, CHINA, AND INDIA: THE SITUATION IN THE FIFTEENTH CENTURY

How were all these speculations about how to reach the spice lands put into effect? To some extent, the question is also *why* were they ultimately realized? Europe was to a certain degree trapped by Islamic control of the traditional routes to India, but after all, the effective Arab or Islamic control of the spice trade did not represent a real crisis. Europe was still obtaining large quantities of spices in the fifteenth century just as before. Although it was once thought that prices were escalating even beyond their already high levels, research conducted in recent decades shows this was not the case except for a few brief periods of volatility. Even though we have dwelled on European frustration with foreign and infidel control of the spice trade, there was no titanic clash of civilizations or ideologies going on. The fact that Pope Pius II couldn't stimulate a crusade even after the shock of the fall of Constantinople shows how little enthusiasm there was for confrontation in Europe. Only at the end of the century, coincident with the first Atlantic journeys, did Castile launch its campaign to wipe out the kingdom of Granada, the last Islamic part of Spain. On the other side, there was no united Muslim front against the Christian West. The attempt at keeping the Europeans away from direct trade with India was an economic, not an ideological, calculation, and was limited to Egypt and perhaps the Turks, not a matter of conviction for the whole world of Islam.

Muslim observers were aware of the European enthusiasm for spices. Zakariya al-Kazwini, a Persian cosmographer who wrote in the mid-thirteenth century, remarked that it was astonishing to see spices being bought and sold in a city "in the land of the Franks on a river called the Rhine" (perhaps Mainz). Here exotic products from the farthest East, such as pepper, ginger, cloves, spikenard, and galangal, were routinely traded in great quantities.[21] There is no sense here, however, of such an observation constituting precious strategic information on the European economy—it is just a curious fact.

No Muslim coalition was determined to keep the Europeans away from India. The Indian Ocean in the fourteenth and fifteenth centuries was busy with Islamic merchants from Arabia, Egypt, and the Persian Gulf handling the westbound trade from India and dealing with many other Muslim peoples farther east, as far as China and Indonesia. Although Arab geographers did not identify the Spice Islands precisely, they were quite familiar with Java and Sumatra and ports along the Straits of Malacca through which most of the commerce with India passed from Indonesia. All these lands had substantial Muslim populations. If one looks at the travel account of Ibn Battutah (1304–68), whose journey of 1325 to 1349 took him from Tangier to East Africa, India, and China, he seems at home everywhere. He is opinionated, sometimes irritated with various peoples and places, but he always finds Muslim communities and his adventures, extensive and varied as they are, occur in an essentially familiar or at least not uncomfortable space. For Christians, on the other hand, the world of the Indian Ocean was marvelous, "an oneiric horizon" in Jacques Le Goff's words.[22] For the Muslims and for others involved in its complex trade, the Indian Ocean was a zone of largely peaceful competition. No single power gained or even sought hegemony over the Indian Ocean and its trade. Islamic traders were found everywhere, but the control exerted by non-Muslims—by China, Indian states, and the sailors and traders of the eastern islands—was compatible with a system of coexistence that ended only with the arrival of the Portuguese.[23]

That the strongest powers in the global spice trade were Islamic was not something that bothered everyone in Europe. For the Venetians, Genoese, and other Mediterranean traders, the system in place had many virtues. They controlled European access to the wholesale markets, such as Alexandria, and had developed a series of relationships in the Muslim entrepôts. Papal prohibitions against such trade had never been an imposing problem and in the fifteenth century were irrelevant. Individual Venetians or Genoese such as the Vivaldis or Columbus might rebel against such complacency, but they did so as free agents, going against the interests of their cities' oligarchies.

The efforts to find the source of spices were therefore not responses to a generally acknowledged crisis. Europe had been paying a lot for spices for centuries, in good times and bad, and in fact it would continue to do so even after the Portuguese took over the profits of the spice trade. Discovery of a water route to the Indies was therefore more of an opportunity than a necessity. Portugal and Spain were the first realms involved in this project for logical reasons, including the commercial complacency of the Italians and the geographical situation of Iberia on the Atlantic and western Mediterranean coasts, yet unpredictable circumstance and accident played important roles in who launched and profited from the discoveries. The voyages of Columbus, da Gama, and their successors were attempts not to find out where India was—the location of India had been known since the time of Marco Polo—but to find an indirect, all-water route to reap the profits of such commerce in defiance of Islam but also of the Venetians and Genoese. New technical accomplishments in cartography were vital, as were such navigational aids as portolan charts and compasses. New kinds of ships were developed that combined the speed of Mediterranean models with the size and durability of northern commercial vessels. But this is a classic example of how technology offers possibilities rather than in itself determining the course of history. Had technology been determinative, the Chinese would have taken over the entire spice enterprise and indeed the entire mercantile system of the Indian Ocean. The fifteenth century is not only the era in which Europe laid the groundwork for its subsequent colonial expansion, but the period when China both attained its greatest reach and then withdrew of its own accord.

Admiral Zheng He (ca. 1371–1430) undertook seven voyages on behalf of the Chinese Ming emperors to Southeast Asia, India, and Africa.[24] A Muslim eunuch, Zheng He commanded an armada vastly more ambitious than anything dreamed of in Europe until the modern era. The first expedition in 1405 to Champa (present-day southern Vietnam) and Indonesia was intended as a demonstration of power to China's neighbors. It certainly was imposing, as it included no fewer than 317 ships, an extraordinary fleet in comparison with the 3 ships Columbus left with and the 4 that da Gama had when he started. The treasure boats that led Zheng He's fleet had nine masts, whereas Columbus' flagship the *Santa Maria* had only three and was no longer than 120 feet. The *Santa Maria* was manned by a crew of 40, and Columbus set sail with about 70 men in all. Zheng He's first armada seems to have had 27,870 men, including scholars, artisans, and naturalists as well as sailors and troops.

Zheng He was especially interested in the islands to the south of China and in India, but we are best informed about his fourth, sixth, and seventh voyages, which reached as far west as Africa, because of an account kept by another Muslim, Ma Huan, who also served as an Arabic translator.[25] Ma Huan gave a systematic inventory of the places visited, their distances from China, and their rulers, customs, valuable products, and exotic animals. According to Ma Huan, the expedition was instructed to visit the lands of the "Western Ocean," to read out the imperial commands, and to bestow gifts in return for items of trade and tribute. Exotic products were brought back, but it was a giraffe from Africa that seems to have caused the greatest stir in China, becoming an occasion for wonder and celebratory poems.

Zheng He died in 1430 on the last of these voyages. The Ming court immediately thereafter lost interest in these extremely expensive ventures and seems to have considered the country already well served by the level and organization of trade, which required no colonial takeover or expansion. Why China didn't pursue its technological and organizational advantages in the fifteenth century is the subject of a lot of dubious speculation focused on entrepreneurship versus insularity, or the supposed lessons of history. China's failure to exploit the opportunities afforded by these voyages is thought to exemplify a fatal unwillingness to engage the world, or a lack of curiosity. It is also brought out as an example of the disadvantages of large-scale government enterprises versus the kind of small start-ups and flexibility typical of Western entrepreneurs. The emperor could establish such huge campaigns or stop them entirely at will, while the comparatively small and informal Western ideas and projects could evolve until they achieved a model that succeeded.

The difference between China and the West at this crucial time was not in level of entrepreneurship but in differing judgment about how to acquire exotic products. China was as enthusiastic for perfumes and spices as anywhere in the world. The Chinese had the same hunger for such marvels as giraffes and peculiar fragrances like ambergris. A thirteenth-century handbook written by Zhao Rugua, a Chinese customs official, describes the same spices that were so much in vogue in medieval Europe: aloe wood, nutmeg, pepper, sandalwood, frankincense, and cardamom, for example. The Ming emperors did not turn their backs on the world, but rather continued to import exotic substances from the south and west.[26] Camphor and cloves entered the kingdom after Zheng He's death just as they had during his life.

Between China and Europe there was a contrasting understanding of commercial circumstances. Unlike the Europeans, the Chinese knew where to find spices at prices that were easily borne. With the exception of the Venetians and Genoese, the Europeans were less content with the circumstances of trade. Even if there wasn't a spice crisis, Europeans were comparatively eager, if not desperate, to increase supply, and comparatively appalled at the prices they had to pay as a result of their dependence on a narrow basis for that supply.

China's decision to cede control of the spice trade to other players reflected a cultural attitude, not a decision based on technology or geographical information. Equally dependent on historical and cultural attitudes was the European persistence in trying to overcome obstacles to profit and direct contact with the spice realms. We come back to a point made earlier, in Chapter 5, concerning the importance of the imagination, misinformation, and exaggeration of potential profits and opportunities. Zheng He's voyages had added to the repertoire of Chinese information about the places where spices and other exotica were produced. The Chinese judged that it wasn't worth trying to take over this far-flung commerce to turn it entirely to their own benefit and that the system in place was adequate for their desires. In Europe, by contrast, all the knowledge of India and the Indies accumulated as a result of the openings for travel provided by the Mongols did little to offset the myths of abundance, the perception of unlimited wealth, and the possibilities for exploiting it. Europe was entranced by the flavor, scent, and aura of spices, obsessed with finding out where they came from, and eager to figure out how to profit from direct contact with those who grew them. Ignorance was as much a spur to commercial adventure as was knowledge.

There is an interesting comparison to be made between how the epic voyage of da Gama was commemorated and the memory of Zheng He's exploits, a comparison that reveals contrasting opinions about colonial ventures. *The Lusiads* by Luís Vaz de Camões, Portugal's national poet, appeared in 1571 and told the story of da Gama as a kind of epic on the order of Virgil's *Aeneid*. Camões regarded da Gama as the instrument of divine favor for Portugal, his exploits opening a new age. The quest for fame and riches was linked to the destiny of Christian expansion sponsored by Portugal. The poem is fragrant with the scent of all the spices acquired and exploited through the Portuguese system. The venture was commercial but also religious.

A novel written in 1597 by Luo Maodeng titled *Voyage of the San Bao Eunuch* gives a less heroic and more picturesque account of Zheng He's adventures. The journeys provided the writer with entertaining and fantastic anecdotes, and even suggestions that the admiral visited the other world, but the flotilla was regarded as a merely historical curiosity, much the way one might now write about blimps or seaplanes. In the novel, Zheng He does not represent the foundation of an empire on the order of da Gama, nor is his accomplishment heralded as a turning point.[27] The Chinese shared with the Europeans an infatuation with spices, but not the hunger to grow rich by controlling their trade. Such global ambitions, poorly backed up logistically though they might be, would inspire the ventures of the Iberian kingdoms, followed soon by many of the other European nations.

EIGHT

*Finding the
Realms of Spices:
Portugal and Spain*

The voyages of Columbus and da Gama obviously *were* historical turning points. It is beyond our purpose to describe in detail how Portugal and
Spain came to be the leaders of a fateful movement out of the old confines
of European influence to disturb the commercial arrangements of Asia
and virtually to destroy and remake the Americas. We want to look at their
contrasting theories of how to find the direct route to the spices and how
these were implemented. This involves more attention to Portugal than to
Spain, because Portugal's projects leading to India were more gradual and
complex than Spain's relatively sudden interest in the plans of Columbus.

The Portuguese spent about seventy years exploring and mapping the coast of Africa and figuring out how to navigate the Atlantic Ocean going north and south. This latter task was difficult because the prevailing winds and currents made it impossible most of the time to sail directly south or north between Portugal and Africa, so elaborate tacking (sailing in a zigzag course) was usually necessary. Ships could not just hug the coast the way they did in the narrow Mediterranean but rather were forced to tack back and forth far out of sight of land.[1] The discovery of the Azores by the Portuguese in 1427 was probably a result of such unavoidable detours into the vastness of the Atlantic, and the first European landing in Brazil in 1500 by Pedro Álvares Cabral was the inadvertent by-product of a long tacking maneuver to the southwest.

The Europeans referred to West Africa south of the Sahara as "Guinea" (following the Arabic name for the region).[2] The gold and opulence of the kingdoms below the desert were known, especially after 1324 when Mansa Mussa, the ruler of Mali, made a pilgrimage to Mecca that involved such a lavish quantity of gold (offered as pious gifts) that it excited comment for decades. The Catalan Atlas depicts the kingdom of "Ginyia" (Guinea) and its capital "Tenoch" (Timbuktu). The ruler is crowned, seated on a throne with a scepter in one hand and either an orb or a gold nugget in the other. The accompanying text states: "This black lord is called Mussa Melly [a conflation of Mansa Mussa and Mali], lord of the blacks of Guinea. This king is the richest and noblest of these parts because of the abundance of gold that is taken from his land."[3]

The regions around the Niger, Senegal, and Volta rivers were the source of much of the gold that reached Europe, so gold was, in the first instance, what the Portuguese sought when they began to explore Africa south of the relatively familiar regions of Mediterranean North Africa. According to the chronicler of early Portuguese exploration, Gomes Eanes de Zurara, what motivated the voyages were trade and the desire to find distant Christians.[4] These two were related in that this was not a missionary project but was based on the assumption that Christians would be friendly trading partners. The quest for Christians and exotic and profitable commodities would be linked throughout the Portuguese efforts in Africa and later in India.

Finding the Realms of Spices

Mansa Mussa ("Mussa Melly"), king of Mali, the land of gold, as depicted in the Catalan Atlas, 1375–77. (Bibliothèque nationale de France, Paris)

Although the Portuguese program of research and experimentation can be seen as culminating in the final circumnavigation of Africa by da Gama at the end of the fifteenth century, the initial curiosity about Africa was powered by gold and slaves rather than immediate ambitions for spices and India. In the era of Prince Henry the Navigator (who lived from 1394 to 1460), Portuguese exploration of Africa was not yet related to a plan to find a route to India. The search for gold was, in effect, another attempt to get around the middlemen who brought it across the Sahara into North Africa, an anticipation of what would later be the project to connect directly with the spice merchants of India. Slaves were particularly useful for the first experiments with cultivating sugar in Madeira and the Azores, a sign of things to come in the following centuries when the West Indies became the center of a world sugar trade.

Unexpectedly, one of the first by-products of African voyages was neither gold nor slaves but a spice, the sharp reddish malagueta pepper, also known as grains of paradise. Malagueta was found shortly after the Portuguese reached the delta of the Gambia River in 1450.[5] South of this river the shore of what is now Sierra Leone and Liberia came to be called the Malagueta

Coast by the Portuguese. By the 1490s, the place where malagueta pepper grew was well known outside Portugal. In 1479–80, Eustache de la Fosse, a merchant from Tournai (now in Belgium), traveled to the so-called Gold Coast and the Malagueta Coast and wrote a description of his voyage. On his globe fashioned in 1492, Martin Behaim states that he accompanied a Portuguese voyage in 1484 that went to the kingdoms of Gambia and Golof where grains of paradise grow, and he also identifies the "land of malagueta" (Terra de Malaguet) in West Africa.[6] Thus the true origin of grains of paradise was known throughout Europe by the late fifteenth century. In later times, European colonial cartographers and entrepreneurs named other sections of the West African shore the "ivory coast," the "slave coast," and the "gold coast." The name "grain coast" for Liberia and Sierra Leone survived until the early twentieth century on English maps of Africa as a recollection of the trade in grains of paradise.[7]

Grains of paradise had been highly regarded for flavoring and for medicine since the late thirteenth century, but the source was assumed to be the vaguely defined India that provided almost all other spices. An Italian pilot serving on a Portuguese expedition to the Malagueta Coast described grains of paradise as looking like Italian sorghum, but with a peppery taste. A French observer in 1479 gave a more detailed account of the plant, saying it grew in lovely profusion on lattices in the manner of hops. The reddish fruit resembles an apple, and within it are the prized seeds, the piquant "grains." Later observers likened the fruit to bright red figs.[8]

This discovery was the first European accomplishment in the effort to find where spices actually came from. The fact that grains of paradise did not grow in India was proof of what Marco Polo had said 150 years earlier, that some spices originate outside India. The presence of malagueta in Guinea also encouraged a developing idea that Africa might be a way station to the riches (and in particular the spices) of Asia. The addition of spices to the list of valuable African goods contributed to the expansion of Portuguese ambitions in the later part of the fifteenth century, even though grains of paradise were already losing some of their fashionable allure and were not such a great source of profit in themselves.

By 1475 the Portuguese had passed the equator. From this time, their plans seem to have been driven more by a desire to find a direct sea route to India than to explore and exploit Africa. The accession of King João II in 1481 (who ruled until 1495) gave a particular impetus to the desire to go around the Egyptian and Venetian control of the Mediterranean spice trade. Writing in 1551, the chronicler Ferrão Lopes Castanheda said that before the Portuguese "discovered" India, the greater part of the spices, drugs, and jewels of Asia came via the Red Sea to Alexandria and were brought to Portugal and the rest of Europe by the Venetians. Desirous of increasing his lordship and reputation, King João accelerated the project of mapping out the coast of Guinea and southern Africa.

Africa was not just an obstacle, however, but an opportunity. The legendary Christian ruler Prester John was still more or less associated with India, but his kingdom had now moved toward or even into Africa, partly because of new knowledge about the Christian kingdom of Ethiopia. Prester John came to be thought of more as a help in clearing the road to India via Africa, not as the ruler of India himself. King João's plan to find the source of spices thus incorporated a sea route and further information about Africa and Prester John, both in order to find India. Especially if it proved impossible to reach India by going around Africa, Prester John might provide another route within Africa, or he might alternatively assist Portuguese ships coming up the eastern coast of Africa on their way to India if circumnavigation worked.[9]

King João II sought the answer to three vital and interrelated questions: Could Africa be circumnavigated in order to find India? Where did the spices come from? Where exactly was Prester John?[10] The search for Christian allies in the East was conceptually joined to the quest for spices. Just as da Gama's crewman had said, the Portuguese came to find Christians and spices. Prester John was not just a chimera or a distraction but part of the grand quest, advancing the arrival of the Portuguese in India.

Prester John's imaginary career and in particular his identification with Africa in the fifteenth century was related to a long-standing confusion between Ethiopia and India and how Asia was separated from Africa. Both places were known to the ancient Greeks and Romans, but according to many authorities India and the northeast part of the African continent adjoined, so that Ethiopia was extended in their imagination from south of Egypt east toward India.[11] The Indian Ocean was sometimes identified as the western border of India, but quite often the Nile was regarded as the frontier between Asia and Africa.

The legend of Prester John was not completely groundless or fantastic. There really was a Christian African kingdom, in Ethiopia (also called Abyssinia), just as there was a substantial Christian population along the western coast of India.[12] Ethiopia was one of the first places to have embraced Christianity (in the third and fourth centuries), but it had little or no connection with Western Europe for the first thousand years after its conversion, and it followed the Monophysite doctrine (that Christ has essentially one divine nature), which had been deemed heretical in the Catholic and Orthodox churches. Ethiopia sent occasional emissaries to Europe beginning in 1306, when a group of Ethiopians visited the papal court in Avignon. In 1400, King Henry IV of England wrote to Prester John as "King of Abyssinia" in response to rumors that the African ruler was planning to recapture Jerusalem from the Muslims. Speculation in this vein, understandably, irritated the real Ethiopians. At Rome in the mid-fifteenth century, members of an Ethiopian delegation responded to inquiries about the legendary priest-king with the bewildered comment, "We are from Ethiopia, our king is Zara Yaqob—why do you call him Prester John?"

Europeans showed up in Ethiopia occasionally, beginning in 1402, but its location in relation to other parts of Africa and to India remained uncertain. If Prester John seemed to have moved from India to Africa, the relationship between the two landmasses needed further research. The Portuguese continued their push to the south, exploring the Gulf of Guinea between 1470 and 1475 and finding that Africa extended farther south after the coastline turned to the east, so that the gulf did not easily connect with the seas of India as they had first hoped. The delta of the Congo River was seen by Diogo Cão in 1483, and it was thought that this represented either a branch of the Nile or the end of the African continent. Five years later, Bartomeu Dias returned to Lisbon having finally found the way around Africa considerably to the south of the Congo. Dias rounded the Cape of Good Hope, but he did not pursue his course up the eastern coast toward India. Even so, Ptolemy had been proved wrong: the Indian Ocean was open.

Why another decade ensued before da Gama made good on the path opened by Dias may have to do with internal Portuguese politics and opposition to expending effort on this seemingly wild venture. Many in the Portuguese royal court advocated paying more attention to North Africa in order to respond to the revived Spanish attacks on Muslim Granada. They feared that while Portugal was preoccupied in chasing the elusive problem of India, it would be threatened by an aggressive and unified Spanish crown nearer to home.[13] For those who remained advocates of the India plan, it is also likely that time was needed to bolster the circumnavigation scheme by finding Prester John in Africa. Some idea of the extent of the African interior was now available and it was not very encouraging. It was still hoped that one of the great rivers of Africa, such as the Congo, the Gambia, or the Senegal, might lead east to Prester John's realm. Arab cartographers and Jewish-Catalan mapmakers in Majorca depicted rivers or canals connecting Guinea with the Red Sea, but of course these were never actually discovered, and in fact inner Africa remained impenetrable for Europeans for another four centuries.

Rather than relying on overland trips into the as yet almost unknown continent, Portuguese representatives were sent via the known routes to Ethiopia and India to see if Prester John could be found, and if his territory bordered the Red Sea or the Indian Ocean. This was the first direct Portuguese contact with India and a kind of scouting mission via the traditional paths in preparation for implementing the nontraditional circumnavigation route. In 1487, the same year that Dias left Portugal on his landmark voyage, two intrepid Portuguese agents named Pêro da Covilhã and Afonso de Paiva were sent to the Red Sea regions. According to the chronicler Francisco de Álvarez, their mission was "to go discover and learn about Prester John and where cinnamon is found along with other spices that are come from those regions to Venice by way of the lands of the Moors."[14] Together Covilhã and Paiva reached Aden. We don't know exactly what the details of the plan were, but Covilhã sailed for India while Paiva set out by boat south for Ethiopia. They presumably were to look for Prester John in both territories and then meet in Cairo at a set time. Covilhã visited Calicut, Goa, and the East African coast, where he ventured as far south as Sofala in what is now Mozambique.

In his mission, Covilhã very likely answered the first two questions of King João. Assuredly he found where the spices came from and probably he also figured out the relation of India to Africa, including confirmation that Africa could be circumnavigated. How much of his research reached Lisbon is unknown, as he never returned. At the rendezvous in Cairo in 1490, he found out that Paiva had died (where is not clear). In the meantime (in 1488), Dias had returned to Portugal with the secret information about the Cape of Good Hope. The urgency of the Prester John mission seemed greater as the sea road to India appeared to be feasible. Since it now appeared possible to sail into the Indian Ocean from the west, an ally on the East African coast on the order of Prester John would be useful to provide a transit base for the long journey and to help repulse any retaliatory attacks on Portuguese ships by regional Islamic powers and traders.

Two new emissaries were sent out by the royal court to talk with Covilhã in Cairo. This new pair were Portuguese Jews, Abraham of Beja and Joseph of Lamego. On behalf of King João, Abraham and Joseph instructed Covilhã to undertake the Ethiopian trip left incomplete by Paiva's death. The emissaries went back to report to the king of Portugal, perhaps bearing information about India and Africa discovered by Covilhã. The fact that da Gama knew that Calicut was a major spice port and that he bore a letter for its ruler from the king of Portugal argues for some communication between Covilhã and the court before he set forth for the kingdom of Prester John.

Pêro da Covilhã probably didn't arrive in Ethiopia until 1494. He was welcomed by its ruler, the "king of kings" Eskender (Alexander), but not allowed to leave. The custom of Ethiopia, he was told, was that travelers who arrived in the kingdom might never depart. Eskender was murdered soon after Covilhã's arrival, but his successors Naod and Lebna Dengel (David) imposed the same conditions, according him honor and a measure of luxury, but not permitting him to return to Portugal. The Ethiopian rulers probably feared the diffusion of information about their realm, so Covilhã spent the rest of his life in Ethiopia, about thirty years altogether. A Portuguese mission arrived in 1520 and found the elderly Covilhã, so that some of our information about him comes from Francisco Álvarez, who accompanied this later embassy and spoke extensively with Covilhã. Another source says that when presented in 1520 with the option to come back to Portugal at long last, Covilhã declined, saying he was too old and too tired.[15]

Under these circumstances it is unlikely that any news about the great Christian kingdom in Africa reached Portugal, so da Gama, although eager to find Prester John en route to India, was little better informed than his predecessors about Ethiopia. Prester John's realm, Ethiopia, and India were still generally confused and all were still regarded somewhat interchangeably as the home of spices. Toward the end of the fifteenth century, the German pilgrim Arnold von Harff visited the Holy Land and claimed in his account of his travels that spices came to the Mediterranean via the Sinai Peninsula from the land of Prester John, a country known as "Little India or Abyssinia." Another German pilgrim named Bernard von Breydenbach wrote in 1486 that spices arrived in Sinai on ships from India, but he believed that the Indians were the same as the Ethiopians and they had been converted by St. Thomas. This misinformation at the time of Portugal's breakthrough discovery of the all-water route to India should not come as a great surprise. In the 1550s, the British were looking for a water route to the Spice Islands via the Arctic Sea, north of Russia, and still searching for a northwest passage through Canada or up the Hudson River throughout the early seventeenth century. Closer to the time of the great explorations, the Milanese ambassador to England reported in about 1500 that John Cabot (an Italian explorer in service to the English) told him that spices came from Japan and were brought to Mecca by boat and then distributed by caravans. Closer to a correct understanding of the situation was the report of a Florentine observer, Girolamo Sernigi, writing about da Gama's expedition almost while it was under way. In a chapter with the title "Of Prester John and Where the Spices and Gems Come From," he distinguishes between Calicut and India generally and the realm of Prester John. Calicut is where the spices are, but there are not many Christians. Prester John's realm is far away, near the "Gulf of Arabia" and to be identified with the black Africans of Ethiopia and Malindi (the coast of modern Kenya).[16]

The failure to make much progress on the Prester John front delayed but did not discourage the Portuguese intention to complete and begin to exploit the way to India. They politely rebuffed suggestions that a westward Atlantic voyage would find the spice lands. Even as news of Columbus' exploits was diffused, they continued to concentrate on their own plan. In July of 1497, da Gama left Lisbon with four ships and 170 sailors.[17] Upon reaching the vicinity of Sierra Leone, he sailed west and south for several weeks, away from the coast into the empty South Atlantic. He finally turned east to reach sight of the African coast just seventy miles north of the Cape of Good Hope. Making progress up the eastern side of Africa, he found, to his surprise, prosperous entrepôts with mostly Muslim traders. Already in Mozambique he found that spices from India were for sale and also, to his dismay, that the beads, clothes, and honey he carried as gifts or possible trading goods that might have passed muster in Guinea were regarded in sophisticated East Africa with derision as worthless. He found no signs of Prester John. Nevertheless, the presence of Indian products showed he was certainly on the right track. At Malindi the local Muslim sultan (not the Christian Prester John) furnished him with a pilot who was familiar with the winds and currents, so that he crossed over to India in the brief space of a month.

On May 18, 1498, da Gama arrived just north of the city of Calicut, one of the great spice ports of the Malabar coast, a place visited about ten years earlier by Pêro da Covilhã. The timing was poor in that the city was inundated by the monsoon, an inauspicious beginning to a tense three-month stay that would be further marred by violence and what might charitably be termed misunderstandings. The fact that the Portuguese brought little or nothing of value exacerbated the problem. The ruler of Calicut furnished enough pepper to make the voyage economically credible and sent a generous but slightly scolding message to the Portuguese king: "Vasco da Gama, *fidalgo* [gentleman] of your household, came to my land, and I rejoiced at that. In my land, there is much cinnamon and much cloves and ginger and pepper and many precious stones. And what I want from your land is gold and silver and coral and scarlet [cloth]."[18] Da Gama's homeward voyage was extremely difficult. The westward crossing of the Indian Ocean took three months because of adverse winds, and thirty men died of scurvy. Two ships made it back to Portugal.

Oddly enough, da Gama stayed in the Azores while one of his captains conveyed the news of the voyage's attainment of India to King Manuel (ruled 1495–1521). The king wasted no time in announcing the discovery to the rest of Europe and in adopting the title "Lord of the Conquest, Navigation, and Commerce of Ethiopia, Arabia, Persia, and India." In a message to the rulers of Spain, Ferdinand and Isabella, the Portuguese king boasted that the expedition had found the great cities of India, "wherein is fully practiced the commerce of spices and gems," and just to make sure they understood, he specified cloves, cinnamon, and pepper, along with rubies and gold. In keeping with the Christians and spices tenor of the Portuguese plan, he also proposed that the profits be used for a blockade of the Red Sea and a joint effort to free the Holy Land from the Muslims.[19]

In Venice, whose fortunes were so closely tied to the spice trade, the disturbing news circulated even before King Manuel's announcement. The Venetian ambassador in Cairo remarked that it would be the cause of the ruination of his state. The diarist Girolamo Priuli, also from Venice, was alarmed but also incredulous. Writing in early August 1499, he reported that news came from Cairo that three Portuguese ships sent out "to enquire after the Spice Islands" had arrived in Calicut and Aden and concluded: "This news appears of the greatest importance to me if it is true, but I don't think it deserves credence." According to the rumor he had received, the commander of the Portuguese fleet was Christopher Columbus!

With the return to Lisbon in 1501 of Pedro Álvares Cabral, commander of the second Portuguese voyage to India, the truth had to be admitted. The Venetian envoy to the Portuguese court wrote to his government confirming Cabral's arrival with a huge quantity of pepper, and the diarist Priuli remarked darkly: "If this route continues—and already it appears to me easy to accomplish—the king of Portugal might be called the king of money. . . . The entire city [Venice] remains astonished that in our day such a new route would be discovered, never known or heard of by our ancestors." Venetian merchants feared they would be ruined, according to Priuli, since the Portuguese would undercut the prices made necessary by the transport and tax costs imposed by the Ottoman Turks and by Venice itself.[20] Venice was threatened by simultaneous crises of a full-fledged war with the Turks and the drying up of its principal source of profit, the spice trade with Egypt, yet the Portuguese were never able to undercut prices so much that the Venetians were driven out of the spice business.

There has been a long-standing debate among historians over how great an effect the Portuguese had on Venice and on spice prices in sixteenth-century Europe. Frederick Lane argued that prices had not been rising in the fifteenth century, that they didn't fall significantly in the sixteenth century, and that the Portuguese did not displace Venice or further the integration of the European spice trade. This analysis is no longer accepted, and a recent evaluation of the economic impact that accounts for inflation seems conclusively to disprove the argument of continuity.[21] The Portuguese did indeed change things forever even if Venice proved itself to be redoubtable against all enemies, Muslim and Christian, and experienced an expansive sixteenth century. Prosperity was now based more on territorial aggrandizement on the Italian peninsula and on Venice's position within Europe than on the long-distance trade of the past, but Venice remained among the greatest commercial powers throughout the sixteenth century.

Along the Indian Ocean the Portuguese found a complex, largely peaceful and efficient network of commerce connecting Indonesia, India, Egypt, the Persian Gulf, Arabia, and East Africa. Traders of various nations and religions had long-standing relations and networks. The ocean was hardly free of pirates or of state-sponsored violence, but the Portuguese had a belligerent idea of how to seize the profits of the spice trade for themselves and an impatience with the existing system. The second Portuguese expedition to reach Calicut arrived in 1500 with cannons. Under the leadership of Pedro Álvares Cabral, this was a considerably more ambitious affair than da Gama's few ships. Cabral had a fleet of thirteen vessels carrying 1,500 men. Only six ships made it back, so the expedition was by no means a complete success. It began with a fortuitous error of great future consequence. By tacking even farther to the west than da Gama in order to hit the southernmost part of Africa, Cabral accidentally stumbled upon Brazil, which he named the Land of the Holy Cross. It quickly became known for its plentiful supply of brazil wood, a particularly useful dyestuff and one of the few medieval spices actually found in the New World—hence the eventual name change for the new land.

The expectation had been that Cabral would establish a commercial base ("factory") in Calicut, seek alliances with the hoped-for numerous Christian kingdoms in India, and put into effect the venerable plan to blockade the Red Sea to choke off the spice trade between India and Egypt. For a time Cabral and his associates engaged in tedious negotiations with the ruler of Calicut (a new one had succeeded since da Gama), but when the Portuguese seized some Muslim ships it led to violence, the Portuguese fired their ships' guns on the city, and its ruler fled. The Portuguese willingness, even eagerness, to use force was further demonstrated when they reached Ceylon, the source of the best cinnamon, in 1505. Their aggressiveness coupled with their quickness in figuring out the geography of the spice trade was shown by the conquest of Malacca, in 1511, where they established a fortress to control the narrow route between Sumatra and Malaya through which all the Indonesian spices had to pass. At the height of Portuguese power the claim was made by the pharmacist and diplomat Tomé Pires that "whoever holds Malacca has his hand on the throat of Venice," an appealing bit of geopolitical wisdom about the global spice trade, but not completely accurate since Venice managed to survive even this Portuguese coup. The Portuguese sent ships to the nutmeg island of Banda that same year, 1511, and to the clove island of Ternate in 1513. A new era had begun, for Europeans had finally mapped the spice lands and could set about trying to plunder them. The passage quoted earlier from Camões' epic in honor of da Gama's voyage is more than a conventional rhapsody on spices, for the poet describes where they come from with unprecedented accuracy.

The Portuguese put together a series of trading stations and fortifications that stretched from Brazil in the New World to Macau off the coast of southern China. This was not an empire in the traditional sense of a land-based territorial complex but resembled more the Venetian pattern of coastal and island commercial and military enclaves. The Portuguese headquarters overseas was Goa on the west coast of India. From here the spice trade was organized and efforts were made to discourage competition and to monopolize the most valuable products of the Indian Ocean.

Despite their possession of advanced weapons and brutal ambition, the Portuguese did not take over the Asian seaborne trade nor did they drive Muslims out of commerce in these areas, even though it was their stated intention to do so. The arrival of Europeans in South and Southeast Asia did not immediately transform societies and economies in the total and traumatizing way that the Spanish presence in the New World did. Even at the height of its power, Portugal simply didn't have the resources to send out more than a few ships a year to keep this vast empire together. Ultimately Brazil was a greater prize than the Indies, as the Portuguese, beginning in the later sixteenth century, were displaced in Asia by European competitors. They kept together the remnants of their conquests even after Brazil's independence was achieved in the nineteenth century. India took over Goa in the 1960s. Only after the democratic revolution of 1974 did the Portuguese give up Guinea-Bissau, Angola, and Mozambique, their former stations in Africa, and East Timor, site of so much suffering in relation to Indonesia, and finally Macau, just recently incorporated into China.

Facing the Atlantic and with a religious and commercial interest in Africa, Portugal was the first European nation to come up with a concerted plan to find a direct route to the spices of India. Spain's interest in the same project developed considerably later, in the 1480s. The Spanish kingdoms of Castile and Aragon spent most of the fifteenth century preoccupied with domestic political and economic upheavals punctuated by civil wars. Until the resolution of these conflicts and the union of the kingdoms through the marriage of Ferdinand of Aragon and Isabella of Castile, there was only intermittent interest in plans for expansion as opposed to Portugal's more consistent and intense efforts in Africa.

Castile did initiate a mission to the new (and, as it turned out, ephemeral) Mongol ruler Tamerlane. The ambassador of King Henry III, Ruy González de Clavijo, reached the court of Tamerlane in Samarkand in 1404 where he met envoys from China.[22] This was one of the few European contacts with Ming China in the fifteenth century, but Clavijo didn't venture east of Samarkand and nothing further was attempted; Tamerlane died in 1405 and his empire quickly fell to pieces.

Even more than Portugal, however, Spain had a long-standing history of commerce and warfare with Islam. There was extensive trade with Muslim North Africa, and until 1492 the Muslim kingdom of Granada survived, a remnant of what had once been Islamic hegemony over the Iberian Peninsula. Islam was on one hand a familiar source of commercial wealth, and on the other a religious enemy regarded with a Crusade antipathy. The decision of Ferdinand and Isabella to support the schemes proposed to them by Columbus was an outgrowth of plans to extend Spain's power beyond its Islamic neighbors and coincided with a campaign to conquer Granada and destroy this last vestige of independent Muslim Spain. Riches, crusade, and exploration were connected, not just in Columbus' imagination but according to the intentions of the Catholic monarchs. It is hardly a coincidence that the fateful year 1492 saw the fall of Granada, the expulsion of the Jews of Spain, and the launching of Columbus' first voyage. A messianic, or at least transformative, atmosphere surrounds all three paradigm-shattering events.

The real personality of Christopher Columbus fits neither the nineteenth-century ideal of heroic voice of science against obscurantist superstition nor the tormented and obsessed figure found in modern biographies. He was a man of grandiose ambition and more than normal stubbornness, but he was an intellectual and an experienced mariner, having sailed all over the Mediterranean and accompanied Portuguese ships to Africa. His view of geography was formed by his travels and extensive reading.[23] He was extraordinarily daring in his willingness to test his theories in four dangerous voyages, but he was not the author of a unique or unprecedented vision of the world.

As with da Gama's expedition, that of Columbus was small-scale and not particularly well funded. The difference was that da Gama was preceded by decades of sustained work on the geography of Africa, while Spain came to this idea at the last moment, with no prior history of great curiosity about Prester John, a route to the Indies, or Africa apart from the connections between Morocco and Granada. Columbus essentially sold his grand plan to Spain after it had been rejected elsewhere, including Portugal. He made his first presentation to Ferdinand and Isabella in 1491 and, although he experienced many tense moments and setbacks, he was able to put his idea into effect before two years had elapsed. That idea was a westward route to the Indies.

The possibility that India could be found more easily by sailing west than by the long and difficult route around Africa and then east was encouraged by both new and old theories. Ptolemy's calculation that the world had a small circumference suggested that the western edge of Europe was relatively (compared to the reality) close to the eastern coast of Asia. In addition, the less landlocked picture of the earth offered by Ptolemy and especially fifteenth-century mapmakers encouraged speculation about a possible water route between the continents. Martin Behaim describes lands in the east, the far north, and southern Africa as all unknown to Ptolemy, but he depicts the continents and islands as mutually accessible following a Ptolemaic model, only more open. He states on his globe "that every part may be reached in ships." This contrasts with the earlier assumption, exemplified by Mandeville, for example, that one could travel mostly overland in one direction and come back to Europe. Everywhere, according to Mandeville, the traveler would find people, lands, islands, and cities but a journey around the world would be essentially by land.[24]

It was of course crucial that the oceans not be so open or extensive that they were impossible to cross. What appeals to the imagination about Columbus is the obvious risk involved in simply sailing west until you hit land, an all-in-one gamble compared with the slow, careful experiments in navigating around Africa undertaken by the Portuguese. Columbus took reassurance from the Ptolemaic calculation of the earth's circumference and perhaps also from the Florentine geographer Toscanelli's theories about the westward route. Toscanelli argued for the neo-Ptolemaic small circumference, hence a short distance separating Europe from Asia, but he also advocated the idea that islands intervened between the mainlands of the two continents, something not envisioned by Ptolemy. These islands would make the period traversed in the open ocean shorter and the discovery of the Indies actually feasible.

Before reaching the Spice Islands or the great cities of China, Columbus anticipated arrival at Atlantic islands lying to the west of Europe.[25] He put in at Gomera in the Canary Islands before setting out for the Indies. While in the Canaries, he mentioned in his journal the story that land could sometimes be seen on the westward horizon from Gomera, but also from the Portuguese islands of Madeira and the Azores. This was not Asia but rather "Antillia," an island lost in the mid-Atlantic, supposedly settled in the early eighth century by Spanish or Portuguese Christians fleeing from the Arab invasions of Spain. Contact with the mainland of Europe was severed and nothing had been heard from the island for centuries. Martin Behaim's globe states that the refugees were led by the archbishop of Porto in Portugal and six other bishops. A Spanish ship approached the island in 1414, he claims, and although it did not land, it also found no danger in approaching. The permanent impact of this legend is the name of Antilles given to the West Indian islands, "West Indian" itself being also the product of the confused mixture of old and new geographical knowledge.

Antillia was extremely important to Toscanelli because it served as a way station on the short route to Asia that he posited. According to reconstructions of Toscanelli's lost chart that accompanied his letter of 1474 to Fernão Martins, Antillia lies midway between the Canary Islands and the large island of Japan (Cipangu). In the letter Toscanelli says: "But from Antilia, known to you, to the far-famed island of Cippangu there are ten spaces [marked out on the map]. . . . So there is not a great space to be traversed over unknown waters." These ten spaces were the equivalent of 2,500 miles.

The Toscanelli letter is fascinating not only for its geographical theories but for the degree to which it dwells on the purpose of all this theorizing: the riches to be found in Asia. Toscanelli begins by saying he has often spoken about a sea route to India, "the land of spices," one that would be shorter than going down the coast of Africa ("via Guinea"). He describes his chart as showing that spices grow in lands lying to the *west* of Europe and Africa. He repeats Marco Polo's observations about the Chinese port of Zaiton and the immense quantities of pepper it imports. Cathay is a populous and peaceful kingdom ruled over by the benevolent Great Khan. It is the richest land in the world, possessing gold, silver, precious stones—and spices. From the golden-roofed island of Cipangu it is an easy trip to the gigantic city of Quinsay in China with its thousands of marble bridges.

Marco Polo had reported the existence of Japan but placed it much farther off the Chinese coast than it really is situated, and he also attributed to it the plethora of gold, as mentioned several times before. Toscanelli relied on both of these crucial inaccuracies, placing Cipangu well to the east of China and a manageable distance from Antillia, even directly from Europe or the Canary Islands. The German mapmakers Martellus and Behaim also located Japan within striking distance of Europe, exaggerating both its size and its distance from the Asiatic mainland.

How much Columbus relied on Toscanelli is unknown, as is how much he was acquainted with the maps of Behaim and Martellus or the works of Marco Polo before setting out on his initial voyage. He certainly shared the picture of a relatively small and island-filled Atlantic across which lay the Asian mainland. In late September and early October 1492, Columbus believed he had passed Antillia and that he was heading directly for Cipangu. When he first reached Cuba, after negotiating the tiny islands of the Bahamas, he was convinced he had indeed arrived in Cipangu, although he later decided it was Cathay and Hispaniola was Cipangu.

In her absorbing and engaging study of Columbus' intellectual background, Valerie Flint gives two contrasting maps that show where Columbus *thought* he was (plotted according to the Behaim map), and the course that we know he actually followed.[26] Between Cipangu and mainland China lie many islands of the "Indies." India itself faces out toward Africa, south and only slightly west of China (so much for William of Rubruck's observations nearly 250 years earlier). As he sailed around the islands later referred to as the West Indies, Columbus was sure he had found various spices, which confirmed his certainty of having arrived in Asia. Rumors of gold, spices, mastic, and medicinal rhubarb convinced Columbus that Haiti was Cipangu. He then entertained the idea that Hispaniola might turn out to be an Arabian or Indian island, but he was sure that it contained substantial quantities of cinnamon, ginger, musk, and rhubarb.[27] Columbus admitted that the mastic trees didn't seem to be producing in winter and that, although he knew aloe wood was nearby, he hadn't actually found any. He did find some interesting botanical items, but he confused New World plants with the sought-after Asian aromatics, mistaking agave for aloe wood; gumbo-limbo for mastic; American plums for Indian myrobolans.[28]

The results of Columbus' first voyage were both spectacular and ambiguous. He had not actually found the cities of Cathay, let alone the court of the Great Khan, and did not return with his ships' holds full of cinnamon or pepper. Nevertheless, clearly he had touched on some kind of western-lying territory and kept in play the competing claims of Spain and Portugal. In 1479, before the unification of Spain with the marriage of Ferdinand and Isabella, Castile and Portugal had concluded a treaty at Alcáçovas that confirmed Spanish possession of the Canary Islands in return for giving Portugal a free hand in exploring the African coast. Portugal was allowed to keep any territory it might in future discover in the direction of "Guinea," so the treaty was a precedent for the notion of partitioning off lands not yet demarcated or even "discovered." In March 1493, Columbus returned to Europe, landing first in Lisbon before visiting the Catholic monarchs in Barcelona. He told King João II of Portugal of his voyage and assured the monarch that his discoveries were nowhere near Africa, the Portuguese sphere of influence as stated in the pact of Alcáçovas. João II was not so sure of this, but promised he would take up the matter of a new demarcation with the rulers of Spain. The Portuguese, convinced that the shorter route to the Indies was east and south around Africa (and Dias had already shown the feasibility of this), were concerned to safeguard their control of Africa and everything to the east of a certain line. The Spanish wanted freedom to follow up whatever it was that they had found in the west. Officially mediated by Pope Alexander VI but in fact arranged by negotiation

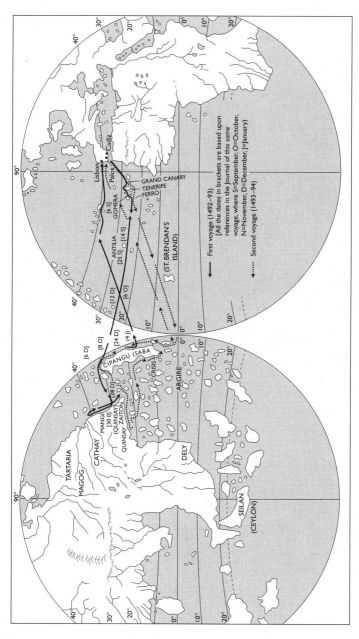

Where Columbus thought he was, according to a projection of his itinerary onto a diagram of Martin Behaim's globe. (Map by William L. Nelson, redrawn from Valerie I. J. Flint, *The Imaginative Landscape of Christopher Columbus,* © 1992 Princeton University Press; used by permission of Princeton University Press)

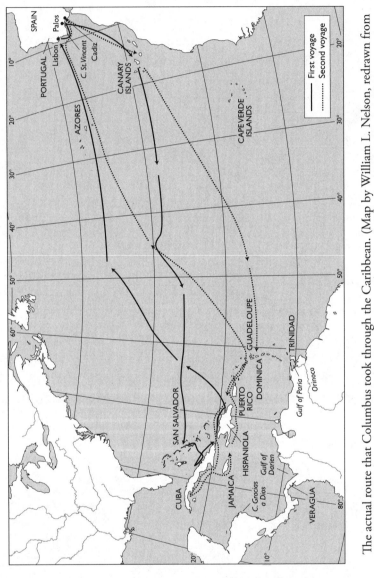

The actual route that Columbus took through the Caribbean. (Map by William L. Nelson, redrawn from Valerie I. J. Flint, *The Imaginative Landscape of Christopher Columbus*, © 1992 Princeton University Press; used by permission of Princeton University Press)

between the two kingdoms, the Treaty of Tordesillas, in June 1494, stated that everything beyond (thus west of) a line three hundred miles from the Cape Verde Islands would belong to Spain, and all lands discovered to the east of that line would be Portugal's. The line was later changed to one thousand miles west of the islands. Given the uncertainty about the earth's size and about what lands Columbus had reached, the treaty was a gamble for both sides, but it did serve to give the Portuguese a clear path to India and allowed them to keep Brazil once the implications of Cabral's wandering off course in 1500 were realized.

The problem became more urgent once the Portuguese reached the Spice Islands of the Moluccas in 1511–13. The Portuguese were the "finders," from the European point of view, but these islands were not off the coast of India as expected—to the Portuguese, they were disturbingly far back around toward what was now widely acknowledged to be a continent previously unknown to Europeans. Far from being positioned near India, the "east Indies" turned out to be quite far east of India—almost, it was thought, off the western coast of Mexico, and possibly even on the other, Spanish side of the thousand-mile line. The size of the earth was still underestimated, only now not because of ignorance of the American continents but rather because of the extent of the Pacific Ocean.

The Spanish were determined to wrest the spice trade away from Portugal. The location of the Spice Islands in relation to the rest of the world and the unexpected size of the earth's circumference were demonstrated in the heroic and horrific journey of Magellan's fleet, in 1519–22. The purpose of this voyage, according to Maximilian Transylvanus, the first to write about it, was "to search for the islands in which the spices grow."[29] Magellan, a Portuguese mariner, was financed by German investors (the Fugger merchant and banking family in particular) and commissioned by Spain, an international complex of entrepreneurs reflecting the rivalries that the spice routes were creating.

Magellan did not survive this voyage, which covered fifteen times more of the earth than Columbus' first round trip. In fact only 18 men from an original crew of 260 managed to return. The expedition did prove that one could reach the Spice Islands sailing west, by going around the southern end of South America, but the distance and difficulty had obviously been underestimated. It is an indication of how lucrative the spice trade really was that even this disastrous trip was at least financially profitable. The one surviving ship, the *Victoria,* brought back about 53,000 pounds of cloves, enough to create a theoretical 2,500 percent profit, split among the handful of survivors, the investors, and the Spanish crown.[30]

Spain now could claim that the Spice Islands and indeed all the East Indies lay on their side of the Tordesillas line, along with most of the American continent. In the years after the exhausted if triumphant return of the remnant of Magellan's crew, the Spanish ruler, Charles I, pursued Spain's interests in Asia energetically, although by an agreement signed in Saragossa in 1529, he recognized Portugal's right to the islands in return for a substantial monetary payment. His successor, Phillip II, attempted to tie together a world empire under Spanish domination. It was in his honor that the only Asian islands Spain retained over the long run, the Philippines, were named. Nonetheless, Spain was willing to relinquish many of its Asian claims because of the success of its New World ventures. The conquests of Mexico and Peru and the discoveries of vast quantities of gold and silver there turned Spain's attention away from Asia. How could the gold of Cipangu, as yet undiscovered, rival that of the Andes?

The Portuguese built an empire on the discovery of the route to the spices of Asia. The Spanish built an empire on a mistaken initial idea about this route and then with less attention to spices than to the wealth of the West Indies (sugar) and the western continents (precious metals). Spain took over Portugal and its empire from 1580 to 1640, at the height of its imperial reach, but because of the difficulty and ultimately the impossibility of maintaining such globe-spanning domains, Spain and Portugal were succeeded by other powers, especially the Dutch and the British, in the quest for spices and their profits.

CONCLUSION
*The Rise and Fall
of Spices*

The crucial role that nutmeg played in
early colonial history is hard to reconcile with the
dusty tin of spice most Americans take out of the rack
at the end of the year to garnish their eggnog.

John Seabrook
"Soldiers and Spice," originally published
in the *New Yorker* (August 31, 2001)

In 1648, the French princess Marie-Louise de Gonzague journeyed to Poland to meet her new husband, King Casimir V, who had just succeeded to the Polish throne. She and members of her entourage were dismayed by the ceremonial meals served to them during their progress through Germany and Poland. The dishes presented at these banquets were showy, but so strongly flavored with spices (especially saffron) as to be inedible, or at least, in the words of one of these unfortunates, "no Frenchman could eat them." A similarly dismissive report was given by the countess of Aulnoy, a French traveler in Spain, in 1691, when she commented on the disparity between beautifully presented dishes and their unpleasant reek of saffron and other spices. France's distinct rejection of spices was noted by a German observer in the early eighteenth century who remarked that his countrymen who like well-spiced food were bound to be disappointed with what they ate in France.[1]

In the era of Louis XIV, France was assuming the position of undisputed gastronomic leadership that it would hold thereafter, or perhaps until just recently. One of the most distinctive features of the French culinary revolution of the seventeenth century was the rejection of spices. In part this was because new flavors were introduced, so that sauces were no longer the thin, vinegary affairs of the Middle Ages and the Renaissance but thicker, based on butter and egg yolks or on mayonnaise-like combinations. The sweet-and-sour effect formerly desired was now despised. Sauces were becoming richer but simpler, flavored with indigenous tastes furnished by capers, anchovies, mushrooms (or truffles), and scallions, not with nutmeg and cinnamon. Spices were also losing their importance as treats, snacks, or flavorings for wine. New World and other recently discovered imports, such as tea, coffee, and chocolate were preferred to old-fashioned luxury standbys on the order of hippocras or candied spices. The tropical beverages were drunk with lots of sugar, and indeed sugar went from being one spice among many to a staple product in its own category, while almost all the rest of its former associates in the realm of spices sank into obscurity.

We'll have more to say about sugar, but for the moment the important aspect of the seventeenth-century change is that the eclipse of spices was related to a new desire for letting the natural flavor of the main ingredients of a dish speak for themselves. Butter, shallots, or truffles might enhance these, but there was a rejection of artifice, strange colors, and whimsical foolery, all popular features of medieval cookery. Giving advice to household stewards in the mid-seventeenth century, Nicholas de Bonnefons wrote that "cabbage soup should taste of cabbage, leeks of leeks, turnips of turnips."[2] This may seem banal, but in the context of centuries of culinary cleverness, in which mixture and complexity were the desired effects, it had all the disturbing shock of stark modernism in contrast to Victorian ornamentation. The year 1615 saw the last edition of the *Viandier* of Taillevent as a work of reference rather than a historical curiosity.[3] Bonnefons and his contemporaries dismissed the elaboration, trickery, and special effects of the fading culinary tradition of the *Viandier*.

"The Ridiculous Meal" (*Le repas ridicule*), a satire written in 1665 by the French poet Nicolas Boileau, shows his harsh take on social ostentation in general and spices in particular. The host of this meal, a newly rich vulgarian, reminiscent of Petronius' Trimalchio, urges his guests to partake of dubious and out-of-fashion dishes: "Do you like nutmeg?" he asks. "It has been put in everything. Smell these wonderful chickens, Monsieur."[4] This critique of pretentious dining was in keeping with Boileau's classicism, his belief that truth to nature and simplicity, not obscurity or cleverness, were the true goals of poetry. Clarity, directness, and a supposedly classical severity rather than medieval ornamentation were extolled, even if, as it turns out, the gastronomy of the classical era was actually as elaborate and highly spiced as that of the Middle Ages.

Outside of France, as the comments of the French travelers cited above demonstrate, change was slower. In Italy, Antonio Latini, author of a seventeenth-century cookbook, explicitly and daringly proposed that it was possible to cook and flavor food without using spices. They could be replaced by herbs such as parsley or thyme, but Latini is not so committed to the new wave that he fails to offer traditional, complicated recipes with "suitable" spices like cinnamon, coriander, nutmeg, cloves, and pepper. Bartolomeo Stefani, the author of *L'arte di ben cucinare* (1662), represents a somewhat more modern aesthetic, from northern Italian Lombardy rather than Spanish-influenced Naples as with Latini. Unlike Latini, who always uses sugar in his sauces, Stefani rarely calls for sugar and recommends a moderate use of spices, employing more butter and anchovies. He still likes cinnamon and sugar in soup, however. Stefani can imagine that beef stew might be made without spices, flavored simply with rosemary and garlic: "Do not add spices, for when it is cooked it will be good." His advice is given with thrift in mind rather than purely a culinary judgment, for cost apart, adding cinnamon, pepper, and nutmeg will make the dish more "dignified." Nevertheless, he is enough of a minimalist to state that strawberries don't need anything to be added, "since one must be able to perceive their natural taste and smell."[5]

It was in this era that vegetables came into prominence in elite dining, beginning with salads, a taste that had been pioneered in the Renaissance but limited to Italy in the sixteenth century. The most dramatic changes were in sauces, however. The new cuisine was quite elaborate, but it emphasized a richer, smoother taste. The classic French sauces were based on butter and flour flavored with meat essences of various concentrations (bouillon, stock, glace de viande). They were seasoned with salt, herbs, and shallots rather than spices. The resulting sauces seemed both more natural (complementing rather than covering up the meat or fish) and more elegant (allowing for endless variation).

Classic French cuisine can hardly be described as a move toward simplicity; no one has ever thought of this style as labor-saving or "no fuss." The new recipes were extravagant, calling for the use of whole sides of meat to be distilled into rich and concentrated sauces, for example. Eighteenth-century English critics of the new French fashions complained about this effort to produce the most concentrated flavors. According to an article in *The Connoisseur:* "It is impossible to conceive, what vast sums are melted down into sauces! We have a cargo of hams every year from Westphalia, only to extract the essence of them for our soups; and we will kill a brace of bucks every week, to make coulis of the haunches."[6]

French chefs proposed to make cuisine conform to nature by imposing rules based on purely culinary judgments about tastes and ingredients rather than medical theories or a desire for dramatic and clashing aromatic shocks. Cinnamon, ginger, and other spices were replaced by herbs, truffles, and foie gras, which provided intense rather than piquant flavors. The taste of meat, fish, or vegetables was complemented and nuanced by sauces and methods of preparation, not transformed into something else by elaborate reshaping or the addition of spices. The change of style is clear from contrasting the recipes of the two periods. In *Pleyn Delit,* a compendium of cuisine from the fourteenth and fifteenth centuries, 70 percent of the recipes call for spices, usually in great variety.[7] In one of the most authoritative cookbooks of classic French cuisine, François Massialot's *Cuisinier roial et bourgeois* (published in 1691), the use of spices has declined dramatically. Cinnamon is used in only 8 percent of the recipes (versus 27 percent in *Pleyn Delit*). Cloves and nutmeg are still fairly common (in 22 percent and 27 percent of the recipes), but in the eighteenth century their role would be reduced to mere cameo appearances. Such medieval prestige spices as galangal, saffron, and grains of paradise are altogether absent in Massialot's book. The *Nouveau dictionnaire* of 1776 stated concisely that "today in France . . . spices, sugar, and saffron etc. are proscribed."[8]

In fact sugar was not entirely forbidden, but rather exiled to the realm of desserts and drinks. No longer was it an essential component of sauces, but it would take on a vigorous new life of its own apart from spices, its original companions. Sugar went from being a luxury to a staple.

In seventeenth-century cookbooks 30 percent of the meat and fish dishes still called for sugar. For the eighteenth century the figure is just 10 percent, and a French observer reflected the taste of the era by dismissing sugared sauces for meat as "impertinent and quite ridiculous."[9] The modern era in fact saw exponential growth in the use of sugar, but in different forms and vehicles. Increasing quantities of sugar became available from the New World as the plantations of Brazil and the Caribbean expanded. Sugar was especially important in sweetening tea, coffee, and chocolate, the new beverages brought from Asia and the New World. Sugar had been prized in the Middle Ages for its use as a drug, to sweeten other medicines, as the basis for various other kinds of quasi-medicinal candies, and as a component in sauces. Sugar was already versatile and important in late-medieval cuisine and medicine, but it was used in relatively small quantities because it was expensive. In Elizabethan England, average per capita sugar consumption was no more than a pound a year. It increased to four pounds per year in the seventeenth century, and by 1720 the average was at eight pounds. The present consumption of sugar in Britain is on the order of eighty pounds per year, and it is 126 pounds in the United States. Modern food processing requires sugar in prepared sauces, cured meats, salad dressings, marinades, snack food—virtually everything prepared commercially.[10]

It was the eighteenth and nineteenth centuries that saw an incredible increase in sugar consumption as tea and sweets became affordable for the working class and fruit pies and tarts surpassed meat pies in popularity. Sugar was a leading source of nutrition for urban workers as well as omnipresent in middle-class rituals of gentility (English tea or German service of coffee and cake). One historian has even credited the entire English Industrial Revolution to the combination of cheap energy provided by sugar and the alertness afforded by the caffeine in the tea it accompanied.[11]

Sugar was therefore both an exception to and an exemplification of the decline of spices in the modern world. Its banishment from main courses was more than made up for by new roles, especially in desserts. Here in the meal's last course, now defined as sweet, the great medieval spices found a kind of modest exile home. Cinnamon, cloves, nutmeg, and ginger are still all used along with sugar in cookies, cakes, and other European and American desserts, from spice cakes to gingersnaps. They are especially important in holiday cuisine with its archaic traditionalism. Christmas features eggnog spiced with nutmeg, mulled wine, plum pudding, gingerbread, and other quasi-medieval preparations made with lots of sugar and a modicum of spices. Pumpkin pie in American Thanksgiving meals is another example of holiday spiced specialties, along with candied yams, cranberry sauce, and other sugary side dishes of New World products dressed up in medieval guise.

The only piquant spice to survive the passing of the old cuisine is pepper. Perhaps because the one extant classical cookbook, attributed to the Roman gourmand Apicius, employs pepper constantly, the spice seemed to have an appropriate pedigree. At any rate, salt and pepper became universal. A few classic dishes like Steak au Poivre call for large quantities of pepper, but usually it is used to season food before cooking and as a last addition: the food is typically not supposed to taste "peppery," so the spice is a kind of expected but modest accompaniment. Chili pepper, another important New World product, would sweep India, Africa, and many other parts of the globe, but not Europe or the Anglicized parts of North America, where until recently it was disdained when not actively feared.

For the most part, the culinary reign of spices ended, sooner in France, later in northern Europe. With a few exceptions, such as saffron in Spanish paella and risotto Milanese or cardamom in Swedish desserts, spices simply lost their long-standing status as fashions by the eighteenth century. What brought about their downfall? The answer has something to do with the arrival of new beverages, stimulants, and flavors. Coffee, tea, chocolate, and tobacco offered new taste sensations but also produced psychological effects that proved to be mildly or, in the case of tobacco, quite seriously addictive.[12] This doesn't completely suffice as the sole explanation, since all these new pleasures were also available in the Middle East, where spices remained prominent in gastronomy and were even incorporated into tea drinking and smoking.

Another possible explanation is that spices became cheaper with colonialism and the opening up of the new trade routes, so their consumption no longer conveyed an adequate sense of privilege and exclusivity. Certainly as they became less expensive, they diminished in importance so that they were relegated to occasional flavorings for special dishes, such as gingerbread or paella. Yet tea, coffee, chocolate, tobacco, and sugar managed to make the transition from luxuries to mass-market staples without losing their commercial power. As these products became common, the way they were consumed signified sufficient social distinction to preserve their reputation among the better sort. Tea in England is the classic example of a common commodity whose service, accoutrements, and rituals denoted status, even down to whether the milk and sugar were added to the tea (middle and upper class) or the tea was added to the milk and sugar (working class).

Increased availability does not inevitably lead to a fall from fashion. Yet spices, as the above-mentioned French remarks attest, certainly *did* become unfashionable before simply disappearing from most European cuisine. There must have been a change in taste, a shift in what was considered pleasant and appropriate in food. The love of spices was more than a passing fad, because it lasted for centuries, really from the Roman Empire to the end of the Renaissance, well over a thousand years. When we look at the Middle Ages the real mystery is not why spices were popular, but why later, after a millennium of continuous popularity, they dropped out of favor.

Another partial explanation has to do with changes in medicine and pharmaceutical preparations. While all societies associate health with diet, gastronomy in the eighteenth century tended to separate itself more clearly from medicine to enter an aesthetic realm of its own. Medicine in turn started to rely on different drugs (some of them from the New World) and less on medieval herbals and antidotaries. Spices began to lose their healthful allure as cookbooks ceased to make claims about their medical importance. In the eighteenth century, the humoral theories that ascribed disease to an imbalance of the basic bodily fluids started to go out of fashion, so the hot and dry benefits of spices were no longer important. The effectiveness of new drugs, such as quinine or opiates, was theorized differently, more specifically and not as part of a universal idea of equilibrium and balance.[13]

Finally it may be that spices were no longer so attractive once their origins were known. The East would remain exotic in Western eyes, but even the Spice Islands were not the earthly paradise. The fading of Prester John, the Garden of Eden, and the Rivers of Paradise meant that spices were ultimately prosaic products, much like tea or chocolate, and less adaptable than these to new patterns of consumption.

It isn't as if one day spices were all the rage, and on the next they suddenly fell from grace. As late as 1667, the tiny nutmeg island of Run in the Banda archipelago was exchanged by the British for the Dutch settlement of New Amsterdam on the American continent, the future heart of New York City. Even though King Charles II of England thought his side had the advantage of this deal, he could not have known just how different the value of the two islands of Manhattan and Run would subsequently be. Not only did succeeding years unveil the economic might of New York, they also revealed the decreasing importance of nutmeg.[14] The decline was gradual, but inexorable and finally quite extreme.

What took place was a seismic shift in taste. The wealthy people of Europe no longer liked fiery and perfumed food. To this day Italian, Spanish, and French foods still use almost no spices. They are anything but bland, but their gastronomic effects, what make them recognizable and tasty, come from sensations and flavors other than those provided by spices—from herbs, methods of cooking, wine, cheese, but not from piquancy, acidity, or sweetness. Elsewhere on the culinary map spices still retain the power to surprise and dazzle. They are prominent in "fusion" cuisines (a combination of Asian and European cooking traditions) and part of the desire for novelty in eclectic "global" trends. In addition, the aura of "natural," botanical means of preserving health and wellness has returned exotic scents and flavors to fashion.

The recent turning away from the richness imparted by butter and meat broths and distillates has meant that spices are becoming relied on more to provide novel taste impressions. A medieval gastronome transported to our era and its cuisine would find it lacking in game and rather simple in preparation style, but would be able to find most of the customary and expected spices. Culinary fashions come around in long arcs, and perhaps the current emphasis on hybrid and multicultural food will produce permanent changes just as it seems to be ending the reign of France as arbiter of culinary standards. Whatever happens, we are not likely to see a return to medieval taste by reason of its multiple ingredients, its labor-intensive methods, and its alien outlook on what constitutes elegant or satisfying food. The Middle Ages had its glories and peculiarities, and while its distinctive theological, architectural, and geographical ideas are widely understood, we continue to discover more about the peculiar notions of food and health that were represented by the vogue for spices.

THE DEMAND FOR SPICES

The decline of spices in the seventeenth and eighteenth centuries shows in relief how important spices were previously. It is worth emphasizing once more that spices were not simply a temporary phenomenon or fad. They were persistently important to medicine and cuisine from the time of the ancient Greeks through the Italian Renaissance. Specific spices, like specific cuisines, might pass in and out of favor. The Romans lacked nutmeg and cloves, whereas the cooks and connoisseurs of the Middle Ages never knew silphium or fish paste, but the desire of the affluent for sharp, piquant food flavors remained constant. We began this book with the question of why there was such a great demand for spices in the Middle Ages and can now see how well we can answer it. The reason this is an important historical puzzle is that the demand for luxury products moved such historical enterprises as the Spanish and Portuguese voyages of discovery and conquest. In addition, the history of tastes and their shifts tells us more about a society and its texture and character than recital of its more obvious socioeconomic facts (per capita GNP or demography). The history of medieval spices is part of the history of culture and taste, but of course spices also moved great political and military events following from the European conception of the world and how its riches might be exploited.

The desire for spices was most obviously related to culinary taste. There is no extraneous reason for the popularity of spicy food—spices were not used to preserve meat or cover up the taste of deterioration. The influence of Islam, long-term preferences going back beyond Roman times, and a taste for elaborate sensations all played a part in ensuring the permanent importance of spices throughout the Middle Ages and across the diverse cuisines and tides of fashion that brought in and carried away particular spices. As has been shown, however, food is not the entire reason for the significance of the spice trade. Spices were also considered drugs, an opinion and practice that went back to antiquity. Spices were believed useful in diet to balance the humors but also recommended as remedies in themselves with various properties to alleviate disease. Beyond these specific medical applications, spices were associated in the mind of medieval scholars and consumers with what we think of as "wellness," with a kind of gracious and healthful manner of life. Their fragrance communicated and signified pleasure, good taste (in the sense of style), and the ability to create a space of refined beauty and purity.

It is this latter symbolic series of images that are perhaps most important and most difficult to grasp, because spices are physically so obvious that their mental and cultural overtones seem to be less important. Spices were enjoyed for the sensations they produced and evoked, but also because they were expensive, exotic, and even mysteriously sacred. That they were costly means that their ostentatious consumption at meals or as drugs conveyed and even became necessary for social distinction. Not everyone could afford them, particularly the high-end spices like cloves and nutmeg or the perfumes of musk and ambergris, so that to be seen to live in their fragrance was to communicate power and prestige, a form of cultural capital.

Nevertheless, as discussed in connection with scarcity, not everything that is expensive is worth boasting about. A commodity has to have an aura that complements its rarity, and it was the exotic nature of spices that provided this allure. Spices were exotic because they came from far away, from mysterious, rich, and magical lands. Real and imaginary, these places—India, the Spice Islands, or Cipangu—were fascinating. To some degree the Orient had always been a source of wonder and was seen by Europeans as teeming with marvels, both strange and appealing. The image of spices in the Middle Ages was more than just a chapter in the history of Orientalism, however, not just another product of the always mysterious East. The lands where they grew were distant and different but also fortunate. Kublai Khan and Prester John supposedly reigned over peaceful kingdoms where crime, poverty, and sickness were uncommon or banished. Either these lands were Christian, and so part of the greater recognizable community to which European Christians affiliated themselves, or they were subject to virtuous pagans whose principles were similar to those of Christianity only more effectively implemented.

The ultimate home of spices and their most alluring symbol was the earthly paradise. Distance, attractiveness, and healthfulness were supplemented by a literal odor of sanctity. Some spices came into the ordinary mortal world out of the Garden of Eden, as Joinville said, brought down by the four Rivers of Paradise. The bulk of what was traded, however, was recognized as coming from India, although what that meant geographically and imaginatively changed over the vast chronological space between the time of Alexander the Great, in the fourth century B.C., and Vasco da Gama.

Spices held a special position as more than merely desirable consumer goods but as sacred objects or at least objects joined to an atmosphere of sanctity. They were virtuous, both in the sense of having healing powers and in an ultimate moral sense, symbolic of a holy death, of rebirth and of surpassing the limits of the temporal. And they were symbols not just in the iconographic sense but in their aromas, which touched the psychological centers of human longing, even if only momentarily. It is impossible to overstate the importance of fragrance itself, of intoxicating and wonderful scents in a world of unpleasant odors, decay, and infirmity.

Not all consumers would have worked out in detail these overtones of meaning, but that is what makes successful consumer products so durable and powerful: the sense they convey of promise, pleasure, and virtue beyond their inevitably mundane uses. Spices were simultaneously valuable commodities, social signifiers of discriminating taste, pleasurable substances, and yet vessels of higher, even sacred meaning. They conveyed this through a fragrance sometimes sweet, sometimes sharp, sometimes rich, sometimes impossible to describe but always delightful. Spices were not addictive, even in the mild way of coffee or tea, not mind-altering like opium or even tobacco. They were simply enchanting, but they created a worldly infatuation with a slightly spiritual aura. This worldliness (after all, they were expensive commodities) would produce an extraordinary impact on historical events. It was the enchantment of their flavor, scent, and allure that made spices such important commodities in the first place.

Notes

INTRODUCTION. SPICES: A GLOBAL COMMODITY

1. Adam Smith, *The Wealth of Nations,* ed. R. H. Campbell and A. S. Skinner, vol. 2 (Indianapolis, 1981), pp. 448–626.

2. Timothy Morton, *The Poetics of Spice: Romantic Consumerism and the Exotic* (Cambridge, 2000), p. 25.

3. A few who have tried to correct this belief: Toby Peterson, "The Arab Influence on Western European Cooking," *Journal of Medieval History* 6 (1980): 317–20; Lorna J. Sass, "Religion, Medicine, Politics, and Spices," *Appetite* 2 (1981): 7–13; Terence Scully, *The Art of Cookery in the Middle Ages* (Woodbridge, 1995), pp. 56–57, 84. Yet it is still often stated as fact even in scholarly publications, such as Julie Bergere Hochstrasser, "The Conquest of Spice and the Dutch Colonial Imaginary: Seen and Unseen in the Visual Culture of Trade," in *Colonial Botany: Science, Commerce, and Politics in the Early Modern World,* ed. Londa Schiebinger and Claudia Swan (Philadelphia, 2005), p. 171; or the article on "Spices and Flavourings" by Hansförg Küster in *The Cambridge World History of Food,* vol. 1 (Cambridge, 2000), p. 46.

4. *Chiquart's 'On Cookery': A Fifteenth-Century Savoyard Culinary Treatise,* ed. and trans. Terence Scully (New York, 1986), p. 9.

5. I thank Christopher Dyer of the University of Leicester for this information, which is taken from an account in the Essex Record office at Chelmsford, D/DP 177.

6. *Accounts of the Stewards of the Talbot Household at Blakemere, 1392–1425,* ed. and trans. Barbara Ross (Keele, 2003), pp. 15, 160.

7. As opposed to the silver cup, which he regarded as "the fruit of Rome" (i.e., worldly). See *Supplement to the Life of Marie d'Oignies by Thomas de Cantimpré,* chapter 3, part 5, trans. Hugh Feiss in *The Life of Marie Oignies by Jacques de Vitry* (Toronto, 1993), p. 204.

8. *Lexikon des Mittelalters,* under "Georg der Reiche" and "Gewürze."

9. Gaston Bachelard, *La psychanalyse du feu* (Paris, 1949), p. 38.

10. *The Anglo-Latin Satirical Poets and Epigrammatists of the Twelfth Century,* ed. Thomas Wright, vol. 1 (Rolls Series 59/1) (London, 1872; repr. Wiesbaden, 1964), p. 265.

11. On medieval saffron, Luise Bardenhewer, *Der Safranhandel im Mittelalter* (Inaugural-Dissertation) (Bonn, 1914).

12. Francesco Balducci Pegolotti, *La pratica della mercatura,* ed. Allen Evans (Cambridge, Mass., 1936), pp. 293–97.

13. *El primer manual hispánico de mercaderia (siglo XIV),* ed. Miguel Gual Camarena (Barcelona, 1981), p. 84.

14. *Roman de la Rose,* lines 1328–44.

15. Paul E. Beichner, "The Grain of Paradise," *Speculum* 36 (1961): 302–7; Bruno Laurioux, "Modes culinaires et mutations du goût à la fin du Moyen Âge," in *Une histoire culinaire du Moyen Âge,* collected essays by Bruno Laurioux (Paris, 2005), pp. 285–93.

16. Tim Richardson, *A History of Candy* (New York, 2002), pp. 67–207; José Pérez Vidal, *Medicina y dulceria en el "Libro de Buen Amor"* (Madrid, 1981), pp. 144–57.

17. What balsam is or was thought to be and the legends surrounding it are described in Stefan Halikowski Smith, "Meanings Behind Myths: The Multiple Manifestations of the Tree of the Virgin at Matarea," forthcoming in the *Journal of Religious Studies.*

18. On ambergris see Karl H. Dannenfeldt, "Ambergris: The Search for Its Origin," *Isis* 73 (1982): 382–97.

19. Marco Polo, *Milione, Le devisament dou monde: Il Milione nelle redazioni toscana e franco-italiana,* ed. Gabriella Ronchi (Milan, 1982), pp. 593–94. A translation of the passage from the Z version, a Latin manuscript that has the description of the whale hunt, is given in Marco Polo, *The Travels,* trans. Ronald Latham (Harmondsworth, 1958), pp. 296–97.

20. See Edward Peters, "The Desire to Know the Secrets of the World," *Journal of the History of Ideas* 62 (2001): 593–610.

CHAPTER 1. SPICES AND MEDIEVAL CUISINE

1. Bruno Laurioux, "De l'usage des épices dans l'alimentation médiévale," *Médiévales* 5 (1983): 16–17.

2. Taillevent, *The Viandier of Taillevent: An Edition of All Extent Manuscripts,* ed. Terence Scully (Ottawa, 1988), recipe no. 170, p. 231.

3. For cookbooks as a particular kind of source for information about the Middle Ages, Bruno Laurioux, *Les livres des cuisine médiévaux* (Typologie des sources du Moyen Âge occidental, fasc. 77) (Turnhout, 1997).

4. Bruno Laurioux, *Manger au Moyen Âge* (Paris, 2002), pp. 38–39.

5. Jean-Louis Flandrin and Carole Lambert, *Fêtes gourmandes au Moyen Âge* (Paris, 1998), pp. 31–32.

6. Walter of Bibbelsworth quoted in *Curye on Inglysch,* ed. Constance B. Hieatt and Sharon Butler (London, 1985), p. 3. For the papal conclave, H. Aliquot, "Les épices à la table des papes d'Avignon au XIV siècle," in *Manger et boire au Moyen Âge,* vol. 1 (Nice, 1984), 132–33.

7. *Sir Gawain and the Green Knight,* in *The Complete Works of the Pearl Poet,* trans. Casey Finch (Berkeley, 1993), lines 892 and 979 (pp. 248, 252); *The Story of the Grail (Perceval) in Arthurian Romances,* trans. and ed. William W. Kibler (New York, 1991), pp. 421–22. "Gingerbread" is in quotation marks because in the Middle Ages this usually meant a chewy candy with a toffeelike consistency made from honey and spices other (perversely) than ginger. See Constance B. Hieatt, "Making Sense of Medieval Culinary Records,"

in *Food and Eating in Medieval Europe,* ed. Martha Carlin and Joel T. Rosenthal (London and Rio Grande, W.Va., 1998), p. 102. It could, however, be related to *Gingibre Conduitt* (preserved ginger made with sugar and parsnips), Flandrin and Lambert, *Fêtes gourmandes,* pp. 156, 160. The prominence of parsnips in this dish seems odd because they were humble, even peasant food, but parsnips were probably of appropriate texture, color, and humoral properties.

8. Mestre Robert, *Libre del coch: Tractat de cuina medieval,* ed. Veronika Leimgruber (Barcelona, 1982).

9. *Viandier of Taillevent,* recipe no. 173, pp. 231–32.

10. As noted in Bruno Laurioux, *Le Moyen Âge à table* (Paris, 1989), p. 40.

11. Fulcher of Chartres, *Fulcheri Carnotensis Historia Hiersolymitana, 1095–1127,* ed. Heinrich Hagenmeyer (Heidelberg, 1913), book 3, chapter 37, 3–8 (pp. 748–49).

12. Pliny, *Natural History* 12.14, ed. and trans. H. Rackham, Loeb Classical Library (Cambridge, Mass., 1960), vol. 4, p. 20. On Roman Egypt and the pepper trade, Gary K. Young, *Rome's Eastern Trade: International Commerce and Imperial Policy, 31 B.C.– A.D. 305* (London, 2001), pp. 27–89.

13. Andrew Dalby, *Dangerous Tastes: The Story of Spices* (Berkeley and Los Angeles, 2000), pp. 54, 78; Robin A. Donkin, *Between East and West: The Moluccas and the Traffic in Spices up to the Arrival of Europeans* (Philadelphia, 2003), pp. 111–16.

14. For: Toby Peterson, "The Arab Influence on Western European Cooking," *Journal of Medieval History* 6 (1980): 317–40. Against: Bruno Laurioux, *Une histoire culinaire du Moyen Âge* (Paris, 2005), pp. 305–35, which concludes succinctly, "le goût médiéval n'est pas arabe" (p. 332).

15. *The Neapolitan Recipe Collection: Cuoco Napolitano,* ed. and trans. Terence Scully (Ann Arbor, 2000), p. 68.

16. Laurioux, *Une histoire culinaire du Moyen Âge,* pp. 313–16.

17. Laurioux, "De l'usage des épices," p. 18; Laurioux, *Le Moyen Âge à table,* p. 18; Maxime Rodinson, "Mamūniyya East and West," in Maxine Rodinson et al., *Medieval Arab Cookery: Essays and Translations* (Totnes, 2001), pp. 185–96.

18. *Viandier of Taillevent,* recipe no. 11, pp. 50–52.

19. Christopher Woolgar, "Fast and Feast: Conspicuous Consumption and the Diet of the Nobility in the Fifteenth Century," in *Revolutions and Consumption in Late Medieval England,* ed. Michael Hicks (Woodbridge, 2001), pp. 7–25.

20. George Benson, *Later Medieval York: The City and County from 1100 to 1603* (York, 1919), pp. 88–90.

21. C. M. Woolgar, *The Great Household in Late Medieval England* (New Haven, 1999), pp. 159–60.

22. *Sir Gawain and the Green Knight,* lines 116–20 (p. 214).

23. Geoffrey Chaucer, *The Canterbury Tales,* "The Franklin's Tale," 1139–45:

> For I am siker that ther be sciences,
> By whiche men make diverse apparences
> Swiche as this subtile tregetoures pleys,
> For ofte at festes have I wel herd seye,
> That tregetours, with-inne an halle large

Have maad come in a water and a barge,
And in the halle rowen up and doun.

24. *Chiquart's 'On Cookery,'* pp. 116–19; "Ane Ordynaunce One Frydaye at Night at the Towre or Wher the King Wilbe the Same Day," in *The Coronation of Richard III, the Extant Documents,* ed. Anne F. Sutton and P. W. Hammond (Gloucester and New York, 1983), p. 291.

25. Woolgar, *Great Household in Late Medieval England,* p. 157.

26. Bridget Ann Henisch, *Fast and Feast: Food in Medieval Society* (University Park, Pa., 1976), pp. 147–205; Flandrin and Lambert, *Fêtes gourmandes,* pp. 45, 55.

27. "The Boke of Kervynge," in *The Babees Book,* ed. Frederick J. Furnivall (London, 1868; repr. New York, 1969), pp. 256–86.

28. John Russell, "The Boke of Nurture Folowyng Englondis Gise," in *The Babees Book,* p. 158.

29. Woolgar, "Fast and Feast," pp. 21–22; Laurioux, *Le Moyen Âge à table,* p. 36; Laurioux, *Les livres des cuisine,* p. 19; Flandrin and Lambert, *Fêtes gourmandes,* pp. 112–13.

30. *Chiquart's 'On Cookery,'* pp. 22–24.

31. *Viandier of Taillevent,* no. 196, p. 251. A reconstruction of what this must have looked like is given in Flandrin and Lambert, *Fêtes gourmandes,* p. 115.

32. Paul Freedman, *Images of the Medieval Peasant* (Stanford, 1999), p. 149.

33. *Formaggi del medioevo: La "Summa lacticiniorum" di Pantaleone da Confienza,* ed. Irma Naso (Turin, 1990).

34. *Llibre de totes maneres de confits,* ed. Joan Santanach i Suñol (Barcelona, 2004).

35. Ken Albala, *Eating Right in the Renaissance* (Berkeley, 2002), pp. 10–12, 96, 181.

36. Flandrin and Lambert, *Fêtes gourmandes,* p. 15.

37. Examples from Massimo Montanari, "L'image du paysan et les codes de comportement alimentaire," in *Le petit peuple dans l'Occident médiéval: Terminologies, perceptions, réalités,* ed. Pierre Boglioni et al. (Paris, 2002), pp. 97–112, esp. 103; Freedman, *Images of the Medieval Peasant,* pp. 149–50, 153.

38. Christopher Dyer, "Did the Peasants Really Starve in Medieval England?" in *Food and Eating in Medieval Europe,* ed. Martha Carlin and Joel Rosenthal (London and Rio Grande, W.Va., 1998), p. 69.

39. Arnau de Vilanova, *Opera nuperrima revisa . . .* (Lyon, 1520), folio 137ra. This particular work on diet and health was falsely attributed to the early-fourteenth-century physician Arnau de Vilanova. I'm grateful to Professor Michael McVaugh of the University of North Carolina for this reference.

40. Eustache Deschamps, *Oeuvres complètes,* ed. Marquis de Queux de Saint-Hilaire and Gaston Raymond, vol. 7 (Paris, 1891), pp. 88–90. I am grateful to Anne Dropick for this information.

41. Montanari, "L'image du paysan," p. 208.

42. Scully, *The Art of Cookery,* p. 57. Augustine, *On the City of God,* book 21, 4, states that despite his previously skeptical attitude, he had personal experience that cooked peacock remains quite edible even after a year of storage. The vowing poem is Jacques de Longuyon, *Les voeux du paon,* ed. Brother Camillus Casey (Ph.D. diss., Columbia University, 1956).

43. Examples from Allen J. Grieco, "Food and Social Classes in Medieval and Renaissance Italy," in *Food: A Culinary History,* ed. Jean-Louis Flandrin and Massimo Montanari, trans. Clarissa Botsford et al. (New York, 1999), pp. 302–12.

44. *Le Ménagier de Paris,* ed. Georgina E. Brereton and Janet M. Ferrier (Oxford, 1981). In their introduction (p. xxi, n. 4), the editors point out that the author himself is often inaccurately referred to as "the Menagier" but this word refers only to the book's title. I am grateful to Agnieszka Rec, a student at Yale University, for her help with references from the *Ménagier.*

CHAPTER 2. MEDICINE: SPICES AS DRUGS

1. Henry of Huntington, *The History of the English People, 1000–1154,* trans. Diana Greenway (Oxford, 2002), p. 64. The idea that King Henry died because he ate too many lampreys ("a surfeit of lampreys") is a modern invention, sanctified by the comical history *1066 and All That.*

2. On medieval cuisine and the theory of humors, see Scully, *The Art of Cookery,* pp. 41–51.

3. In the famous English folk poem "The Ballad of Lord Randall," the protagonist's erstwhile true-love has fed him a dish of eels that has poisoned him.

4. Jean-Louis Flandrin, "Seasoning, Cooking, and Dietetics in the Late Middle Ages," in *Food: A Culinary History,* pp. 320–27; *The Neapolitan Recipe Collection,* p. 88.

5. Albala, *Eating Right in the Renaissance,* pp. 254–55, 266–67.

6. Arnau de Vilanova, *Regimen de sanitat a Jaume II* (version of Berenguer Sarreiera), chapter 17, in *Arnau de Vilanova, Obres catalanes,* vol. 2 (Escrits mèdics), ed. Miquel Batllori (Barcelona, 1947), pp. 186–87.

7. *Chiquart's 'On Cookery,'* pp. 98–99. A more sober version is offered by a Neapolitan cookbook in which the chicken is stuffed with cheese, eggs, fat, herbs, and spices and cooked in a carafe, *The Neapolitan Recipe Collection,* p. 58.

8. Flandrin and Lambert, *Fêtes gourmandes,* p. 142.

9. Lynn Thorndike, "A Mediaeval Sauce-Book," *Speculum* 9 (1934), p. 186. On this text and its different versions, Terence Scully, "The *Opusculum de saporibus* of Magninus Mediolanensis," *Medium Aevum* 54 (1985): 178–207.

10. The text is Francesc Eiximenis, *Lo Cresità (selecció),* ed. Albert Hauf (Barcelona, 1983), pp. 142–45. See also Paul Freedman, "Medieval Clichés of Health and Diet According to Francesc Eiximenis," in *Sociedad y memoria en la Edad Media: Estudios en homenaje de Nilda Guglielmi,* ed. Ariel Guiance and Pablo Obierna (Buenos Aires, 2005), pp. 127–34.

11. Francesc Eiximenis, *Terç del Crestià,* ed. Father Martí and Father Feliu, O.F.M. Cap. (Barcelona, 1932), vol. 3, c. 304, p. 183.

12. On medieval pharmacological knowledge and theories, see Jean-Pierre Bénézet, *Pharmacie et médicament en Méditerranée occidentale (XIIIe–XVIe siècles)* (Paris, 1999); Walton Orvyl Schalick, III, "Add One Part Pharmacy to One Part Surgery and One Part Medicine: Jean de Saint-Amand and the Development of Medical Pharmacology in Thirteenth-Century Paris" (Ph.D. diss., Johns Hopkins University, 1997); John M. Riddle, *Quid pro Quo: Studies in the History of Drugs* (Aldershot, 1992).

13. John M. Riddle, *Eve's Herbs: A History of Contraception in the West* (Cambridge, Mass., 1997), pp. 44–63, esp. 52.

14. Franck Collard, *Le crime de poison au Moyen Âge* (Paris, 2003), pp. 59–65.

15. *Obras médicas de Pedro Hispano,* ed. Maria Helena da Rocha Pereira (Coimbra, 1973).

16. Peter Dilg, "Materia medica und therapeutische Praxis um 1500: Zum Einfluss der arabischen Heilkunde auf den europäischen Arzneischatz," in *Kommunikation zwischen Orient und Okzident: Alltag und Sachkultur* (Vienna, 1994), pp. 353–77.

17. Mattheus Platearius, *Das Arzneidrogenbuch "Circa instans" in einer Fassung des XIII. Jahrhunderts aus der Universitätsbibliothek Erlangen,* ed. Hans Wölfel (Berlin, 1939), pp. 33–34, 85, 91–92. These observations are repeated in the *Livre des simples médecines. Codex Bruxellensis IV. 1024: A 15th-Century French Herbal,* commentary by Carmélia Opsomor and William T. Stearn, English trans. Enid Roberts and William T. Stearn (Antwerp, 1984), pp. 110, 219, 229.

18. L.-A. Michon, *Documents inédits sur la Grande Peste de 1348* (Paris, 1860), pp. 67–68; John M. Riddle, "Pomum Ambrae: Amber and Ambergris in Plague Remedies," *Sudhoffs Archiv für Geschichte der Medizin und der Naturwissenschaften* 48 (1964): 111–22, reprinted in Riddle, *Quid pro quo.*

19. *Libro de los medicamentos simples* (facsimile edition of the *Livre des simples médecines* held in St. Petersburg), ed. Natacha Elaguina et al. (Barcelona, 2002), fols. 166r and 166v. On the illustrator, see Kathrin Giogoli and John Block Friedman, "Robinet Testard, Court Illuminator: His Manuscripts and His Debt to the Graphic Arts," *Journal of the Early Book Society for the Study of Manuscripts and Printing History* 8 (2005): 142–88.

20. John M. Riddle, *Marbode of Rennes' De Lapidibus Considered as a Medical Treatise* (Wiesbaden, 1977), pp. 24, 34, 92.

21. R. A. Donkin, *Beyond Price: Pearls and Pearl-Fishing: Origins to the Age of Discoveries* (Philadelphia, 1998), p. 260.

22. Jean-Pierre Albret, *Odeurs de sainteté: La mythologie chrétienne des aromates,* 2nd ed. (Paris, 1996), p. 121.

23. Gail Kalinoski, "Healing Gems: Entrepreneurs Unleash Power of Precious Stones," *Fairfield County Business Journal,* July 14, 2003, pp. 1, 8.

24. *The Tabula Antidotarii of Armengaud Blaise and Its Hebrew Translation,* ed. Michael McVaugh and Lola Ferre (Philadelphia, 2000).

25. François Granel, "La Thériaque de Montpellier," *Revue d'histoire de la pharmacie* 64, no. 228 (1976): 75–83. See also a description and recipe in *The Trotula: An English Translation of the Medieval Compendium of Women's Medicine,* ed. Monica H. Green (Philadelphia, 2002), pp. 132–33. The English word "treacle" has, since 1700, meant the uncrystallized syrup from the first stage of sugar refining (molasses in the U.S.), but before then it was the English form of the word "theriac."

26. *The Story of the Grail (Perceval),* pp. 421–22; Girart de Roussillon as cited in Andrew Dalby, *Flavours of Byzantium* (Totnes, 2003), pp. 110–11.

27. Carmélia Opsomer, "La pharmacie du Paradis," in *Saveurs du Paradis: Les routes des épices* (Antwerp, 1992), p. 55.

28. Olivier de la Haye, *Poème sur la Grande Peste de 1348,* ed. Georges Guigue (Lyons, 1888), lines 1658–64, 2960–3121.

29. Carmélia Opsomer-Halleux, "The Medieval Garden and Its Role in Medicine," in *Medieval Gardens,* ed. Elisabeth B. MacDougall (Washington, 1986), p. 105.

30. For information on John of Arderne I have relied on an unpublished paper by Peter Murray Jones of King's College, Cambridge, "Herbs and the Medieval Surgeon," presented at a conference at Pennsylvania State University in April 2003. I am very grateful to him for letting me cite his paper.

31. *Constantini liber de coitu: El tratado de andrología de Constantino el Africano,* ed. and trans. Enrique Montero-Cartelle (Santiago de Compostela, 1983), pp. 151–85.

32. *Canterbury Tales,* "The Merchant's Tale," lines 1807–11.

33. A point made in Jack Turner, *Spice: The History of a Temptation* (New York, 2004), p. 186: "If there is a single, solid conclusion to be drawn from the deeply bizarre study of aphrodisiacs, it is that practically everything remotely edible has at some time or another been credited with sexually enhancing powers—and many inedible substances besides."

34. Mattheus Platearius, *Das Arzneidrogenbuch "Circa instans,"* p. 85.

CHAPTER 3. THE ODORS OF PARADISE

1. Susan Ashbrook Harvey, *Scenting Salvation: Ancient Christianity and the Olfactory Imagination* (Berkeley, 2006), pp. 172–73.

2. Béatrice Caseau, "Enodia: The Use and Meaning of Fragrances in the Ancient World and Their Christianization, 100–900 A.D." (Ph.D. diss., Princeton University, 1994), pp. 82–90; *Encyclopedia of Judaism,* "havdalah," "spices."

3. Petronius, *Satyricon,* trans. Michael Heseltine (Cambridge, 1969), cap. 78 (p. 180).

4. Agostino Paravicini-Bagliani, *The Pope's Body,* trans. David S. Peterson (Chicago, 2000), pp. 47–48.

5. Albret, *Odeurs de sainteté,* p. 29.

6. Koran 76:5, 76:17–18, 83:26. Nerina Rustomji, "The Garden and the Fire: Materials of Heaven and Hell in Medieval Islamic Culture" (Ph.D. diss., Columbia University, 2003), pp. 165–66.

7. Harvey, *Scenting Salvation,* pp. 190–91.

8. Caseau, "Enodia," pp. 117–22.

9. Avicenna, *Avicennae Liber Canonis* (Venice, 1582), cited in Arthur Groos, *Romancing the Grail: Genre, Science, and Quest in Wolfram's Parzival* (Ithaca, 1995), p. 204.

10. *Picatrix: Un traité de magie médiéval,* trans. Béatrice Bakhouche et al. (Turnhout, 2003), p. 371.

11. Harvey, *Scenting Salvation,* p. 12; W. Deonna, "Enodia: Croyances antiques et modernes: L'odeur suave des Dieux et des élus," *Genava* 17 (1939): 185–87.

12. Deonna, "Enodia," p. 187.

13. Richer of Saint-Denis, *Gesta Senoniensis Ecclesie,* in Monumenta Germaniae Historica, Scriptores, vol. 25, book 4, chapter 19 (pp. 308–9). I am grateful to Professor Dyan Elliott of Northwestern University for this account.

14. Harvey, *Scenting Salvation,* p. 180.

15. Patrick Geary, *Furta Sacra: Thefts of Relics in the Central Middle Ages,* 2nd ed. (Princeton, 1990).

16. *Acta Sanctorum,* July, vol. 5, p. 208; Migne, *Patrologia Latina* 126, 1011–24.

17. An incident noted in John A. Arnold, *Belief and Unbelief in Medieval Europe* (London, 2005), p. 83.

18. Caseau, "Enodia," p. 258.

19. Examples from *Visions of Heaven and Hell Before Dante,* ed. Eileen Gardiner (New York, 1989), pp. 43–157, 210; Thomas H. Seiler, "Filth and Stench as Aspects of the Iconography of Hell," in *The Iconography of Hell,* ed. Clifford Davidson and Thomas H. Seiler (Kalamazoo, 1992), pp. 132–40; and C. M. Woolgar, *The Senses in Late Medieval England* (New Haven, 2006), p. 114.

20. The above-mentioned story of the martyrdom of Polycarp likens his body in the flames, which did not consume his flesh, to bread baking in an oven. It doesn't say it actually smelled like bread in an oven, however, but rather like incense and perfume (Harvey, "Scenting Salvation," p. 12).

21. Jean de Joinville, *History of Saint Louis,* in *Chronicles of the Crusades,* trans. M. R. B. Shaw (Harmondsworth, 1963), p. 212. Joinville probably took this idea from the thirteenth-century Crusade preacher Jacques de Vitry. For this and other versions of the windfall of paradise, see Heimo Reinitzer, "Zeder und Aloe: Zur Herkunft des Bettes Salomos im 'Moritz von Craûn,'" *Archiv für Kulturgeschichte* 58 (1976): 24–26.

22. Harvey, *Scenting Salvation,* pp. 225–26, 235–36.

23. Jean Delumeau, *History of Paradise: The Garden of Eden in Myth and Tradition,* trans. Matthew O'Connell (New York, 1995), pp. 46–52; Scott Westrem, *Broader Horizons: A Study of Johannes Witte de Hese's "Itinerarius" and Medieval Travel Narratives* (Cambridge, 2001), lines 398–402, p. 223.

24. Augustine, *De Genesi ad litteram* 8.7. St. Ephrem makes the following observation: "The four are the Nile, the Danube, the Tigris, and the Euphrates. Although we know the places where they arise, these are not their original source. The reason is that paradise is situated on a great height; the rivers sink into the ground around paradise and drop into the midst of the sea as through an aqueduct; then the land allows them to rise to the surface each in its own place" (Delumeau, *History of Paradise,* p. 40).

25. Reinhold Grimm, *Paradisus coelestis, Paradisus terrestris: Zur Auslegungsgeschichte des Paradieses im Abendland bis zum 1200* (Munich, 1977), p. 124.

26. Stefan Halikowski Smith, "The Mystification of Spices in the Western Tradition," *European Review of History* 8 (2001): 128.

27. Donkin, *Between East and West,* p. 115.

28. Natalia Lozovsky, *"The Earth Is Our Book": Geographical Knowledge in the Latin West, ca. 400–1000* (Ann Arbor, 2000), p. 60.

29. Ctesias, *Indika,* section 36 in *Ctésias de Cnide, La Perse, l'Inde, autres fragements,* ed. and trans. Dominique Lenfant (Paris, 2004), p. 179.

30. Pliny, *Natural History,* 37.11.42 (vol. 10, p. 194).

31. *Alexandri Magni iter ad Paradisum,* cited in Delumeau, *History of Paradise,* p. 46.

32. I am very grateful for the help of Brian Skinner, my Geology Department colleague at Yale University.

33. Mattheus Platearius, *Das Arzneidrogenbuch "Circa instans,"* p. 4; the illustration appears in two manuscripts, *Livre des simples médecines d'après le manuscrit français 12322 de la Bibliothèque Nationale de Paris,* trans. and commented on by Ghislaine Malandin et al.

(Paris, 1986), p. 41, and the facsimile edition of the St. Petersburg manuscript, *Libro de los medicamentos simples,* ed. Natacha Elaguina et al. (Barcelona, 2002), f. 28r. I thank John Friedman for this information.

34. John Mandeville, *Le livre des merveilles du monde,* ed. Christiane Deluz (Paris, 2000), p. 468; *Mandeville's Travels,* ed. M. C. Seymour (Oxford, 1967), p. 220; John of Marignolli, *Relatio,* ed. Anastasius Van den Wyngaert, in *Sinica Franciscana,* vol. 1 (1929), p. 539; Sérgio Buarque de Holanda, *Visão do paraíso: Os motivos edênicos no descobrimento e colonização do Brasil* (São Paulo, 1969), p. 119.

35. Wolfram von Eschenbach, *Parzival,* vol. 1, ed. Karl Lachmann, revised by Eberhard Nellmann (Frankfurt, 1994), book 9, stanza 481. On exotic medicines in *Parzival,* see Groos, *Romancing the Grail,* pp. 203–19.

36. Friedrich Zarncke, "Der Priester Johannes," in *Abhandlungen der königlichen Sächsischen Gesellschaft der Wissenschaften,* Phil.-Hist. Classe 7 (1879), pp. 912–13.

37. *Navigatio Sancti Brendani Abbatis from Early Latin Manuscripts,* ed. Carl Selmer (Notre Dame, 1959; repr. Dublin, 1989), 1.15–85 (pp. 4–8).

38. Athanasius, *Quaestiones ad Antiochum,* 47, cited in Howard Rollin Patch, *The Other World According to Descriptions in Medieval Literature* (Cambridge, Mass., 1950), p. 135. On debates in the early church over the location of paradise, see Ildefonsus Ayer, "Où plaça-t-on le paradis terrestre?" *Études Franciscaines* 36 (1924): 117–40; Anna-Dorothee von den Brincken, *Fines Terrae: Die Enden der Erde und der vierte Kontinent auf mittelalterlichen Weltkarten,* Monumenta Germaniae Historica, Schriften 36 (Hanover, 1992); Alessandro Scafi, "Mapping Eden: Cartographies of the Earthly Paradise," in *Mappings,* ed. Denis E. Cosgrove (London, 1999), pp. 50–70.

39. Isidore, *Etymologies,* 14.3.2.

40. For European impressions of India, see Thomas Hahn, "The Indian Tradition in Western Intellectual History," *Viator* 9 (1978): 214–34; Helmut Gregor, *Das Indienbild des Abendlandes (bis zum Ende des 13. Jahrhunderts)* (Vienna, 1964); Giuseppe Tardiola, *Le meraviglie dell'India* (Rome, 1961); Ulrich Knefelmap, "Das Indienbild in Resieberichten," in *Die Begegnung des Westens mit dem Osten,* ed. Odilo Engels and Peter Schreiner (Sigmaringen, 1993), pp. 99–112.

41. Brunetto Latini, *Li livres dou tresor,* ed. Francis J. Carmody (Berkeley and Los Angeles, 1948; repr. Geneva, 1975), book 1, chapter 122, part 26 (p. 114).

42. Ibid., 1.122.19–26 (pp. 113–14).

43. Michèle Guéret-Laferté, *Sur les routes de l'Empire Mongol: Ordre et rhétorique des relations de voyage aux XIIIe et XIVe siècles* (Paris, 1994), p. 216; Odoric of Pordenone, *Relatio,* in *Cathay and the Way Thither,* ed. Henry Yule and Henri Cordier, vol. 2 (London, 1916), p. 308.

44. On legends about Alexander in the classical and medieval periods, D. J. A. Ross, *Alexander Historiatus* (London, 1963); *Alexander the Great in the Middle Ages,* ed. W. J. Aerts et al. (Nijmegen, 1978).

45. The definitive treatment of these peoples is John Friedman, *The Monstrous Races in Medieval Art and Thought* (Cambridge, Mass., 1981; repr. Syracuse, 2000).

46. Pliny, *Natural History,* book 7.

47. Henri Baudet, *Paradise on Earth: Some Thoughts on European Images of Non-European Men,* trans. Elizabeth Wentholt (New Haven, 1965), pp. 26–27; William D. Phillips,

Jr., and Carla Rahn Phillips, *The Worlds of Christopher Columbus* (Cambridge, 1992), pp. 164–67.

48. On Prester John, Zarncke, "Der Priester Johannes," in *Abhandlungen der königlichen Sächsischen Gesellschaft der Wissenschaften*, Phil.-Hist. Classe 7 (1879), pp. 831–1028, and 8 (1883), pp. 1–184; Vsevolod Slessarev, *Prester John: The Letter and the Legend* (Minneapolis, 1959).

CHAPTER 4. TRADE AND PRICES

1. Janet L. Abu-Lughod, *Before European Hegemony: The World System, A.D. 1250–1350* (Oxford, 1989), pp. 260–86.

2. Piero Falchetta, *Fra Mauro's World Map* (Turhout, 2006), p. 255. Fra Mauro follows Marco Polo, but with more and different details about the products and routes.

3. For Venetian merchants in Delhi, Robert Lopez, "Da Venezia a Delhi nel Trecento," in Lopez, *Su e giù per la storia di Genova* (Genoa, 1973), pp. 137–59.

4. Sanjay Subrahmanyam, *The Career and Legend of Vasco da Gama* (Cambridge, 1997), p. 184.

5. Liutprand of Cremona, *Relatio de legatione Constantinopolitane,* in Liutprandi Cremonensis, *Antapodosis etc.,* Corpus Christianorum, Continuatio medievalis, vol. 156 (Turnhout, 1998), pp. 217–18.

6. On the fondaco, see Olivia Remie Constable, *Housing the Stranger in the Mediterranean World: Lodging and Travel in Late Antiquity and the Middle Ages* (Cambridge, 2003).

7. Damien Coulon, *Barcelone et le grand commerce d'orient au Moyen Âge: Un siècle de relations avec l'Égypte et la Syrie-Palestine, ca. 1330–ca. 1430* (Madrid and Barcelona, 2004), pp. 62–87.

8. *Merchant Culture in Fourteenth Century Venice: The Zibaldone da Canal,* trans. John E. Dotson (Binghamton, 1994), pp. 127–28.

9. Ibid., pp. 114–16.

10. John Larner, *Marco Polo and the Discovery of the World* (New Haven, 1999), p. 70.

11. Eliyahu Ashtor, *Histoire des prix et des salaires dans l'Orient médiéval* (Paris, 1969), pp. 324–25.

12. David Bulbeck et al., *Southeast Asian Exports Since the Fourteenth Century: Cloves, Pepper, Coffee, and Sugar* (Leiden, 1998), p. 26.

13. Josep Planes i Borràs, "The Accounts of Joan Benet's Trading Ventures from Barcelona to Famagusta, 1343," *Epeteris* 19 (1992): 105–18; Eliyahu Ashtor, "Profits from Trade with the Levant in the Fifteenth Century," *Bulletin of the School of Oriental and African Studies* 38 (1975): 265–67, repr. Ashtor, *Studies on the Levantine Trade in the Middle Ages* (London, 1978); Peter Spufford, *Power and Profit: The Merchant in Medieval Europe* (New York, 2002), p. 312.

14. Eliyahu Ashtor, "The Volume of Mediaeval Spice Trade," *Journal of Economic History* 9 (1980): 753–63, especially 757, repr. in Ashtor, *East–West Trade in the Medieval Mediterranean* (London, 1986); K. S. Mathew, *Portuguese Trade with India in the Sixteenth Century* (New Delhi, 1983), p. 22. The huge cargoes in 1496 seem exaggerated, as the total pepper production of the Malabar region in 1500 or so seems to have been on the order of 8

million pounds; Jan Kieniewicz, "Pepper Gardens and Market in Precolonial Malabar," in *Spices in the Indian Ocean World,* ed. M. N. Pearson (Aldershot, 1996), p. 211.

15. *The Diary of Samuel Pepys* for November 16–17, 1665.

16. Flandrin and Lambert, *Fêtes gourmandes,* p. 157.

17. T. F. Whittet, "Pepperers, Spicers, and Grocers—Forerunners of the Apothecaries," *Proceedings of the Royal Society of Medicine* 61 (1968): 802. I thank Jennifer Sisk of Yale University for this reference.

18. Pamela Nightingale, *A Medieval Mercantile Community: The Grocers' Company and the Politics of Trade of London, 1000–1485* (New Haven, 1995); Leslie Matthews, *The Pepperers, Spicers, and Apothecaries of London During the Thirteenth and Fourteenth Centuries* (London, 1980); Whittet, "Pepperers, Spicers, and Grocers," pp. 801–6.

19. Bénézet, *Pharmacie et médicament,* pp. 170–72.

20. Ibid., pp. 60–62. According to Bénézet (p. 178), wax candles were in a certain sense considered medicines as they were lit to symbolize vows made in aid of cures for illness.

21. Rita Staccini, "L'inventario di una speziera del Quattrocento," *Studi medievali,* 3rd ser., 22 (1981): 377–420; J. Barbaud, "Les formulaires médicaux du Moyen-Âge," *Revue d'histoire de la pharmacie* 35 (1988): 1401.

22. Tomás López Pizcueta, "Los bienes de un farmacéutico barcelonés del siglo XIV: Francesc de Camp," *Acta Medievalia* 13 (1992): 17–73.

23. Sylvia Thrupp, "The Grocers of London: A Study in Distributive Trade," in *Studies in English Trade in the Fifteenth Century,* ed. Eileen Power and M. M. Postan (London, 1933), pp. 247–92.

24. Carles Vela i Aulesa, *L'obrador d'un apotecari medieval segons el llibre de comptes de Francesc ses Canes, Barcelona, 1378–1381* (Barcelona, 2003), pp. 125, 136.

25. Ibid., pp. 293–94.

26. Bénézet, *Pharmacie et médicament,* pp. 176–78.

27. Tarrgona, Archivo Histórico Provincial, manual 3669/1, fols. 224v–227r. I am grateful to Michael McVaugh of the University of North Carolina for telling me about this record and giving me a copy of his transcription.

28. On these poems, John Friedman, "Chaucer's Pardoner, Rutebeuf's 'Dit de l'Herberie,' the 'Dit du Mercier,' and Cultural History," *Viator* 38 (2007): 289–319.

29. William Langland, *Piers Plowman,* version B, book 5, lines 282–307.

30. "London Lickpenny," in *Medieval English Political Writings,* ed. James M. Dean (Kalamazoo, 1996), p. 224.

31. Friedman, "Chaucer's Pardoner," p. 300.

32. C. Anne Wilson, *Food and Drink in Britain from the Stone Age to the 19th Century* (Chicago, 1991), pp. 282–83.

33. Pegolotti, *La pratica della mercatura,* pp. 298–300.

34. Langland, *Piers Plowman,* version B, book 2, lines 226–27.

35. George Earlie Shankle, *State Names, Flags, Seals, Songs, Birds, Flowers and Other Symbols* (New York, 1934), pp. 105–6. Connecticut's role in the spice trade is at least symbolically reinforced by the career of the original benefactor of Yale University, Elihu Yale (1649–1721), an English trader born in New Haven who dealt in spices and became governor of Madras and eventually of the entire British East India Company.

36. Wilson, *Food and Drink,* pp. 282–83.

37. Mattheus Platearius, *Das Arzneidrogenbuch,* pp. 14, 56; *Livre des simples médecines* (Opsomer ed.), pp. 75, 163.

38. Pere Verdés i Pijuan, "Una espècia autòctona: El comerç del safrà a Catalunya durant el segle XV," *Anuario de estudios medievales* 31, no. 2 (2001): 758–85, esp. 766–67 and 779–82.

39. *Quellen zur Geschichte des Kölner Handels und Verkehrs im Mittelalter,* vol. 1 (Bonn, 1917), no. 1031, vol. 2 (Bonn, 1923), no. 754, 755, 974, 1139, vol. 4 (Bonn, 1934), no. 49; Johannes Müllner, *Die Annalen der Riechstadt Nürnberg von 1623,* part 2, 1351–1469, ed. Gerhard Hirschmann (Nuremberg, 1984), pp. 353, 373, 390, 510. I am grateful to Dr. Christine Reinle of the University of Giessen for these references.

40. Kathryn L. Reyerson, "Commercial Fraud in the Middle Ages: The Case of the Dissembling Pepperer," *Journal of Medieval History* 8 (1982): 63–73.

41. Antoni Riera, "'Transmarina vel orientali especies magno labore quaesita, multo precio empta': Especias y sociedad en el Mediterráneo noroccidental en el siglo XII," *Anuario de estudios medievales* 30, no. 2 (2000): 1031–49; Woolgar, *Great Household in Late Medieval England,* p. 129.

42. John Munro, "Oriental Spices and Their Costs in Medieval Cuisine: Luxuries or Necessities?" talk given at University College, Toronto, 1988, posted at www.chass.utoronto .ca./~munro5/SPICES1.htm.

43. Vela i Aulesa, *L'obrador d'un apotecari medieval,* passim. For the Manresa apothecary, see the Tarrgona document cited above in n. 27.

CHAPTER 5. SCARCITY, ABUNDANCE, AND PROFIT

1. On mastic in its historical setting, see Andrew Dalby, "Mastic for Beginners," *Petits propos culinaires* 65 (2000): 38–45. Columbus' letter is in Christopher Columbus, *A Synoptic Edition of the Log of Columbus' First Voyage,* ed. Francesca Lardicci et al. (Turnhout, 1999), vol. 6 of *Repertorium Columbianum,* pp. 67, 86, 224.

2. Donkin, *Between East and West,* p. xix.

3. Philip D. Curtin, *Cross-Cultural Trade in World History* (Cambridge, 1984), p. 142. In general on the risks and rewards of the early-modern spice trade, Peter Musgrave, "The Economics of Uncertainty: The Structural Revolution in the Spice Trade, 1480–1640," in *Shipping, Trade, and Commerce: Essays in Memory of Ralph Davis,* ed. P. L. Cottrell and D. H. Aldcroft (Leicester, 1981), pp. 9–21.

4. Jeffrey G. Williamson and Kevin H. O'Rourke, "Did Vasco da Gama Matter for European Markets? Testing Frederick Lane's Hypothesis Fifty Years Later," Economic Papers, Trinity College, Dublin, 2006, at http://ideas.repec.org/p/tcd/tcduee/tep2007.html. Pierre Delaveau, *Les épices: Histoire, description et usage des différents épices, aromates et condiments* (Paris, 1987), p. 72.

5. Mattheus Platearius, *Das Arzneidrogenbuch "Circa Instans,"* p. 91.

6. Herodotus, *Histories* 3.107 and 110–11.

7. Pausanias, *Description of Greece* 9.28.1.

8. Pliny, *Natural History* 12.81, 12.85; Theophrastus, *Enquiry into Plants* 9.5.1, and examples from M. Laurent, "Le phénix, les serpents et les aromates dans une miniature du XIIe siècle," *L'antiquité classique* 4 (1935): 381.

9. Christel Meier, *Gemma spiritalis: Methode und Gebrauch der Edelsteinallegorese vom frühen Christentum bis ins 18. Jahrhundert,* part 1 (Munich, 1977), pp. 99–138, 353–58; Berthold Laufer, *The Diamond: A Study in Chinese and Hellenistic Folk-Lore* (Chicago, 1915), pp. 6–28.

10. Lynn Thorndyke, *A History of Magic and Experimental Science,* 8 vols. (New York, 1923–58), vol. 2, p. 262.

11. Marco Polo, *Milione, Le devisament dou monde: Il Milione nelle redazioni toscana e franco-italiana,* ed. Gabriella Ronchi (Milan, 1982), chapter 175, pp. 562–63.

12. A few examples for pepper: the Old English "Wonders of the East," noted in Andy Orchard, *Pride and Prodigies: Studies in the Monsters of the "Beowulf" Manuscript* (Woodbridge, Eng., 1995), p. 188; the purported letter of Alexander the Great to Aristotle (probably from the ninth century), *Epistola Alexandri ad Aristotelem ad codicum fidem edita et commentario critico instructa,* ed. W. W. Boer (The Hague, 1953), p. 53; Gervase of Tilbury, *Otia Imperialia: Recreation for an Emperor,* ed. and trans. S. E. Banks and J. W. Binns (Oxford, 2002), p. 187 (dating from the early thirteenth century); and Johannes Witte de Hese's fictitious "voyage" of the fifteenth century, Westrem, *Broader Horizons,* p. 138.

13. As described in Guéret-Laferté, *Sur les routes de l'Empire Mongol,* pp. 241–44.

14. Joinville quoted above in Chapter 3 (at n. 21); Odoric of Pordenone, *Relatio,* in *Cathay and the Way Thither,* vol. 2, p. 342; Marco Polo, *Milione,* p. 532.

15. Jerome, Letter 146.2, in *Epistulae,* vol. 3, ed. Isidor Hilberg, Corpus Scriptorum Ecclesiasticorum Latinorum, vol. 56 (Vienna, 1918), p. 311. Walafrid Strabo, *De cultura hortorum,* 302–4, in Monumenta Germaniae Historica, Poetae, vol. 2, p. 346.

16. Hetoum, King of Armenia, *La flor des estoires de la terre d'Orient,* in *Recueil des historiens des croisades: Documents arméniens,* vol. 2 (Paris, 1906), p. 261, and *The Defective Version of Mandeville's Travels,* ed. M. C. Seymour, *Early English Text Society,* Old Series 319 (Oxford, 2002), 105.

17. Marco Polo, *Milione,* p. 579; Odoric of Pordenone, *Relatio,* ed. Anastasius van den Wyngaert, in *Sinica Franciscana,* vol. 1 (1929), pp. 439–40, and another version in *Cathay and the Way Thither,* vol. 2, p. 295, n. 8.

18. *Mirabilia descripta: Les merveilles de l'Asie par le Père Jourdain Catalani de Sévérac,* ed. Henri Cordier (Paris, 1925), pp. 439–40; John Mandeville, *Le livre des merveilles du monde,* pp. 318–20; *Mandeville's Travels,* pp. 123–24.

19. John of Marignolli, *Relatio,* p. 530.

20. Pierre d'Ailly, *Imago mundi,* ed. Edmond Buron, vol. 1 (Paris, 1930), 16; Aeneas Sylvius Piccolomini, *Historia rerum ubique gestarum* in *Aeneae Sylvii Piccolominei . . . opera quae extant omnia* (Basel, 1551, repr. Frankfurt, 1967), p. 288.

21. Poggio Bracciolini, *De l'Inde: Les voyages en Asie de Niccolò de' Conti,* ed. and trans. Michèle Guéret-Laferté (Turnhout, 2004), pp. 97, 121, 155.

22. For what follows, see E. G. Ravenstein, *Martin Behaim, His Life and His Globe* (London, 1908), pp. 84–90. On Behaim's career, see Armin M. Brandt, *Martin Behaim* (Regensburg, 1989).

23. Folker Reichert, "Columbus und Marco Polo—Asien in Amerika: Zur Literaturgeschichte der Entdeckungen," *Zeitschrift für Historische Forschung* 15 (1988): 45–46.

24. Larner, *Marco Polo,* p. 154.

25. Phillips and Phillips, *Worlds of Christopher Columbus,* pp. 157–70.

1. Christine R. Johnson, "Bringing the World Home: Germany in the Age of Discovery" (Ph.D. diss., Johns Hopkins University, 2000), pp. 215–17.

2. Ibid.

3. Johanna Maria van Winter, "Kochen und Essen im Mittelalter," in *Mensch und Umwelt im Mittelalter,* ed. Bernd Hermann (Stuttgart, 1986), p. 92.

4. Bernard of Clairvaux, *Apologia ad Guillelmum Abbatum,* trans. Conrad Rudolph, *"The Things of Greater Importance": Bernard of Clairvaux's Apologia and the Medieval Attitude Toward Art* (Philadelphia, 1990), pp. 264–69.

5. Ibid., p. 265.

6. Bernard's letter to his cousin Robert, *S. Bernardi Opera,* vol. 7, *Epistolae* I (Rome, 1974), letter 1, cap. 12 (p. 9).

7. Alain de Lille, *Plaint of Nature,* trans. James J. Sheridan (Toronto, 1980), p. 174.

8. *Twelfth-Century Statutes from the Cistercian General Chapter,* ed. Chrysogonus Waddell (Brecht, 2002), no. 65 (p. 354).

9. Pérez Vidal, *Medicina y dulceria,* pp. 33–36, 157–226.

10. On monks who drink spiced wine, Wycliffe, "Of the Leaven of the Pharisees," cap. 4, in *The English Works of Wyclif Hitherto Unprinted,* ed. F. D. Matthew, Early English Text Society 74, 2nd ed. (London, 1902), pp. 13–14. On the Antichrist, Wycliffe, "Of Antichrist and His Meynee," in *Three Treatises by John Wycklyffe, D.D., Now First Printed from a Manuscript in the Library of Trinity College, Dublin,* ed. James Henthorn Todd (Dublin, 1851), p. 130.

11. C. Stephen Jaeger, *The Origins of Courtliness: Civilizing Trends and the Formation of Courtly Ideals, 939–1210* (Philadelphia, 1985), p. 186.

12. Odile Redon and Lucia Bertolini, "La diffusione in Italia di una tradizione culinaria senese tra due e trecento," *Bolletino Senese di Storia Patria* 100 (1993): 35–81.

13. Nicola Masciandaro, *The Voice of the Hammer: The Meaning of Work in Middle English Literature* (Notre Dame, 2006), pp. 94–116.

14. *The Harley Lyrics: The Middle English Lyrics of MS. Harley 2253,* ed. G. L. Brook (Manchester, 1964), no. 3, cited in Mary Carruthers, "Sweetness," *Speculum* 81 (2006): 1010–11.

15. I am very grateful to Traugott Lawler of Yale University for his observations on spices and pleasure in Chaucer's works.

16. The distinction between use and enjoyment is discussed in Augustine's *On Christian Doctrine.*

17. Langland, *Piers Plowman,* version B, book 10, 289–90.

18. As noted in Turner, *Spice,* p. 285.

19. *The Libelle of Englyshe Polycye, A Poem on the Use of Sea Power, 1436,* ed. George Warner (Oxford, 1926), especially chapters 6 and 7, pp. 17–23.

20. Jordi Bolòs i Masclans, "Un territori en temps de guerra," in *Hug Roger III, senyor en les muntanyes: Procés al darrer comte del Pallars, 1491* (Lleida, 2002), p. 174.

21. Verdés i Pijuan, "Una espècia autòctona," pp. 758–85.

22. Pliny, *Natural History,* 16.59.136 (vol. 4, p. 476).

1. The conversation is reported in an anonymous chronicle attributed to Álvaro Velho. See Subrahmanyam, *Career and Legend of Vasco da Gama,* p. 129; Joaquim Romero Magalhães, *Portugueses no mundo do século XVI: Espaços e productos* (Lisbon, 1998), pp. 24–25; Vitorino Magalhães Godinho, *Os descobrimentos e a economia mundial,* 2nd ed. (Lisbon, 1985), vol. 2, p. 159.

2. Christopher Columbus, *Journals and Other Documents on the Life and Voyages of Christopher Columbus,* trans. Samuel Eliot Morison (New York, 1963), pp. 13–14; João Paulo Oliveira Costa and Victor Luís Gaspar Rodrigues, *Portugal y Oriente: El proyecto indiano del rey Juan* (Madrid, 1992), p. 35.

3. William of Rubruck, *The Mission of Friar William of Rubruck,* ed. Peter Jackson and David Morgan (London, 1990), 36.3 (p. 247).

4. For European ideas about the Mongols, see Folker E. Reichert, *Begegnungen mit China: Die Entdeckung Ostasiens im Mittelalter* (Sigmaringen, 1992), pp. 65–111; I. de Rachewiltz, *Papal Envoys to the Great Khan* (London, 1971); Kurt Villads Jensen, "Devils, Noble Savages, and the Iron Gate: Thirteenth-Century European Concepts of the Mongols," *Bulletin of International Medieval Research* 6 (2000): 1–20.

5. One doesn't want to exaggerate just how peaceful conditions were at any given time across this expanse. The Mongols often feuded among themselves, and even as peacemakers they weren't by any means the first to permit trade across Central Asia. See the cautious remarks in Reichert, *Begegnungen mit China,* pp. 83–84. Nevertheless, the fact that before the seventeenth century, as Reichert goes on to demonstrate, European contact with China and East Asia was confined to this period, 1240–1360, shows the historical importance of the Mongols.

6. Rory Maclean, author of *Magic Bus: On the Hippie Trail from Istanbul to India* (New York, 2006), did manage to follow the overland road popular with young travelers in the 1960s, but he required some help from the American military in Afghanistan.

7. Pegolotti, *La pratica della mercatura,* pp. 21–23.

8. Robert S. Lopez, "L'extrême frontière du commerce de l'Europe médiévale," *Le Moyen Âge* 69 (1963): 479–90.

9. On Europeans in India, see Robert S. Lopez, "European Merchants in the Medieval Indies," *Journal of Economic History* 5 (1943): 164–84.

10. Falchetta, *Fra Mauro's World Map,* p. 335: "Although in the nearby note I say that the spices travel as far as the Black Sea, today the roads are in such a poor state that they no longer reach that far." The annotation is placed in Arabia.

11. On medieval maps and the impact of Asian travel, Ingrid Baumgärtner, "Weltbild und Empire: Die Erweiterung des Kartographischen Weltbilds durch die Asienreisen des apäten Mittelalters," *Journal of Medieval History* 23 (1997): 227–53.

12. C. F. Beckingham, "The Quest for Prester John," *Bulletin of the John Rylands Library* 62 (1980): 296, repr. in Beckingham, *Between Islam and Christendom: Travellers, Facts, and Legends in the Middle Ages and Renaissance* (London, 1983), article no. 2, also in Beckingham and Bernard Hamilton, *Prester John, the Mongols and the Ten Lost Tribes* (Aldershot, 1996), article no. 14.

13. J. R. S. Phillips, *The Medieval Expansion of Europe* (Oxford, 1988), pp. 104–5.

14. Marinus Sanatus, *Liber secretorum fidelium crucis . . .* (Toronto, 1972, repr. of Hanau, 1591 ed.). The map is reproduced on the endpapers of the reprint. See also Evelyn Edson, "Reviving the Crusade: Sanudo's Schemes and Vesconte's Maps," in *Eastward Bound: Travel and Travellers, 1050–1550,* ed. Rosamund Allen (Manchester, 2004), pp. 131–55.

15. Nathalie Bouloux, *Cultures et savoirs géographiques en Italie au XIVe siècle* (Turnhout, 2002), pp. 53–56.

16. Valerie Flint, *The Imaginative Landscape of Christopher Columbus* (Princeton, 1992), pp. 10–15, 24–25.

17. Poggio Bracciolini, *De l'Inde,* p. 117. Marco Polo had mentioned Indonesian islands called "Sondur" and "Condur," *Milione,* pp. 540–41.

18. Falchetta, *Fra Mauro's World Map,* annotation no. 23 (p. 181), no. 178 (p. 219), no. 215 (p. 225), no. 589 (p. 303), no. 594 (p. 303), no. 601 (p. 305).

19. Ibid., no. 53 (p. 193): "Some authors write that the Sea of India is enclosed like a pond and does not communicate with the ocean. However Solinus claims that it is itself part of the ocean and that it is navigable in the southern and south-western parts."

20. Ibid., no. 149 (pp. 211–13).

21. Cited in John Keay, *The Spice Route: A History* (Berkeley, 2006), p. 108.

22. Jacques Le Goff, "The Medieval West and the Indian Ocean: An Oneiric Horizon," in Le Goff, *Time, Work, and Culture in the Middle Ages,* trans. Arthur Goldhammer (Chicago, 1980), pp. 189–200.

23. Abu-Lughod, *Before European Hegemony,* pp. 248–90; K. N. Chaudhuri, *Trade and Civilisation in the Indian Ocean: An Economic History from the Rise of Islam to 1750* (Cambridge, 1985).

24. On these voyages, see Edward Dreyer, *Zheng He: China and the Oceans in the Early Ming Dynasty, 1404–1433* (London, 2006).

25. Ma Huan, *Ying-yai Sheng-lan: The Overall Survey of the Ocean's Shores, 1433,* trans. J. V. G. Mills (Cambridge, 1970). Another contemporary account is that of Fei Xin, *Hsing ch'a sheng-lan: The Overall Survey of the Star Raft,* trans. J. V. G. Mills, rev. Roderick Ptak (Wiesbaden, 1996).

26. *Chau Ju-kua, His Work on the Chinese and Arab Trade in the Twelfth and Thirteenth Centuries, Entitled Chu-fan-chi,* trans. Friedrich Hirth and W. W. Rockhill (St. Petersburg, 1911).

27. Robert Finlay, "Portuguese and Chinese Maritime Imperialism: Camões's *Lusiads* and Luo Maodeng's *Voyage of the San Bao Eunuch,*" *Comparative Studies in Society and History* 34 (1992): 225–41.

CHAPTER 8. FINDING THE REALMS OF SPICES:
PORTUGAL AND SPAIN

1. These and other navigational problems are discussed by Francisco Contente Domingues, "A prática de navegar," in *História da expansão portuguesa,* ed. Francisco Bethencourt and Kirti Chaudhuri, vol. 1 (Lisbon, 1998), pp. 62–87.

2. On the economic aspects of Portuguese exploration of the African coast, see Ivana Elbl, "Cross-Cultural Trade and Diplomacy: Portuguese Relations with West Africa, 1441–1521," *Journal of World History* 3 (1992): 165–204.

3. *Mappamundi: The Catalan Atlas of the Year 1375,* ed. Georges Grosjean (Zurich, 1978), panel 3, sheet 2.1.51.

4. Robert S. Wolf, "Da Gama's Blundering: Trade Encounters in Africa and Asia During the European 'Age of Discovery,' 1450–1520," *The History Teacher* 31 (1998): 302.

5. On the Portuguese and the discovery of the origins of malagueta pepper, Francisco Manuel Carlos de Mello, Conde de Ficalho, *Memoria sobre a malagueta* (Lisbon, 1878).

6. Eustache de la Fosse's account in *Europeans in West Africa, 1450–1560* (Hakluyt Society, Second Series, vol. 86, 1941), no. 101, p. 240. Behaim in Ravenstein, *Martin Behaim, His Life, His Globe,* pp. 71–72 and map insert no. 4.

7. Keay, *The Spice Route,* p. 150.

8. Vitorinho Magalhães Godinho, *Os descobrimentos e a economia mundial,* 2nd ed., vol. 2 (Lisbon, 1985), p. 151.

9. Ibid., pp. 159–74.

10. The questions as formulated in C. F. Beckingham, "The Travels of Pero da Covilhã," in Beckingham, *Between Islam and Christendom,* p. 11.

11. Pierre Schneider, *L'Éthiopie et l'Inde: Interférences et confusions aux extérmités du monde antique* (Rome, 2004), pp. 429–71.

12. On the later career of Prester John in relation to the Portuguese, see articles by C. F. Beckingham, *Between Islam and Christendom,* especially "The Travels of Pero da Covilhã," "The Quest for Prester John," and "The Achievements of Prester John." Also Moritz Trebeljahr, "Pêro da Covilhãs Indien- und Äthiopienreise und die Expansionspolitik Johannes II. von Portugal" (M.A. thesis, University of Freiburg-im-Breisgau, 2003).

13. Subrahmanyam, *Career and Legend of Vasco da Gama,* p. 50.

14. Trebeljahr, "Pêra da Covilhãs Indien- und Äthiopienreise," p. 12.

15. Ibid., pp. 70–95.

16. Giuseppe Tardiola, *Atlante fantastico del medioevo* (Rome, 1990), p. 86.

17. On da Gama's voyage, see Subrahmanyam, *Career and Legend of Vasco da Gama,* esp. pp. 76–161.

18. Ibid., p. 144.

19. Max Justo Guedes and Gerald Lombardi, eds., *Portugal–Brazil: The Age of Atlantic Discoveries* (Milan, 1990), pp. 44–45, 267.

20. Vitorinho Magalhães Godinho, "Le repli Vénitien et Égyptien et la route du Cap, 1496–1533," in *Éventail de l'histoire vivante: Hommage à Lucien Febvre,* vol. 1 (Paris, 1953), repr. in *Spices in the Indian Ocean World,* pp. 283–300 (esp. 283); Robert Finlay, "Crisis and Crusade in the Mediterranean: Venice, Portugal, and the Cape Route to India, 1498–1509," *Studi Veneziani* n.s. 28 (1994): 45–90 (esp. 45, 57).

21. Williamson and O'Rourke, "Did Vasco da Gama Matter for European Markets?"

22. Ruy González de Clavijo, *Embaja a Tamorlán,* ed. Francisco López Estrada (Madrid, 1999).

23. The latter point effectively proven by Flint, *Imaginative Landscape of Christopher Columbus.*

24. Ravenstein, *Martin Behaim, His Life, His Globe,* p. 71; John Mandeville, *Le livre des merveilles du monde,* p. 335; *Mandeville's Travels,* p. 134.

25. For what follows, Flint, *Imaginative Landscape of Christopher Columbus,* pp. 39–41, 87–90.

26. Ibid., pp. 147–48.

27. Columbus, *Journals and Other Documents on the Life and Voyages of Christopher Columbus,* trans. Samuel Eliot Morison (New York, 1963), pp. 50–54, 141, 242; Columbus, *A Synoptic Edition of the Log of Columbus' First Voyage,* pp. 67, 86, 224, 242.

28. Reichert, "Columbus und Marco Polo—Asien in Amerika," pp. 41–42.

29. Lisa Jardine, *Worldly Goods: A New History of the Renaissance* (New York, 1996), pp. 292–93.

30. Laurence Bergreen, *Over the Edge of the World: Magellan's Terrifying Circumnavigation of the Globe* (New York, 2003); Donkin, *Between East and West,* p. ix.

CONCLUSION. THE RISE AND FALL OF SPICES

1. Jean-Louis Flandrin et al., introduction to François Pierre de la Varenne, *Le cuisinier françois* (Paris, 1983; original ed. 1651), pp. 14–15.

2. Françoise Sabban and Silvano Serventi, *La gastronomie au Grand Siècle* (Paris, 1998), p. 67.

3. Laurioux, *Les livres de cuisine,* p. 66, n. 7.

4. As noted in Delaveau, *Les épices,* p. 160.

5. Examples of Italian cookery from Alberto Capatti and Massimo Montanari, *Italian Cuisine, A Cultural History* (New York, 2003), pp. 111–13.

6. Quoted in T. Sarah Peterson, *Acquired Taste: The French Origins of Modern Cooking* (Ithaca, 1994), pp. 193–94.

7. Constance B. Hieatt et al., *Pleyn Delit: Medieval Cookery for Modern Cooks,* 2nd ed. (Toronto, 1996).

8. The comparison is from Jean-Louis Flandrin, *Chroniques de Platine: Pour une gastronomie historique* (Paris, 1992), pp. 20–21; Peterson, *Acquired Taste,* p. 201.

9. Jean-Louis Flandrin, "Diététique et gastronomie, XIVe–XVIIIe siècles," in *Voeding en geneeskunde/Alimentation et médecine,* ed. Ria Jansen-Sieben and Frank Daelemans (Brussels, 1993), pp. 177–92; Johanna Maria van Winter, "Kookboeken, medisch of culinair?" in ibid., pp. 153–65.

10. Sidney Mintz, *Sweetness and Power: The Place of Sugar in Modern History* (New York, 1985).

11. Alan McFarlane, *Green Gold: The Empire of Tea: A Remarkable History of the Plant that Took Over the World* (London, 2003), p. 179.

12. For spices compared to coffee, tobacco, chocolate, etc., see Wolfgang Schivelbusch, *Tastes of Paradise: A Social History of Spices, Stimulants, and Intoxicants,* trans. David Johnson (New York, 1992). See also the caution about regarding these as interchangeable in Marcy Norton, "Tasting Empire: Chocolate and the European Internalization of Mesoamerican Aesthetics," *American Historical Review* 111 (2006): 660–91.

13. Pérez Vidal, *Medicina y dulceria,* pp. 55–62.

14. Giles Milton, *Nathaniel's Nutmeg, or the True and Incredible Adventures of the Spice Trader Who Changed the Course of History* (New York, 1999), pp. 356–63.

Bibliography

PRIMARY SOURCES

Aeneas Sylvius Piccolomini. *Historia rerum ubique gestarum.* In *Aeneae Sylvii Piccolominei . . . opera quae extant omnia* (Basel, 1551, repr. Frankfurt, 1967).

d'Ailly, Pierre. *Imago mundi.* Ed. Edmond Buron, vol. 1 (Paris, 1930).

Alain de Lille. *Plaint of Nature.* Trans. James J. Sheridan (Toronto, 1980).

Arnau de Vilanova. *Opera nuperrima revisa . . .* (Lyon, 1520).

———. *Regimen de sanitat a Jaume II* (version of Berenguer Sarreiera). In *Arnau de Vilanova, Obres catalanes,* vol. 2 (Escrits mèdics), ed. Miquel Batllori (Barcelona, 1947), 199–200.

The Babees Book. Ed. Frederick J. Furnivall (London, 1868; repr. New York, 1969).

Bernard of Clairvaux. *Apologia ad Guillelmum Abbatum.* Trans. Conrad Rudolph, *"The Things of Greater Importance": Bernard of Clairvaux's Apologia and the Medieval Attitude Toward Art* (Philadelphia, 1990), 264–69.

———. *S. Bernardi Opera,* vol. 7, *Epistolae* 1 (Rome, 1974).

Chau Ju-kua, His Work on the Chinese and Arab Trade in the Twelfth and Thirteenth Centuries, Entitled Chu-fan-chi. Trans. Friedrich Hirth and W. W. Rockhill (St. Petersburg, 1911).

Chiquart's 'On Cookery': A Fifteenth-Century Savoyard Culinary Treatise. Ed. and trans. Terence Scully (New York, 1986).

Clavijo, Ruy González de. *Embaja a Tamorlán.* Ed. Francisco López Estrada (Madrid, 1999).

Columbus, Christopher. *Journals and Other Documents on the Life and Voyages of Christopher Columbus.* Trans. Samuel Eliot Morison (New York, 1963).

———. *A Synoptic Edition of the Log of Columbus' First Voyage.* Ed. Francesca Lardicci et al., vol. 6 of *Repertorium Columbianum* (Turnhout, 1999).

Constantine the African. *Constantini liber de coitu: El tratado de andrología de Constantino el Africano.* Ed. and trans. Enrique Montero-Cartelle (Santiago de Compostela, 1983).

The Coronation of Richard III, the Extant Documents. Ed. Anne F. Sutton and P. W. Hammond (Gloucester and New York, 1983).

Ctesias. *Indika.* In *Ctésias de Cnide, La Perse, l'Inde, autres fragements,* ed. and trans. Dominique Lenfant (Paris, 2004).

Deschamps, Eustache. *Oeuvres complètes.* Ed. Marquis de Queux de Saint-Hilaire and Gaston Raymond, vol. 7 (Paris, 1891).

Eiximenis, Francesc. *Lo Cresità (selecció).* Ed. Albert Hauf (Barcelona, 1983).

———. *Terç del Cresià.* Ed. Father Martí and Father Feliu, O.F.M. Cap. (Barcelona, 1932).

Epistola Alexandri ad Aristotelem ad codicum fidem edita et commentario critico instructa. Ed. W. W. Boer (The Hague, 1953).

Eustache de la Fosse. *Europeans in West Africa, 1450–1560* (Hakluyt Society, Second Series, vol. 86, 1941), no. 101.

Fei Xin. *Hsing ch'a sheng-lan: The Overall Survey of the Star Raft.* Trans. J. V. G. Mills, rev. Roderick Ptak (Wiesbaden, 1996).

Formaggi del medioevo: La "Summa lacticiniorum" di Pantaleone da Confienza. Ed. Irma Naso (Turin, 1990).

Fulcher of Chartres. *Fulcheri Carnotensis Historia Hiersolymitana, 1095–1127.* Ed. Heinrich Hagenmeyer (Heidelberg, 1913).

Sir Gawain and the Green Knight. In *The Complete Works of the Pearl Poet,* trans. Casey Finch (Berkeley, 1993).

Gervase of Tilbury. *Otia imperialia: Recreation for an Emperor.* Ed. and trans. S. E. Banks and J. W. Binns (Oxford, 2002).

The Harley Lyrics: The Middle English Lyrics of MS. Harley 2253. Ed. G. L. Brook (Manchester, 1964).

Henry of Huntington. *The History of the English People, 1000–1154.* Trans. Diana Greenway (Oxford, 2002).

Hese, Johannes Witte de, "*Itinerarius.*" In *Broader Horizons: A Study of Johannes Witte de Hese's "Itinerarius" and Medieval Travel Narratives,* ed. Scott D. Westrem (Cambridge, 2001).

Hetoum, King of Armenia. *La flor des estoires de la terre d'Orient.* In *Recueil des historiens des croisades: Documents arméniens,* vol. 2 (Paris, 1906).

Isidore of Seville. *Etymologiae.* Ed. Marc Reydellet, book 9 (Paris, 1984) and book 17 (Paris, 1981).

———. *Isidori Hispalensis Episcopi, Etymologiarum sive originum libri XX,* 2 vols. Ed. W. M. Lindsay (Oxford, 1911).

Jacques de Longuyon. *Les voeux du paon.* Ed. Brother Camillus Casey, Ph.D. diss., Columbia University, 1956.

Jerome. *Epistulae,* vol. 3. Ed. Isidor Hilberg, Corpus Scriptorum Ecclesiasticorum Latinorum, vol. 56 (Vienna, 1918).

John of Marignolli. *Relatio.* In *Sinica Franciscana,* vol. 1, ed. Anastasius Van den Wyngaert (1929).

Joinville, Jean de. *History of Saint Louis.* In *Chronicles of the Crusades,* trans. M. R. B. Shaw (Harmondsworth, 1963).

Jordanus. *Mirabilia descripta: Les merveilles de l'Asie par le Père Jourdain Catalani de Sévérac.* Ed. Henri Cordier (Paris, 1925).

Latini, Brunetto. *Li livres dou trésor.* Ed. Francis J. Carmody (Berkeley and Los Angeles, 1948; repr. Geneva, 1975).

The Libelle of Englyshe Polycye, A Poem on the Use of Sea Power, 1436. Ed. George Warner (Oxford, 1926).

Libro de los medicamentos simples (facsimile of the St. Petersburg ms.). Ed. Natacha Elaguina et al. (Barcelona, 2002).

Liutprand of Cremona. *Relatio de legatione Constantinopolitane.* In Liutprandi Cremonensis, *Antapodosis etc.,* Corpus Christianorum, Continuatio medievalis, vol. 156 (Turnhout, 1998).

Livre des simple médecines. Codex Bruxellensis IV. 1024: A 15th-Century French Herbal. Commentary by Carmélia Opsomer and William T. Stearn, English trans. Enid Roberts and William T. Stearn (Antwerp, 1984).

Livre des simples médecines d'après le manuscrit français 12322 de la Bibliothèque Nationale de Paris. Trans. and commented on by Ghislaine Malandin et al. (Paris, 1986).

Llibre de totes maneres de confits. Ed. Joan Santanach i Suñol (Barcelona, 2004).

"London Lickpenny." In *Medieval English Political Writings,* ed. James M. Dean (Kalamazoo, 1996).

Ma Huan. *Ying-yai Sheng-lan: The Overall Survey of the Ocean's Shores (1433).* Trans. J. V. G. Mills (Cambridge, 1970).

Mandeville, John. *Le livre des merveilles du monde.* Ed. Christiane Deluz (Paris, 2000).

———. *Mandeville's Travels.* Ed. M. C. Seymour (Oxford, 1967).

———. *The Defective Version of Mandeville's Travels.* Ed. M. C. Seymour, *Early English Text Society,* Old Series 319 (Oxford, 2002).

Mappamundi: The Catalan Atlas of the Year 1375. Ed. Georges Grosjean (Zurich, 1978).

Marie d'Oignies. *Supplement to the Life of Marie d'Oignies by Thomas de Cantimpré,* from Hugh Feiss, in *The Life of Marie Oignies by Jacques de Vitry* (Toronto, 1993).

Marinus Sanatus. *Liber secretorum fidelium crucis . . .* (Toronto, 1972, repr. of Hanau, 1591 ed.).

Mattheus Platearius. *Das Arzneidrogenbuch "Circa instans" in einer Fassung des XIII. Jahrhunderts aus der Universitätsbibliothek Erlangen.* Ed. Hans Wölfel (Berlin, 1939).

Le Ménagier de Paris. Ed. Georgina E. Brereton and Janet M. Ferrier (Oxford, 1981).

Merchant Culture in Fourteenth Century Venice: The Zibaldone da Canal. Trans. John E. Dotson (Binghamton, 1994).

Navigatio Sancti Brendani Abbatis from Early Latin Manuscripts. Ed. Carl Selmer (Notre Dame, 1959; repr. Dublin, 1989).

The Neapolitan Recipe Collection: Cuoco Napoletano. Ed. Terence Scully (Ann Arbor, 2000).

Odoric of Pordenone. *Relatio.* In *Cathay and the Way Thither,* ed. Henry Yule and Henri Cordier, vol. 2 (London, 1916).

———. *Relatio.* In *Sinica Franciscana,* vol. 1, ed. Anastasius van den Wyngaert (1929).

Olivier de la Haye. *Poème sur la Grande Peste de 1348.* Ed. Georges Guigue (Lyons, 1888).

Pegolotti, Francesco Balducci. *La pratica della mercatura.* Ed. Allan Evans (Cambridge, Mass., 1936).

Perceval. In *Arthurian Romances,* trans. and ed. William W. Kibler (New York, 1991).

Petronius. *Satyricon.* Trans. Michael Heseltine (Cambridge, 1969).

Petrus Hispanus. *Obras médicas de Pedro Hispano.* Ed. Maria Helena da Rocha Pereira (Coimbra, 1973).

Picatrix: Un traité de magie médiéval. Trans. Béatrice Bakhouche et al. (Turnhout, 2003).

Pliny. *Natural History.* Ed. and trans. H. Rackham, Loeb Classical Library (Cambridge, Mass., 1960).

Poggio Bracciolini. *De l'Inde: Les voyages en Asie de Niccolò de' Conti.* Ed. Michèle Guéret-Laferté (Turnhout, 2004).

Polo, Marco. *Le devisement du monde.* Ed. Philippe Ménard et al., 4 vols. [to date] (Paris, 2001–6).

————. *Milione, Le devisament dou monde: Il Milione nelle redazioni toscana e franco-italiana.* Ed. Gabriella Ronchi (Milan, 1982).

————. *The Travels.* Trans. Ronald Latham (Harmondsworth, 1958).

El primer manual hispánico de mercaderia (siglo XIV). Ed. Miguel Gual Camarena (Barcelona, 1981).

Quellen zur Geschichte des Kölner Handels und Verkehrs im Mittelalter. Ed. Bruno Kuske (Bonn, 1917–34).

Richer of Saint-Denis. *Gesta Senoniensis Ecclesie.* In Monumenta Germaniae Historica, Scriptores, vol. 25.

Mestre Robert. *Libre del coch: Tractat de cuina medieval.* Ed. Veronika Leimgruber (Barcelona, 1982).

The Tabula Antidotarii of Armengaud Blaise and Its Hebrew Translation. Ed. Michael McVaugh and Lola Ferre (Philadelphia, 2000).

Taillevent. *The Viandier of Taillevent: An Edition of All Extent Manuscripts.* Ed. Terence Scully (Ottawa, 1988).

Theophrastus. *Enquiry into Plants.* Trans. Arthur F. Hort (London, 1916).

The Trotula: An English Translation of the Medieval Compendium of Women's Medicine. Ed. Monica H. Green (Philadelphia, 2002).

Twelfth-Century Statutes from the Cistercian General Chapter. Ed. Chrysogonus Waddell (Brecht, 2002).

Walafrid Strabo. *De cultura hortorum.* In Monumenta Germaniae Historica, Poetae, vol. 2.

William of Rubruck. *The Mission of Friar William of Rubruck: His Journey to the Court of the Great Khan Möngke, 1253–1255.* Ed. Peter Jackson and David Morgan (London, 1990).

Wolfram von Eschenbach. *Parzival,* vol. 1. Ed. Karl Lachmann, revised by Eberhard Nellmann (Frankfurt, 1994).

Wycliffe, John. "Of Antichrist and His Meynee." In *Three Treatises by John Wycklyffe, D.D., Now First Printed from a Manuscript in the Library of Trinity College, Dublin,* ed. James Henthorn Todd (Dublin, 1851).

————. *The English Works of Wyclif Hitherto Unprinted.* Ed. F. D. Matthew, *Early English Text Society* 74, 2nd ed. (London, 1902).

SECONDARY LITERATURE

Abu-Lughod, Janet L. *Before European Hegemony: The World System, A.D. 1250–1350* (Oxford, 1989).

Aerts, W. J., et al., ed. *Alexander the Great in the Middle Ages* (Nijmegen, 1978).

Albala, Ken. *Eating Right in the Renaissance* (Berkeley, 2002).

Albret, Jean-Pierre. *Odeurs de sainteté: La mythologie chrétienne des aromates,* 2nd ed. (Paris, 1996).

Aliquot, H. "Les épices à la table des papes d'Avignon au XIVe siècle." In *Manger et boire au Moyen Âge,* vol. 1 (Nice, 1984), 131–50.

Arnold, John A. *Belief and Unbelief in Medieval Europe* (London, 2005).

Ashtor, Eliyahu. *Histoire des prix et des salaires dans l'Orient médiéval* (Paris, 1969).

———. "Profits from Trade with the Levant in the Fifteenth Century." *Bulletin of the School of Oriental and African Studies* 38 (1975): 250–75; repr. Ashtor, *Studies on the Levantine Trade in the Middle Ages* (London, 1978).

———. "The Volume of Mediaeval Spice Trade." *Journal of European Economic History* 9 (1980): 753–63; repr. Ashtor, *East–West Trade in the Medieval Mediterranean* (London, 1986).

Ayer, Ildefonsus. "Où plaça-t-on le paradis terrestre?" *Études Franciscaines* 36 (1924): 117–40.

Bachelard, Gaston. *La psychanalyse du feu* (Paris, 1949).

Barbaud, J. "Les formulaires médicaux du Moyen-Âge." *Revue d'histoire de la pharmacie* 35 (1988): 138–53.

Bardenhewer, Luise. *Der Safranhandel im Mittelalter* (Inaugural-Dissertation) (Bonn, 1914).

Baudet, Henri. *Paradise on Earth: Some Thoughts on European Images of Non-European Men.* Trans. Elizabeth Wentholt (New Haven, 1965).

Baumgärtner, Ingrid. "Weltbild und Empire: Die Erweiterung des Kartographischen Weltbilds durch die Asienreisen des späten Mittelalter." *Journal of Medieval History* 23 (1997): 227–53.

Beckingham, C. F. *Between Islam and Christendom: Travellers, Facts, and Legends in the Middle Ages and Renaissance* (London, 1983).

Beckingham, C. F., and Bernard Hamilton. *Prester John, the Mongols, and the Ten Lost Tribes* (Aldershot, 1996).

Beichner, Paul E. "The Grain of Paradise." *Speculum* 36 (1961): 302–7.

Bejczy, István. *La lettre du Prêtre Jean: Une utopie médiévale* (Paris, 2001).

Bénézet, Jean-Pierre. *Pharmacie et médicament en Méditerranée occidentale, XIIIe–XVIe siècles* (Paris, 1999).

Benson, George. *Later Medieval York: The City and County from 1100 to 1603* (York, 1919).

Bergreen, Laurence. *Over the Edge of the World: Magellan's Terrifying Circumnavigation of the Globe* (New York, 2003).

Bober, Phyllis Pray. *Art, Culture, and Cuisine: Ancient and Medieval Gastronomy* (Chicago, 1999).

Bolòs i Masclans, Jordi. "Un territori en temps de guerra." In *Hug Roger III, senyor en les muntanyes: Procés al darrer comte del Pallars, 1491* (Lleida, 2002).

Bouloux, Nathalie. *Culture et savoirs géographiques en Italie au XIVe siècle* (Turnhout, 2002).

Brandt, Armin M. *Martin Behaim* (Regensburg, 1989).

Brincken, Anna-Dorothee von den. *Fines Terrae: Die Enden der Erde und der vierte Kontinent auf mittelalterlichen Weltkarten.* Monumenta Germaniae Historica, Schriften 36 (Hanover, 1992).

Brown, Russell Vernon. "Enrique de Villena's *Arte Cisoria*: A Critical Edition." Ph.D. diss., University of Wisconsin, 1974.

Bruce, Scott. *Cerealizing America: The Unsweetened Story of American Breakfast Cereal* (Boston, 1995).

Buarque de Holanda, Sérgio. *Visão do paraíso: Os motivos edênicos no descobrimento e colonização do Brasil* (São Paulo, 1969).

Bulbeck, David, et al. *Southeast Asian Exports Since the Fourteenth Century: Cloves, Pepper, Coffee, and Sugar* (Leiden, 1998).

Camille, Michael. "The Corpse in the Garden: *Mumia* in Medieval Herbal Illustrations." *Micrologus* 7 (1999): 297–318.

Capatti, Alberto, and Massimo Montanari. *Italian Cuisine, A Cultural History* (New York, 2003).

Caseau, Béatrice. "Enodia: The Use and Meaning of Fragrances in the Ancient World and Their Christianization, 100–900 A.D." Ph.D. diss., Princeton University, 1994.

Chaudhuri, K. N. *Trade and Civilisation in the Indian Ocean: An Economic History from the Rise of Islam to 1750* (Cambridge, 1985).

Collard, Franck. *Le crime de poison au Moyen Âge* (Paris, 2003).

Constable, Olivia Remie. *Housing the Stranger in the Mediterranean World: Lodging and Travel in Late Antiquity and the Middle Ages* (Cambridge, 2003).

Coulon, Damien. *Barcelone et le grand commerce d'orient au Moyen Âge: Un siècle de relations avec l'Égypte et la Syrie-Palestine, ca. 1330–ca. 1430* (Madrid and Barcelona, 2004).

Crossley-Holland, Nicole. *Living and Dining in Medieval Paris: The Household of a Fourteenth-Century Knight* (Cardiff, 1996).

Curtin, Philip D. *Cross-Cultural Trade in World History* (Cambridge, 1984).

Dahl, Christiane. *Chinesische Unterweltvorstellungen: Die Jenseitsreise des Wang Ming im Roman 'Die Reise in die Westmeere unter dem Eunuchen Sanbao'* (Dortmund, 1998).

Dalby, Andrew. *Dangerous Tastes, the Story of Spices* (Berkeley, 2000).

———. *Flavours of Byzantium* (Totnes, 2003).

———. "Mastic for Beginners." *Petits propos culinaires* 65 (2000): 38–45.

Dannenfeldt, Karl H. "Ambergris: The Search for Its Origin." *Isis* 73 (1982): 382–97.

Delaveau, Pierre. *Les épices: Histoire, description et usage des différents épices, aromates et condiments* (Paris, 1987).

Delumeau, Jean. *History of Paradise: The Garden of Eden in Myth and Tradition.* Trans. Matthew O'Connell (New York, 1995).

Deluz, Christiane. "Le paradis terrestre, image de l'Orient lointain dans quelques documents géographiques médiévaux." *Senefiance* 11 (1982): 145–61.

Deonna, Waldemar. "Enodia: Croyances antiques et modernes: L'odeur suave des dieux et des élus." *Genava* 17 (1939): 167–263.

Dilg, Peter. "Materia medica und Therapeutische Praxis um 1500: Zum Einfluss der arabischen Heilkunde auf den europäischen Arzneischatz." In *Kommunikation zwischen Orient und Okzident: Alltag und Sachkultur* (Vienna, 1994).

Dillon, Patrick. *Gin: The Much-Lamented Death of Madame Geneva* (Boston, 2003).

Domingues, Francisco Contente. "A prática de navegar." In *História da expansão portuguesa,* ed. Francisco Bethencourt and Kirti Chaudhuri (Lisbon, 1998), 1:62–87.

Donkin, Robin A. *Between East and West: The Moluccas and the Traffic in Spices up to the Arrival of Europeans* (Philadelphia, 2003).

———. *Beyond Price: Pearls and Pearl-Fishing: Origins to the Age of Discoveries* (Philadelphia, 1998).

———. *Dragon's Brain Perfume: An Historical Geography of Camphor* (Leiden, 1999).

Dreyer, Edward L. *Zheng He: China and the Oceans in the Early Ming Dynasty, 1404–1433* (London, 2006).

Dyer, Christopher. "Did the Peasants Really Starve in Medieval England?" In *Food and Eating in Medieval Europe,* ed. Martha Carlin and Joel Rosenthal (London and Rio Grande, W.Va., 1998), pp. 53–71.

Edson, Evelyn. "Reviving the Crusade: Sanudo's Schemes and Vesconte's Maps." In *Eastward Bound: Travel and Travellers, 1050–1550,* ed. Rosamund Allen (Manchester, 2004), 131–55.

Elbl, Ivana. "Cross-Cultural Trade and Diplomacy: Portuguese Relations with West Africa, 1441–1521." *Journal of World History* 3 (1992): 165–204.

———. "Henry 'the Navigator.'" *Journal of Medieval History* 27 (2001): 79–99.

———. "Man of His Time (and Peers): A New Look at Henry the Navigator." *Luso-Brazilian Review* 28 (1991): 73–89.

Falchetta, Piero. *Fra Mauro's World Map* (Turnhout, 2006).

Febvre, Lucien. *Life in Renaissance France.* Ed. and trans. Martin Rothstein (Cambridge, Mass., 1977).

Ficalho, Francisco Manuel Carlos de Melo, Conde de. *Memória sôbre a malagueta* (Lisbon, 1878).

Finlay, Robert. "Crisis and Crusade in the Mediterranean: Venice, Portugal, and the Cape Route to India, 1498–1509." *Studi Veneziani* n.s. 28 (1994): 45–90.

———. "Portuguese and Chinese Maritime Imperialism: Camões's *Lusiads* and Luo Maodeng's *Voyage of the San Bao Eunuch.*" *Comparative Studies in Society and History* 34 (1992): 225–41.

Flandrin, Jean-Louis. *Chronique de Platine: Pour une gastronomie historique* (Paris, 1992).

———. "Diététique et gastronomie, XIVe–XVIIIe siècles." In *Voeding en geneeskunde/Alimentation et médicine,* ed. Ria Jansen-Sieben and Frank Daelemans (Brussels, 1993), 177–92.

———. "Seasoning, Cooking, and Dietetics in the Late Middle Ages." In *Food: A Culinary History,* ed. Flandrin and Massimo Montanari (New York, 1999).

Flandrin, Jean-Louis, et al. Introduction. In *Le cuisinier françois,* by François Pierre de la Varenne (Paris, 1983; original ed. 1651).

Flandrin, Jean-Louis, and Carole Lambert. *Fêtes gourmandes au Moyen Âge* (Paris, 1998).

Flint, Valerie I. J. *The Imaginative Landscape of Christopher Columbus* (Princeton, 1992).

Franco, Hilario, Jr. "La construction d'une utopie: L'empire de Prêtre Jean." *Journal of Medieval History* 23 (1997): 211–25.

Freedman, Paul. *Images of the Medieval Peasant* (Stanford, 1999).

———. "Medieval Clichés of Health and Diet According to Francesc Eiximenis." In *Sociedad y Memoria en la Edad Media: Homenaje a Nilda Guglielmi,* ed. Ariel Guiance y Pablo Ubierna (Buenos Aires, 2005), 125–39.

Friedman, John. "Chaucer's Pardoner, Rutebeuf's 'Dit de l'Herberie,' The 'Dit du Mercier,' and Cultural History." *Viator* 38 (2007): 289–319.

———. *The Monstrous Races in Medieval Art and Thought* (Cambridge, Mass., 1981; repr. Syracuse, 2000).

Friedman, John, and Kathrin Giogoli. "Robinet Testard, Court Illuminator: His Manuscripts and His Debt to the Graphic Arts." *Journal of the Early Book Society for the Study of Manuscripts and Printing History* 8 (2005): 142–88.

Friedman, John, and Kristen Mossler Figg, eds. *Trade, Travel, and Exploration in the Middle Ages, an Encyclopedia* (New York and London, 2000).

Gardiner, Eileen, ed. *Visions of Heaven and Hell Before Dante* (New York, 1989).

Geary, Patrick J. *Furta Sacra: Thefts of Relics in the Central Middle Ages,* 2nd ed. (Princeton, 1990).

Goody, Jack. *Cooking, Cuisine, and Class: A Study of Comparative Sociology* (Cambridge, 1982).

Graf, Arturo. *Miti, leggende e superstizioni del medioevo* (Turin, 1892–93, repr. Pordenone, 1993).

Granel, François. "La Thériaque de Montpellier." *Revue d'histoire de la pharmacie* 64, no. 228 (1976): 75–83.

Greenblatt, Stephen. *Marvelous Possessions: The Wonder of the New World* (Chicago, 1991).

Grieco, Allen J. "Food and Social Classes in Medieval and Renaissance Italy." In *Food: A Culinary History,* ed. Jean-Louis Flandrin and Massimo Montanari, trans. Clarissa Botsford et al. (New York, 1999), 302–12.

Grimm, Reinhold. *Paradisus coelestis, Paradisus terrestris: Zur Auslegungsgechichte des Paradieses im Abendland bis zum 1200* (Munich, 1977).

Groos, Arthur. *Romancing the Grail: Genre, Science, and Quest in Wolfram's Parzival* (Ithaca, 1995).

Guedes, Max Justo, and Gerald Lombardi, eds. *Portugal–Brazil: The Age of Atlantic Discoveries* (Milan, 1990).

Guéret-Laferté, Michèle. *Sur les routes de l'Empire Mongol: Ordre et rhétorique des relations de voyages aux XIIIe et XIVe siècles* (Paris, 1994).

Hahn, Thomas. "The Indian Tradition in Western Medieval Intellectual History." *Viator* 9 (1978): 219–34.

Harvey, Susan Ashbrook. *Scenting Salvation: Ancient Christianity and the Olfactory Imagination* (Berkeley, 2006).

Hayes, Constance. *Pop: Truth and Power at the Coca-Cola Company* (New York, 2004).

Henisch, Bridget Ann. *Fast and Feast: Food in Medieval Society* (University Park, Pa., 1976).

Hieatt, Constance B. "Making Sense of Medieval Culinary Records." In *Food and Eating in Medieval Europe,* ed. Martha Carlin and Joel T. Rosenthal (London and Rio Grande, W.Va., 1998).

Hieatt, Constance B., et al. *Pleyn Delit: Medieval Cookery for Modern Cooks,* 2nd ed. (Toronto, 1996).

Hochstrasser, Julie Bergere. "The Conquest of Spice and the Dutch Colonial Imaginary: Seen and Unseen in the Visual Culture of Trade." In *Colonial Botany: Science, Commerce, and Politics in the Early Modern World,* ed. Londa Schiebinger and Claudia Swan (Philadelphia, 2005), 169–86.

Hofmann, Hans. *Die Heiligen Drei Könige: Zur Heiligenverehrung im kirchlichen, gesellschaftlichen und politischen Leben des Mittelalters* (Bonn, 1975).

Hunt, Alan. *Governance of the Consuming Passions: A History of Sumptuary Laws* (New York, 1996).

Jaeger, C. Stephen. *The Origins of Courtliness: Civilizing Trends and the Formation of Courtly Ideals, 939–1210* (Philadelphia, 1985).

Jardine, Lisa. *Worldly Goods: A New History of the Renaissance* (New York, 1996).

Jensen, Kurt Villads. "Devils, Noble Savages, and the Iron Gate: Thirteenth-Century European Concepts of the Mongols." *Bulletin of International Medieval Research* 6 (2000): 1–20.

Johnson, Christine R. "Bringing the World Home: Germany and the Age of Discovery." Ph.D. diss., Johns Hopkins University, 2000.

Kalinoski, Gail. "Healing Gems: Entrepreneurs Unleash Power of Precious Stones." *Fairfield County Business Journal*, July 14, 2003.

Keay, John. *The Spice Route: A History* (Berkeley, 2006).

Kehrer, Hugo. *Die Heiligen drei Könige in Literatur und Kunst*, 2 vols. (Leipzig, 1908).

Kieniewicz, Jan. "Pepper Gardens and Market in Precolonial Malabar." In *Spices in the Indian Ocean World*, ed. M. N. Pearson (Aldershot, 1996), 209–44.

Knefelkamp, Ulrich. "Das Indienbild in Reiseberichten." In *Die Begegnung des Westens mit dem Osten,* ed. Odilo Engels and Peter Schreiner (Sigmaringen, 1993), 99–112.

Küster, Hansförg. "Spices and Flavourings." In *The Cambridge World History of Food,* vol. 1 (Cambridge, 2000).

Lafortune-Martel, Agathe. *Fête noble en Bourgogne au XVe siècle: Le Banquet du Faisan (1454), aspects politiques, sociaux et culturels* (Montreal and Paris, 1984).

Larner, John. *Marco Polo and the Discovery of the World* (New Haven, 1999).

Laufer, Berthold. *The Diamond: A Study in Chinese and Hellenistic Folk-Lore* (Chicago, 1915).

Launert, Edmund. *Scents and Scent Bottles* (London, 1974).

Laurent, M. "Le phénix, les serpents et les aromates dans une miniature du XIIe siècle." *L'antiquité classique* 4 (1935): 375–401.

Laurioux, Bruno. "De l'usage des épices dans l'alimentation médiévale." *Médiévales* 5 (1983): 15–31.

———. "Identités nationales, particularismes régionaux et 'koiné' européenne dans la cuisine du Moyen Âge." In *Une histoire culinaire du Moyen Âge,* collected essays by Bruno Laurioux (Paris, 2005), 337–55.

———. "Le goût médiéval est-il Arabe? À propos de la 'Saracen Connection.'" In *Une histoire culinaire du Moyen Âge,* collected essays by Bruno Laurioux (Paris, 2005), 305–35.

———. *Les livres de cuisine médiévaux,* Typologies des sources du Moyen Âge occidental (Turnhout, 1997).

———. *Manger au Moyen Âge* (Paris, 2002).

———. "Modes culinaires et mutations du goût à la fin du Moyen Âge." In *Une histoire culinaire du Moyen Âge,* collected essays by Bruno Laurioux (Paris, 2005), 285–93.

———. *Le Moyen Âge à table* (Paris, 1989).

———. *Le règne de Taillevent: Livres et pratiques culinaires à la fin du Moyen Âge* (Paris, 1997).

———. "Table et hiérarchie sociale à la fin du Moyen Âge." In *Du manuscrit à la table: Essais sur la cuisine au Moyen Âge et répertoire des manuscrits médiévaux contenant des recettes culinaires,* ed. Carole Lambert (Montreal, 1992), 87–108.

———. *Une histoire culinaire du Moyen Âge* (Paris, 2005).

———. "Vins musqués et flaveurs de paradis: L'imaginaire médiéval des épices." In *Le monde végétal (XIIe–XVIIe siècles): Savoirs et usages sociaux,* ed. Allen J. Grieco et al. (Saint-Denis, 1993), 157–74.

Le Goff, Jacques. "The Medieval West and the Indian Ocean: An Oneiric Horizon." In *Time, Work, and Culture in the Middle Ages,* by Jacques Le Goff, trans. Arthur Goldhammer (Chicago, 1980), 189–200.

Levtzion, Nehemia. *Ancient Ghana and Mali* (London, 1973).

Little, Lester K. *Benedictine Maledictions: Liturgical Cursing in Romanesque France* (Ithaca, 1993).

Longuyon, Jacques de. *Les voeux du paon*. Ed. Brother Camillus Casey. Ph.D. diss., Columbia University, 1956.

Lopez, Robert S. "European Merchants in the Medieval Indies." *Journal of Economic History* 3 (1943): 164–84.

———. "L'extrême frontière du commerce de l'Europe médiévale." *Le Moyen Âge* 79 (1963): 479–90.

———. "'In quibuscumque mondi partibus.'" In *Miscellanea di storia italiana e mediterranea per Nino Lamboglia* (Genoa, 1978), 345–54.

———. "Da Venezia a Delhi nel Trecento." In *Su e giù per la storia di Genova,* by Robert S. Lopez (Genoa, 1973), 137–59.

López Pizcueta, Tomás. "Los bienes de un farmacéutico barcelonés del siglo XIV: Francesc de Camp." *Acta Medievalia* 13 (1992): 17–73.

Lozovsky, Natalia. *"The Earth Is Our Book": Geographical Knowledge in the Latin West ca. 400–1000* (Ann Arbor, 2000).

McFarlane, Alan. *Green Gold: The Empire of Tea: A Remarkable History of the Plant that Took Over the World* (London, 2003).

Magalhães, Joaquim Romero. *Portugueses no mundo do século XVI: Espaços e productos* (Lisbon, 1998).

Magalhães Godinho, Vitorino. *Os descobrimentos e a economia mundial,* 2nd ed. (Lisbon, 1985).

———. "Le repli Vénitien et Égyptien et la route du Cap, 1496–1533." In *Éventail de l'histoire vivante: Hommage à Lucien Febvre,* vol. 1 (Paris, 1953), repr. in *Spices in the Indian Ocean World,* ed. M. N. Pearson (Aldershot, 1996), 283–300.

Masciandaro, Nicola. *The Voice of the Hammer: The Meaning of Work in Middle English Literature* (Notre Dame, 2006).

Mathew, K. S. *Portuguese Trade with India in the Sixteenth Century* (New Delhi, 1983).

Matthew, Leslie G. "King John of France and the English Spicers." *Medical History* 5 (1961): 65–76.

———. *The Pepperers, Spicers, and Apothecaries of London During the Thirteenth and Fourteenth Centuries* (London, 1980).

Meier, Christel. *Gemma spiritalis: Methode und Gebrauch der Edelsteinallegorese vom frühen Christentum bis ins 18. Jahrhundert* (Munich, 1977).

Melis, Federigo. *Documenti per la storia economica dei secoli XIII–XVI* (Florence, 1972).

Milton, Giles. *Nathaniel's Nutmeg, or the True and Incredible Adventures of the Spice Trader Who Changed the Course of History* (New York, 1999).

Mintz, Sidney. *Sweetness and Power: The Place of Sugar in Modern History* (New York, 1985).

Monneret de Villard, Ugo. *Le leggende orientali sul magi evangelici* (Vatican City, 1952).

Montanari, Massimo. "L'image du paysan et les codes de comportement alimentaire." In *Le petit peuple dans l'Occident médiéval: Terminologies, perceptions, réalités,* ed. Pierre Boglioni et al. (Paris, 2002), 97–112.

Morton, Timothy. *The Poetics of Spice: Romantic Consumerism and the Exotic* (Cambridge, 2000).

Munro, John H. "The Consumption of Spices and Their Costs in Late-Medieval and Early-Modern Europe: Luxuries or Necessities?" (lecture given in 1983, rev. in 1988 and 2001), available at www.economics.utoronto.ca/munro5/lecnot201.htm.

————. "Oriental Spices and Their Costs in Medieval Cuisine: Luxuries or Necessities?" talk given at University College, Toronto, 1988, posted at www.chass.utoronto.ca/~munro5/SPICES1.html.

Musgrave, Peter. "The Economics of Uncertainty: The Structural Revolution in the Spice Trade, 1480–1640." In *Shipping, Trade, and Commerce: Essays in Memory of Ralph Davis*, ed. P. L. Cottrell and D. H. Aldcroft (Leicester, 1981), 9–21.

Nederman, Cary J. *Worlds of Difference: European Discourses of Toleration, c. 1100–1550* (University Park, 2000).

Niane, Djibril Tamsir. *Le Soudan occidental au temps des grands empires, XIe–XVIe siècle* (Paris, 1975).

Nightingale, Pamela. *A Medieval Mercantile Community: The Grocers' Company and the Politics and Trade of London, 1000–1485* (New Haven, 1995).

Norton, Marcy. "Tasting Empire: Chocolate and the European Internalization of Mesoamerican Aesthetics." *American Historical Review* 111 (2006): 660–91.

Oliveira e Costa, João Paulo, and Victor Luís Gaspar Rodrigues. *Portugal y Oriente: El proyecto indiano del rey Juan* (Madrid, 1992).

Orchard, Andy. *Pride and Prodigies: Studies in the Monsters of the Beowulf Manuscript* (Woodbridge, 1995; revised ed., Toronto, 2003).

Paravicini-Bagliani, Agostino. *The Pope's Body.* Trans. David S. Peterson (Chicago, 2000).

Patch, Howard Rollin. *The Other World According to Descriptions in Medieval Literature* (Cambridge, Mass., 1950).

Pérez Vidal, José. *Medicina y dulcería en el "Libro de Buen Amor"* (Madrid, 1981).

Peters, Edward. "The Desire to Know the Secrets of the World." *Journal of the History of Ideas* 62 (2001): 593–610.

Peterson, T. Sarah. *Acquired Taste: The French Origins of Modern Cooking* (Ithaca, 1994).

Peterson, Toby. "The Arab Influence on Western European Cooking." *Journal of Medieval History* 6 (1980): 317–40.

Phillips, J. R. S. *The Medieval Expansion of Europe* (Oxford, 1988).

Phillips, William D., Jr., and Carla Rahn Phillips. *The Worlds of Christopher Columbus* (Cambridge, 1992).

Pifarré Torres, Dolors. *El comerç internacional de Barcelona i el mar del Nord (Bruges) al final del segle XIV* (Montserrat, 2002).

Planes i Borràs, Josep. "The Accounts of Joan Benet's Trading Ventures from Barcelona to Famagusta, 1343." *Epeteris* 19 (1992): 105–18.

Ptak, Roderich. "China and the Trade in Cloves, Circa 960–1435." *Journal of the American Oriental Society* 113 (1993): 1–13.

Rachewiltz, I. de. *Papal Envoys to the Great Khan* (London, 1971).

Ravenstein, E. G. *Martin Behaim, His Life and His Globe* (London, 1908).

Redon, Odile, and Lucia Bertolini. "La diffusione in Italia di una tradizione culinaria senese tra due e trecento." *Bollettino Senese di Storia Patria* 100 (1993): 35–81.

Reichert, Folker E. *Begegnungen mit China: Die Entdeckung Ostasiens im Mittelalter* (Sigmaringen, 1992).

———. "Columbus und Marco Polo—Asien in Amerika: Zur Literaturgeschichte der Entdeckungen." *Zeitschrift für Historische Forschung* 15 (1988): 1–63.

———. *Erfahrung der Welt: Reisen und Kulturbegegnung im späten Mittelalter* (Stuttgart, 2001).

Reinitzer Heimo. "Zeder und Aloe: Zur Herkunft des Bettes Salomos im 'Moritz von Craûn.'" *Archiv für Kulturgeschichte* 58 (1976): 1–34.

Reyerson, Kathryn L. "Commercial Fraud in the Middle Ages: The Case of the Dissembling Pepperer." *Journal of Medieval History* 8 (1982): 63–73.

Richard, Jean. "Les navigations des occidentaux sur l'Océan Indien et la mer Caspienne, XIIe–XVe siècles." In *Sociétés et compagnies de commerce en Orient* (Paris, 1970).

Richardson, Tim. *A History of Candy* (New York, 2002).

Riddle, John M. "Albert on Stones and Minerals." In *Albertus Magnus and the Sciences: Commemorative Essays, 1980,* ed. James A. Weisheipl (Toronto, 1980).

———. *Eve's Herbs: A History of Contraception in the West* (Cambridge, Mass., 1997).

———. *Marbode of Rennes' De Lapidus Considered as a Medical Treatise* (Wiesbaden, 1977).

———. "Pomum Ambrae: Amber and Ambergris in Plague Remedies." *Sudhoffs Archiv für Geschichte der Medizin und der Naturwissenschaften* 48 (1964): 111–22.

———. *Quid pro Quo: Studies in the History of Drugs* (Aldershot, 1992).

Riera, Antoni. "'Transmarina vel orientalis especies magno labore quaesita, multa precio empta': Especias y sociedad en el Mediterráneo noroccidental en el siglo XII." *Anuario de estudios medievales* 30, no. 2 (2000): 1030–49.

Rodinson, Maxime. "Mamūniyya East and West." In *Medieval Arab Cookery: Essays and Translations,* by Maxime Rodinson et al. (Totnes, 2001), 185–96.

Ross, D. J. A. *Alexander Historiatus* (London, 1963).

Rubiés, Joan-Pau. *Travel and Ethnology in the Renaissance: South India Through European Eyes, 1250–1625* (Cambridge, 2000).

Russell, P. E. *Prince Henry "The Navigator," A Life* (New Haven, 2000).

Rustomji, Nerina. "The Garden and the Fire: Materials of Heaven and Hell in Medieval Islamic Culture." Ph.D. diss., Columbia University, 2003.

Ryan, James D. "European Travellers Before Columbus: The Fourteenth Century's Discovery of India." *Catholic Historical Review* 79 (1993): 648–70.

Sabban, Françoise, and Silvano Serventi. *La gastronomie au Grand Siècle* (Paris, 1998).

Sass, Lorna J. "Religion, Medicine, Politics, and Spices." *Appetite* 2 (1981): 7–13.

Scafi, Alessandro. "Mapping Eden: Cartographies of the Earthly Paradise." In *Mappings,* ed. Denis E. Cosgrove (London, 1999), 50–70.

Schafer, Edward. *The Golden Peaches of Samarkand: A Study in T'ang Exotics* (Berkeley, 1963).

Schalick, Walton Orvyl, III. "Add One Part Pharmacy to One Part Surgery and One Part Medicine: Jean de Saint-Amand and the Development of Medical Pharmacology in Thirteenth-Century Paris." Ph.D. diss., Johns Hopkins University, 1997.

Schivelbusch, Wolfgang. *Tastes of Paradise: A Social History of Spices, Stimulants, and Intoxicants.* Trans. David Jacobson (New York, 1992).

Schneider, Pierre. *L'Éthiopie et l'Inde: Interférences et confusions aux extrémités du monde antique* (Rome, 2004).

Scully, Terence. *The Art of Cookery in the Middle Ages* (Woodbridge, 1995).

————. "The *Opusculum de Saporibus* of Magninus Mediolanensis." *Medium Aevum* 54 (1985): 179–207.

Seiler, Thomas H. "Filth and Stench as Aspects of the Iconography of Hell." In *The Iconography of Hell,* ed. Clifford Davidson and Thomas H. Seiler (Kalamazoo, 1992), 132–40.

Shankle, George Earlie. *State Names, Flags, Seals, Songs, Birds, Flowers, and Other Symbols* (New York, 1934).

Siraisi, Nancy G. *Medieval and Early Renaissance Medicine: An Introduction to Knowledge and Practice* (Chicago, 1990).

Slessarev, Vsevolod. *Prester John: The Letter and the Legend* (Minneapolis, 1979).

Smith, Stefan Halikowski. "Meanings Behind Myths: The Multiple Manifestations of the Tree of the Virgin at Matarea." *Journal of Religious Studies* (forthcoming).

————. "The Mystification of Spices in the Western Tradition." *European Review of History–Revue européenne d'histoire* 8 (2001): 119–36.

Spufford, Peter. *Power and Profit: The Merchant in Medieval Europe* (New York, 2002).

Staccini, Rita. "L'inventario di una spezieria del Quattrocento." *Studi medievali,* 3rd ser., 22 (1981): 377–420.

Subrahmanyam, Sanjay. *The Career and Legend of Vasco da Gama* (Cambridge, 1997).

Tannahill, Reay. *Food in History* (New York, 1988).

Tardiola, Giuseppe. *Atlante fantastico del medioevo* (Rome, 1990).

————. *Le meraviglie dell'India* (Rome, 1991).

Thorndike, Lynn. "A Mediaeval Sauce-Book." *Speculum* 9 (1934): 183–90.

Thrupp, Sylvia. "The Grocers of London: A Study in Distributive Trade." In *Studies in English Trade in the Fifteenth Century,* ed. Eileen Power and M. M. Postan (London, 1933), 247–92.

Trebeljahr, Moritz. "Pêro da Covilhãs Indien- und Äthiopienreise und die Expansions-politik Johannes II. von Portugal." M.A. thesis, University of Freiburg in Breisgau, 2003.

Turner, Jack. *Spice: The History of a Temptation* (New York, 2004).

Tzanaki, Rosemary. *Mandeville's Medieval Audiences: A Study on the Reception of the Book of Sir John Mandeville, 1371–1550* (Aldershot, 2003).

Uebel, Michael. "Imperial Fetishism: Prester John Among the Natives." In *The Postcolonial Middle Ages,* ed. Jeffrey Jerome Cohen (New York, 2001), 261–82.

Vela i Aulesa, Carles. *L'obrador d'un apotecari medieval segons el llibre de comptes de Francesc ses Canes, Barcelona, 1378–1381* (Barcelona, 2003).

Verdés i Pijuan, Pere. "Una espècia autòctona: El comerç del safrà a Catalunya durant el segle XV." *Anuario de estudios medievales* 31, no. 2 (2001): 758–86.

Warner, Jessica. *Gin and Debauchery in an Age of Reason* (New York, 2003).

Westrem, Scott D. *Broader Horizons: A Study of Johannes Witte de Hese's "Itinerarius" and Medieval Travel Narratives* (Cambridge, 2001).

————. *The Hereford Map* (Turnhout, 2001).

White, David Gordon. *Myths of the Dog-Man* (Chicago, 1991).

Whittet, T. D. "Pepperers, Spicers, and Grocers: Forerunners of the Apothecaries." *Proceedings of the Royal Society of Medicine* 61 (1968): 801–6.

Williamson, Jeffrey G., and Kevin H. O'Rourke. "Did Vasco da Gama Matter for European Markets? Testing Frederick Lane's Hypothesis Fifty Years Later." Economic Papers, Trinity College, Dublin, 2006, at http://ideas.repec.org/p/tcd/tcduee/tep2007.html.

Wilson, C. Anne. *Food and Drink in Britain from the Stone Age to the 19th Century* (Chicago, 1991).

Winter, Johanna Maria van. "Kochen und Essen im Mittelalter." In *Mensch und Umwelt im Mittelalter,* ed. Bernd Herrmann (Stuttgart, 1986), 88–100.

———. "Kookboeken, medisch of culinair?" In *Voeding en geneeskunde/Alimentation et médécine,* ed. Ria Jansen-Sieben and Frank Daelmans (Brussels, 1993), 153–65.

Wittkower, R. "Marco Polo and the Pictorial Tradition of the Marvels of the East." In *Oriente Poliano: Studi e conferenze all'Istituto Italiano per il medio ed estremo orientei* (Rome, 1957), 155–72.

Wolf, Robert S. "Da Gama's Blundering: Trade Encounters in Africa and Asia During the European 'Age of Discovery,' 1450–1520." *The History Teacher* 31 (1998).

Woolgar, Christopher M. "Fast and Feast: Conspicuous Consumption and the Diet of the Nobility in the Fifteenth Century." In *Revolution and Consumption in Late Medieval England,* ed. Michael Hicks (Woodbridge, 2001).

———. *The Great Household in Late Medieval England* (New Haven, 1999).

———. *The Senses in Late Medieval England* (New Haven, 2006).

Wortis, S. Bernard, et al. "Monobromated Camphor: A Standardized Convulsant," *Archives of Neurology* 26 (1931), 156–61.

Wright, Thomas, ed. *The Anglo-Latin Satirical Poets and Epigrammatists of the Twelfth Century,* vol. 1 (Rolls Series 59/1) (London, 1872; repr. Wiesbaden, 1964).

Young, Gary K. *Rome's Eastern Trade: International Commerce and Imperial Policy, 31 B.C.–A.D. 305* (London, 2001).

Yule, Henry, and Henri Cordier, eds. *Cathay and the Way Thither,* 3 vols. (London, 1913–16).

Zarncke, Friedrich. "Der Priester Johannes." *Abhandlungen der königlichen Sächsischen Gesellschaft der Wissenschaften,* Phil.-Hist. Class. 7 (1879), 871–1028, and 8 (1883), 1–184.

Index

Aristotle, 136
Arnau de Vilanova, 57, 67
Aromatherapy, 5, 87–88
Aromatics: ritual use of, 5, 78, 80, 82; and spice trade, 8; and domestic spices, 10; botanical and nonbotanical substances, 63–65; and prevention of plague, 72; and Christianity, 79–80; Arabia as source of, 80, 135; and indoor climate, 82; and Garden of Eden, 92; cost of, 131; snakes guarding, 135. *See also* Fragrance; Perfumes
Arsenic, 62
Artemesia, 61
Artifice, in medieval cuisine, 27, 28, 38
Artificial rarity, 131–32, 141
Asfetida, 26
Asia: as source of spices, 5, 8, 26, 61, 76, 78, 91, 104; and aromatherapy, 88; paradise associated with, 89, 91, 95–96, 97, 98, 160; economic networks of, 105, 193; and spice trade, 106, 110, 170, 186, 196, 197; European knowledge of, 110, 166, 167, 169, 172, 174, 179, 186; and cost of spices, 114, 137, 141; and saffron, 128; and supply of spices, 130–31, 133, 137, 143, 160, 167; geography of, 140, 165, 166, 172, 174, 177, 179, 181–82, 183, 197, 207, 208, 209; and tales of wealth, 140, 143–44, 145, 165, 166; and Hereford Map, 174; and Turks, 178; and Portugal, 205; and Columbus, 210; and Spain, 214. *See also* East Asia; South Asia
Assidios, 95
Athanasius, St., 97
Atlantic Ocean, 194, 209
Augustine, St., 44, 91, 159, 230n42
Aulnoy, countess of, 216
Avicenna, 82
Avignon, 178, 198
Azores, 194, 208

Bachelard, Gaston, 6
Balsam, 14, 63, 69, 80, 90, 135

Banda, 182, 183, 205, 222
Banquets: descriptions of, 21, 28–32; hierarchical seating of, 29, 32; spices prominent in, 39, 150; and hierarchy of foods, 44; and *Le Ménagier de Paris,* 47–48
Barind (abbot), 97
Beatrice of Hungary, 25
Beatus of Liebana, 98
Becket, Thomas, St., 85
Behaim, Martin, 141–42, 172, 186, 196, 207, 208, 209, *211*
Beirut, and spice trade, 105, 113, 123, 172
Benedict, St., 150
Bernard of Clairvaux, St., 150–52, 153
Beverages, 219, 221
Biblical lands, 89
Biblical lore, 143, 180–81
Bilious temperament, 54
Birds: and banquets, 29, 30; and meals, 34, 35; and carving, 36; and trompe l'oeil, 37; and spectacle, 38; and hierarchy of foods, 44; and sumptuary legislation, 45; humoral qualities of, 55. *See also* Poultry
Black Death, 64, 65
Black pepper: as edible spice, 11; and sharp black sauce, 22; humoral properties of, 63
Black Sea, and spice trade, 110, 173
Blaise, Armengaud, 68
Bloodstone, 67
Bodily equilibrium: and humors, 49, 52–53, 54, 88; and paramedical fashions, 74–75
Boileau, Nicolas, "The Ridiculous Meal" (*Le repas ridicule*), 217
Boke of Kervynge, 36
Bonaventure, St., 119
Bonnefons, Nicholas de, 217
Books of advice, 21
Brazil, 194, 204, 205, 213, 219
Bread, and hierarchy of foods, 40
Brendan, St., 97
Brie, 41

and Persia as source of, 80; and indoor climate, 82; snakes guarding, 134

Frederick Barbarossa (emperor), 102

Frederick II (German emperor), 25

French cuisine, impact on spices, 216–23

Fruit: effects of raw fruit, 41, 51; and hierarchy of foods, 41; humoral properties of, 55

Frumenty, 30

Fuggers, 147, 148, 213

Fulcher of Chartres, 25

Fumigation, 82

Galangal: dried form of, 8; Pegolotti on, 11; in medieval cuisine, 22; first mentions of, 26; price of, 128

Galen, 53, 63, 82

Game animals, 29, 30, 35, 40, 44, 55

Ganges, 91

Garbling, 124

Garden of Eden: as perfumed by spices, 5, 77, 89–95; as true home of spices, 81; four primary rivers of, 89, 91, 92, 94; location of, 89, 95, 97; nourishing fragrance of, 90; and other sources of spices, 90–91; as paradise on earth, 90–91; depicted on Hereford Map, 91, *93;* and location of India, 97, 98; and effortless access to spices, 160. *See also* Paradise

Gaveston, Piers, 35

Geary, Patrick, 85

Gems: curative powers of, 65, 67; rivers of paradise as source of, 94, 95, 102; Epiphanius on, 135–36; and European voyages, 165. *See also* Jewels

Genesis, book of, 89, 91–92, 97

Genghis Khan (Mongol ruler), 167, 168

Genoese traders: and spice trade, 110, 112, 116, 129, 173, 178, 188, 190; and economics, 161; in Crimea, 169; and Muslim traders, 175, 188

Geography: Catalan Atlas (1375–77) and, 100, *101,* 174, 179, *180;* Fra Mauro and, 106, 183, 185; of Asia, 140, 165, 166, 172, 174, 177, 179, 181–82, 183, 197, 207, 208, 209; and European voyages, 165–66, 175, 180, 188; William of Rubruck and, 166–67; Hereford Map and, 173–74, 180; of Indian Ocean, 175, 186, 197; Vesconte Map and, 177, 178; Ptolemy and, 179–82, 207; and land-sea ratio, 180–81, 207–8; and earth's circumference, 181, 182, 207, 208, 213; Behaim and, 186, 207; of spice trade, 186, 204–5; Arab geographers and, 187, 199; of Africa, 197, 198, 199, 200; Toscanelli and, 208–9

George "the Rich" (duke of Bavaria), 6, 10

Ginger: dried form of, 8; as edible spice, 11; and medieval cuisines, 21; sauces, 22; English and French use of, 27; humoral properties of, 56; as aphrodisiac, 72, 73; quality of, 114; price of, 116, 127, 128; and retail trade, 116; irreplaceable nature of, 131

Gingerbread, 24, 116, 228–29n7

Girart de Roussillon, 69

Glazed "hedgehogs," 38

Gluttony: and books of advice, 21; and seven deadly sins, 50–51; and moralists, 59–60, 148, 149, 151, 152–53, 154, 156, 157, 160; sexual desire linked with, 152–53, 157

Gold: and Japan, 138, 142, 144, 209; and Africa, 194, 195

Gold leaf, 35, 37

Grains of paradise, 12, 20, 22, 196. *See also* Malagueta pepper

Grammaticus, Saxo, 153

Granada, 179, 187, 198, 206

Great Britain, 160–61, 201, 214, 219

Greek medical theory, 52–53, 58, 82

Greek medical works, 62, 73

Grocers, 116, 117, 120

Grocers' Company of London, 117

Guinea, 194, 196, 197, 199, 210

Index

266

Index